PRAISE FOR
Writing to Win

"Stark ranks as one of the country's leading authorities in the field of effective legal writing. . . . *Writing to Win* is not the stuff of law school training in the art of legal writing. And that's what makes it so good."

—*Trial*

"*Writing to Win* joins the shelf of that small group of the best style books about legal writing. Don't let it sit there. Use it to make some of your own legal/literary silver bullets."

—*New York Law Journal*

"An excellent primer on writing persuasively."

—*Illinois Bar Journal*

"A practical and down-to-earth guide . . . *Writing to Win* offers so much distilled wisdom that even the skilled writer should learn something new."

—*Lawyers Weekly*

"At once practical and thought provoking . . . instead of focusing single-mindedly on legal writing, Stark provides related insights into lawyers, law practice, ethics, and popular culture."

—*Scribes Journal of Legal Writing*

"Entertaining and useful . . . superbly organized and easy to read . . . a great book."

—*Legalwriting.net*

Writing to Win

THE LEGAL WRITER

Completely Updated and Revised

Steven D. Stark

THREE RIVERS PRESS
NEW YORK

All rights reserved.
Published in the United States by Three Rivers Press,
an imprint of the Crown Publishing Group,
a division of Random House, Inc., New York.
www.crownpublishing.com

THREE RIVERS PRESS and the Tugboat design
are registered trademarks of Random House, Inc.

Originally published in hardcover in slightly different form in the United
States by Main Street Books, St. Charles, Missouri, in 1999 and in
paperback in slightly different form in the United States by Broadway
Books, a division of Random House, Inc., New York, in 2000.

Library of Congress Cataloging-in-Publication Data
is available upon request.

ISBN 978-0-307-88871-6
eISBN 978-0-307-88874-7

PRINTED IN THE UNITED STATES OF AMERICA

Cover design by Deanna Destefano .

14th Printing

First Revised Edition

In memory of Robert Wald—a great writer and a greater friend

Acknowledgments

This book never would have been possible without the help of a lot of people. I owe my teaching career at Harvard to the late Jim Vorenberg, Charlie Nesson, and David Shapiro, all of whom showed a lot of confidence in me when I was still very green. The same holds true of Jack Reilly of Massachusetts Continuing Legal Education, who first persuaded me to start teaching practicing lawyers more than two decades ago. As far as this work goes, I never could have gotten it off the ground without the help of all my students and researchers over the years, not to mention Dwight Golann, whose patience and legal skills helped me out immensely when some of my original research materials were accidentally destroyed. Parts of the book first found their way into print in articles in the *Harvard Law Review*, the *Scribes Journal of Legal Writing*, *Connecticut Law Review*, the *Docket*, *National Law Journal*, and *Legal Times of Washington*; the editors there deserve my thanks. In the writing of the text, my editors, Gerald Howard and Liz Duvall, were a terrific help, as was Charlie Conrad this time around. I also benefited immeasurably from the copious editorial comments and corrections of David Shapiro, the late Frank Connors, and my mother-in-law, Judge Patricia Wald. All read an earlier version of the manuscript, in some cases on only the earlier edition. The usual caveat: Though

I couldn't have done this without any of them, the mistakes that remain are mine, and mine alone. Finally, my wife, Sarah Wald, read every word and at every step offered valuable encouragement and advice. As my sons, Harry and Jake, often say, "She is the best."

Contents

Writing to Win

Introduction to the New Edition

Good writing is timeless. Except, of course, when it's not.

Periodically over the last ten years, I thought about revising my original book on legal and professional writing—*Writing to Win: The Legal Writer.* But as egocentric as it might seem, for a while I never found much I would change. Sure, some of the references marked the book as a product of a slightly earlier time—the references to the O. J. Simpson trial, Kenneth Starr, or "vice-president Al Gore." But for the most part, the book seemed to illustrate the maxim that the principles of good writing don't change all that much over time. A good brief in 1965—much less in the late 1990s when the book was written—is still a good brief today. Ditto for complaint writing, contracts, and even judicial opinions.

And yet: In a variety of ways, writing in many parts of the legal and business worlds has changed more since that book was written about a decade ago than in any comparable period over the last five centuries. "We shape our tools and then our tools shape us," wrote the media theorist Marshall McLuhan a generation ago. Technological changes transform not only the methods of communication but their style as well. The invention of the printing press centuries ago not only altered the dissemination of information in Western cultures, it changed the way people spoke and the way they wrote—and there were constant complaints about it then, just like now.

In our time, of course, the recent development of computers, the Internet, and then smart phones (and all their manifestations, such as the iPad) has begun to do much the same thing. It's undeniable that writing within the office and for clients is dramatically different than it was a decade ago. Whether we recognize it or not, that means that legal analysis and the ways we approach business problems have shifted as well.

These revolutionary changes are one of the subjects of this new edition of the book. In part, that makes this volume a primer on how to communicate successfully in this brave new world. Writing effective e-mails and shorter memos are skills very much at odds with the tools we acquire in school—where the goal is usually to be expansive and detailed as we display our knowledge in all its minutiae. These new forms of communication are also very different from the written and oral tools one needed to master to be a good lawyer or executive, circa 1990 and before.

Yet it's not just these new forms one needs to master. Litigation and contract writing may not have begun to change much since the rise of e-culture. But they will, since it is inevitable that these documents will also be read differently as the years pass, as will even judicial opinions. Some courts now require e-filings. Justices Antonin Scalia and Elena Kagan read briefs on either an iPad or a Kindle, and they will soon be joined by many others.

It means, too, that a lawyer's role and habits of mind will change as they have begun to do already. If the Internet, Twitter, and Facebook are altering the way we do our jobs and how well we do them, they're changing the way we think as well. It was Professor Kingsfield in *The Paper Chase* who kept dwelling on the importance of "thinking like a lawyer." How that's changed at the beginning of the twenty-first century because of these technological shifts is the subject of this new edition too.

Perhaps unsurprisingly, this new focus reinforces many of the fundamental principles that writing teachers and books (including my previous volume) have been stressing for decades—use strong verbs or be concise—though the rationales for doing so have changed somewhat. Yet other suggestions are novel, as one might expect at the dawn of a new epoch.

This updated edition also has an increased spotlight on creative writing as it relates to the presentation of facts and argument, as well as a new section on how affidavits need to be better drafted so that they reflect the true voice of the person they are supposed to represent. And, throughout the text, there are new ideas and examples of both what to do and avoid.

There is an old Chinese curse: May you live in interesting times. Whether it's a curse or not, we live in just such an era. So let's begin to figure out how to adapt—the sooner the better.

Introduction

If you don't need a weatherman to know which way the wind blows, you don't need a literary critic to know how badly most lawyers write. You only need to turn to any page of most legal memos, briefs, judicial opinions, law review articles, and even e-mail to find convoluted sentences, tortuous phrasing, and boring passages filled with passive verbs. Charles Dickens was neither the first nor the last to complain about lawyers' "liking for the legal repetitions and prolixities." In fact, the term "legal writing" has become synonymous with poor writing: specifically, verbose and inflated prose that reads like . . . well, like it was written by a lawyer. Like the late Justice Potter Stewart on obscenity, we know it when we see it, and we see it all the time.

Here is an example. Several decades ago, Joel Henning, a legal consultant and writer, noted a little-publicized case. In *David v. Heckler*, 591 F. Supp. 1033 (E.D.N.Y. 1984), United States District Court Judge Jack Weinstein, one of the federal judiciary's more distinguished judges and better writers, ruled that bad writing in government documents violates the due process clause of the Fourteenth Amendment of the Constitution. Judge Weinstein took the highly laudable step of ordering the Department of Health and Human Services to rewrite its review letters to Medicare claimants because they were "incomprehensible" and contained "insufficient and misleading" information.

One of the sentences in the letters that so upset Judge Weinstein read:

> The amounts are based on statistics covering customary charges of an individual physician and prevailing rates by all physicians rendering similar services in a given locality.

Given the dismal level of a lot of legal writing, that hardly seems so bad. It looks especially good in comparison to this sentence, which comes from Judge Weinstein's own opinion in the matter:

> Doubt as to whether this type of claim should be construed as barred by section 205(h), 42 U.S.C. §405(h), should be resolved in favor of finding jurisdiction since the availability of judicial review for constitutional questions is generally "presumed."

The point isn't simply that we might find Judge Weinstein himself in violation of the Constitution. "Whenever I read something and I can't understand it," Will Rogers said in a line that never failed to draw a laugh, "I know it was written by a lawyer." Robert D. White, in his book *Trials and Tribulations: Appealing Legal Humor,* identified these ten unfortunate characteristics of legal writing:

1. Never use one word where ten will do.
2. Never use a small word where a big one will suffice.
3. Never use a simple statement where it appears that one of substantially greater complexity will achieve comparable goals.
4. Never use English where Latin, *mutatis mutandis,* will do.
5. Qualify virtually everything.

6. Do not be embarrassed about repeating yourself. Do not be embarrassed about repeating yourself.
7. Worry about the difference between "which" and "that."
8. In pleadings and briefs, that which is defensible should be stated. That which is indefensible but you wish were true should merely be suggested.
9. Never refer to your opponent's "argument"; he only makes "assertions," and his assertions are always "bald."
10. If a layperson can read a document from beginning to end without falling asleep, it needs work.

Yet legal writing doesn't have to be this way, and this revised edition is my small attempt to continue to try to turn things around. It's based on an advanced legal writing seminar I taught to third-year students at Harvard Law School for twelve years and continue to give in various versions to practicing lawyers, judges, and paralegals all around the country, and the world.

Numerous eminent books and blogs on legal writing are already out there, so I've tried to make this different. First, as an attorney and former litigator myself, I've tried to focus on the writing of lawyers, not judges. Most writers, after all, learn by emulation. Budding poets read Yeats, Eliot, and Stevens; young novelists immerse themselves in the works of Fitzgerald, Faulkner, and Austen. Law students and lawyers are the great exception; they train for a lifetime of advocacy or corporate practice by reading thousands of opinions of the sort they will never write, but few briefs or memos of the sort they will. Attorneys who can write like Cardozo or Holmes may become brilliant judges, but unfortunately, they are utterly unprepared for their work as practicing lawyers.

This book seeks to remedy that, first by providing dozens of good examples that lawyers can follow, written by other lawyers. Many of the rules I provide also come from interviews with judges and lawyers. When I practiced as a litigator and had to write a brief in, say, an administrative case, the first thing I wanted to see was a selection from a comparable brief by a David Boies or a Kathleen Sullivan. Yet there was nowhere to find such examples easily. Not all such selections here, I should add, are from winning briefs—a reminder, perhaps, that even the best advocates can play only the hand they've been dealt.

Second, as in my courses, I've tried to include examples and maxims from the worlds of journalism, advertising, and fiction writing. Anyone who can write a good ad can probably write a good legal argument, just as any good journalist probably knows how to compose a good statement of facts in an appellate brief. My view is that good writing tends to be pretty much the same everywhere. Sure, there are things that make legal writing different from other types of writing—especially if you have to do a lot of drafting of contracts and legislation or you are a judge crafting rules and decisions. Yet the differences tend to be exaggerated by lawyers and legal educators. Almost everything students learn in law school convinces them that legal prose is a domain unto itself. They hear their professors laud judicial opinions that often seem closer to a foreign language than to English. And unlike most other professionals, who entrust their written products to competent editors, legal academics give their articles to third-year students serving on law reviews, with the predictable consequence that no one but other legal academics will read them.

The key to good writing in school—and even on the bar exam—is often very much at odds with what makes good writing as a lawyer. That's why, if I were designing a law school curriculum, I'd teach intensive legal writing in the last year—the bridge between academic and work life—and I'd focus far more than schools currently do on the essentials of argument and narrative writing. In firms and legal offices, I'd also insist that legal writing and argument be taught by someone who has actively practiced and litigated. Writing is not an academic exercise that can be cleverly taught through a series of PowerPoint slides. It's a labor-intensive craft.

The discerning reader will notice dozens of writing "rules" scattered throughout the text. Of course, the best writers know that writing is not a dogmatic enterprise and the rules are made to be broken. The problem for those of us who have yet to achieve greatness, however, is that it's hard to break the rules effectively without knowing them. Picasso couldn't have become Picasso without learning to sketch a simple still life first.

I've attempted to make the organization of the book simple. Rather than provide dozens of pages of straight text, I've organized each chapter around a set of rules that, though lengthy at times, lawyers and students can apply easily. In Part I, I deal with the problems lawyers face as writers (organizing, strengthening prose, adapting to the new world of e-writing, and editing). In Part II, I address how lawyers can improve their written arguments, whether they are litigators or not. Part III treats litigation writing in all its manifold varieties (writing facts, arguments, complaints, affidavits, and in discovery). Part IV encompasses the everyday writing most lawyers must do (technical writing, memos, e-mails, letters, and the drafting of rules and contracts). In the conclusion, I discuss some of the philosophical reasons that lawyers have traditionally been poor writers. I've written the book so that one can read it straight through, or consult a specific chapter if one needs to write a specific type of legal document, such as a complaint. That means I've been repetitive at times. Every jurisdiction, of course, also has its own idiosyncrasies. So, while I've attempted to provide general principles for legal writing, *always check your local rules before filing any document.*

Many of my examples of both good and bad writing were given to me over the years by lawyers and judges who were assured they would remain anonymous. In many cases, I have identified the authors of my examples and the cases in which the examples appeared. In other instances, however, I cannot do so without disclosing too much about who sent me what, or unduly humiliating the author of a shabby document. In some examples, I have changed the names of the parties to avoid embarrassing them unnecessarily. In no case is the omitted information relevant; it is the writing, not the individual, that is important.

One final caveat: I have tried to inject a note of practicality where necessary, especially in reminding readers how judges read legal documents in the real world. At times my views may seem a little disrespectful. Yet after years of discussing the subject with dozens of lawyers, clerks, and members of the judiciary, I think it's helpful to remind readers that judges were once lawyers, which means they suffer from all the occupational faults we have—if not more.

Like any writer, I stand on the tall shoulders of those who have addressed this subject previously. That's particularly true when you write a book based on lecture notes compiled over several decades that seem to have suggestions from half the lawyers in America attached. Moreover, the blogs dealing with this topic have multiplied in recent years. I've tried to be accurate and credit everyone whose ideas crept into the text, and I have also provided an extensive bibliography. To those who have given me an idea or example somewhere along the line that remains unacknowledged—including my numerous research assistants at Harvard—I apologize, and thank you again.

But enough blabbering. The place to begin the process of improvement is with the basics that confront all legal writers: organization, the rules of the road, adapting to the "new age," and editing. It is to these that we now turn.

PART I

The Fundamentals of Legal Writing

CHAPTER 1 Organizing Your Material

CHAPTER 2 The Rules of the Road

CHAPTER 3 The Mechanics of Editing

CHAPTER I

Organizing Your Material

I. The Overview: Getting Started by
Leading with Your Conclusion

II. Organizing Your Workplace Around Eight Rules

1. Remember that most writing difficulties are organizational difficulties.

2. Writing is something that most people do best alone.

3. Turn off the Internet.

4. Most writers need a regular time to compose.

5. The person who does the research should do the writing.

6. Don't divide the drafting of a document among many writers.

7. Don't stop when you're stuck; instead stop when you don't want to.

8. Keep a notebook and learn from other lawyers.

I. The Overview: Getting Started by Leading with Your Conclusion

For supposedly logical thinkers, lawyers often write surprisingly disorganized prose. Ask a lawyer what he or she intends to say, and you usually get a crisp, simple answer. Somehow, though, in the process of transferring that thought to writing, the clarity vanishes. Take this opening to a brief, filed in the U.S. Court of Appeals for the Fifth Circuit and cited in Tom Goldstein and Jethro Lieberman's *The Lawyer's Guide to Writing Well:*

> Appellee initially filed a motion to strike appendices to brief for appellant. . . . Appellant filed a brief in response, which appellee replied to. Appellant has subsequently filed another brief on this motion, Appellant's Reply to Appellant's Brief in Response to Appellee's Motion to Strike Appendices to Brief for Appellant (appellant's most recent brief), to which the appellee herein responds.

A large part of the problem is the way lawyers organize and compose their material. Like everyone else, lawyers write in many ways. Some older lawyers still dictate off the top of their heads and then edit. Others ponder the matter and draw up a lengthy outline. Still others discuss the issue with a colleague and try several lead sentences before finally hitting the screen and dashing off a few paragraphs in a blaze of glory. Many just write in a kind of stream-of-consciousness style.

If a method works for you and you can't conceive of doing things any other way, stick with your habit. Tradition has it that Ernest Hemingway used to sharpen close to twenty pencils and then go for a walk before writing. That said, however, one method of organization has tended to work well for legal writers in the past.

First, you must have a clear idea of what you're going to say before you begin to write. Compare it to driving: If you're going to travel from New York to Washington and you get into the car without having figured out what route you're taking, you may still eventually arrive in Washington. The problem is that you may take your passengers to Albany or Providence before you finally get your bearings and head for Washington in the most direct fashion.

To get your direction straight, outlining can help. Yet not just any outline will do. Rather, before you sit down to write anything, whether it's a four-line e-mail or a thirty-page brief, you should ask: If I had to condense my message to two or three sentences, what would those sentences be? If the judge or reader stopped me on the street and said, "I only have about a half a minute, so who are you, what do you want, and why?" Having figured out those two or three sentences, you're ready to write and something more. Those first few sentences should be the first paragraph of any document. *In legal writing, we should always lead with our conclusions or a summary.*

Good lawyers do this all the time. Here's how one advocate appealing a criminal conviction began her brief (the names have been changed):

> The State's entire case against Max Hugo turned on Trooper
> Dora Clayhorn's testimony about her success in disguising

herself as a college student, entering the enclosed porch of appellant's home uninvited, proceeding into his living room, and there soliciting the sale of a quarter-gram of cocaine for only $25.00. That evidence was admitted only because the district court declined to suppress it as the fruit of an unlawful search, ruling that the New York police may target an individual and invite themselves to his residence for an undercover sting operation within the sanctity of his own home without a warrant and without any probable cause to believe either that appellant was selling drugs from his home or that he was even selling drugs at all.

Whether the government may roam at large in people's homes as freely as it did in this case is an issue of first impression in this Court.

Or, take this introductory paragraph of the Statement in a Supreme Court brief filed by Andrew Frey and Evan Trager, among others, in *Wachovia Bank, National Association v. Daniel Schmidt III, et al.*, 546 US 1001 (2005):

This case concerns the meaning of 28 U.S.C. §1348, which provides that, for purposes of diversity jurisdiction, national banks are treated as citizens "of the states in which they are respectively located." At the time that Section 1348 and its predecessor statutes were enacted, all corporations, including state-chartered banks, were regarded as citizens of only a *single* state for diversity purposes. Here, however, the Fourth Circuit held that Section 1348 treats national banks as "located" in, and therefore as citizens of, *all* states in which they operate branches. Under its analysis, national banks may be citizens of multiple states across the country, and therefore have an access to the diversity jurisdiction of the federal courts that is uniquely *limited* as compared to their state-chartered competitors and other corporations. This holding is not dictated by the statutory language, was not intended by Congress, and is wholly illogical. It should be set aside.

Most lawyers find it terribly difficult to come up with an approximation of these initial sentences. After all, we're taught from day one in law school that nothing is black or white—everything is a shade of gray. "If you want to understand this, Your Honor," we seem to say, "please sit down for four hours while I explain to you every nuance, detail, and comma." There's no truth but the whole truth, or so we think. Moreover, the essence of an academic paper is to take a two-page idea and write about it for twenty-five pages. In law school, we are trained to write like law professors composing law review articles. That's the genre, as the late Judge Harold Leventhal of the U.S. Court of Appeals for the D.C. Circuit once said, that spends thirty pages describing a problem you never knew existed and then spends fifty pages explaining why it will never be solved.

It's not just law school that reinforces this tendency. Throughout our schooling, almost all of us are taught to compose using a version of what might be called "the Western scientific method." Like a scientist, we see our job as sifting through all the evidence objectively, eventually delivering an impartial conclusion at the end.

Of course, the method makes sense in science, where we don't want our prejudices to cloud our findings. But communication isn't a science, even if economists and lawyers try to pretend their analysis is grounded in something equally pure. Moreover, in the real world, no one would think of presenting information that way. If you're trying to tell me a book to read or movie to see, you begin by saying, "You should read *Catcher in the Rye*," explain why, and then go home. You don't begin, "The question is what book should you read?" then analyze the history of books, literary taste, and other topics before concluding with a recommendation on page 75—unless you're writing an academic paper or exam, of course. Law school merely reinforces these tendencies.

The more highly educated and the older you are, the more you've been trained to write linearly—from beginning to middle to end. By and large, however, people don't read that way anymore—at least on computers and at least in the legal-business world. In those worlds, the core of effective communication and argument, at least initially, is simplification. Unless readers know right up front where you're heading and why, it's very difficult for them to follow what you're saying, much less be convinced by it.

I understand lawyers' reluctance to commit themselves to those first few sentences. However, even though it seems difficult at first, anything can be condensed to such a summary. Take the U.S. Department of Justice antitrust action against Microsoft in the late 1990s. It was complicated by many issues, and there was probably enough discovery in the case to fill hundreds of boxes. Still, if you were arguing that case for the government, you could try to boil it down to this issue: Can Microsoft use its near monopoly on one product, Windows, to force consumers to take another, integrated product they may not want?

Or take Herman Melville's *Moby-Dick*. Sure it's long, but essentially it's a novel about a group of sailors from Massachusetts who chase a giant white whale, eventually find it, and harpoon it while Captain Ahab gets chained to it. I know Melville would be terribly upset with such a condensation, yet even this one sentence gives us a rough sense of the novel.

What we're doing here is similar to what journalists are supposed to do when they apply the "pyramid style" to a story, leading with the five "w's"—*who, what, when, where, why*—plus *how.* Not all six will be relevant each time, of course, but they provide a good starting point. Or, think of it as an upside-down triangle.

After the first paragraph, the reader has gotten, say, 50 percent of the meaning; after the next paragraph, another 20 percent, and so on with diminishing returns until the story finishes.

Or, take an example from your own legal experience. When you read a case in a bound legal reporter, undoubtedly you look at the headnotes first. They give you a brief idea of what the case means, which makes it easier to read. By leading with your conclusion as you write, you give readers a similar set of headnotes.

Why is it important for legal writers to lead with their conclusions? There are four main reasons.

It's more convincing. Basically, writers have two ways to present an argument or explanation to a reader. With the first method—the one lawyers usually use because it's the way they were trained to write academic papers—you lay out your evidence or examples and then draw a definitive conclusion at the end. In contrast, using our recommended second method, you tell the reader the bottom line briefly up front and go on to explain how the evidence supports this conclusion.

This is precisely what University of Minnesota Law School professor Judith Younger did in an excellent *amicus* brief filed in the Minnesota Supreme Court in the case of *In Re the Marriage of: McKee-Johnson v. Johnson,* 444 N.W.2d 259 (1989). She began:

> I submit this brief at the invitation of the Court (Order of Dec. 1, 1988). It deals with a single issue: the meaning of Minn. Stat. §519.11. The Court of Appeals held that the statute precludes antenuptial agreements dealing with marital property. That holding is wrong. The language of the statute, its legisla-

tive history, and the failure of the legislature to repeal Minn. Stat. §518.54 (5) (e) all support the opposite conclusion, that is that antenuptial agreements dealing with marital property are still permissible in Minnesota if they comply with the requirements set forth in §519.11 and the common law. If the Court of Appeals' interpretation of §519.11 is allowed to stand the usefulness of antenuptial agreements in Minnesota will be severely diminished, the freedom of Minnesota couples to contract will be impaired, and Minnesota law will be inconsistent with that of most other states.

You can see that this second form of argument or explanation is more convincing and understandable to a first-time reader. After all, each argument seems to head in the same direction. In contrast, with the first method, you have to read the analysis once to see what it means and then several more times to see if it makes sense. Legal arguments or explanations should not be like an O. Henry or Maupassant short story, where you get to page 19 and suddenly exclaim, "Now I know what he meant— what a surprise!" Yet legal documents frequently read that way because they back into their main points.

You've probably heard the truism "First impressions leave the strongest impressions." Like most truisms, that's true. It's reminiscent of a story old lawyers like to tell about the late Judge Henry Friendly of the U.S. Court of Appeals for the Second Circuit. "I've got five arguments I'd like to make," a lawyer began in oral argument. Judge Friendly put up his hand. "Just give me your best one," he said. That's the way our readers think: They want the key information in the beginning, and it's important for you to give it to them.

Thus, if you're writing a memo or e-mail and begin a middle paragraph, "Most important . . ." you've written a bad memo or e-mail. If it's "most important," put it first; don't bury it.

It's easier to read the first time. As lawyers, we often get too close to our material. We've been living with it for months, sometimes even years, so we forget what it's like for someone else to read about this unfamiliar matter. Forcing yourself to condense your material to your conclusion and then explain further is a good grounding mechanism. It puts you in a mode of explication where you don't lose the proverbial forest for the trees but you also don't leave out key facts a first-time reader needs to understand the matter.

A hasty or distracted reader can still understand it. In school, we get the impression that our readers will carefully savor each sentence we write. This is hardly true, especially in the electronic age. Numerous studies have shown that online—and especially on smart phones—people no longer read linearly as they once did, nor do they read with nearly the same engagement. In the "old days" (ten years ago), it was said that it was hard to read and do anything else. Today, we read while we're talking on the phone, or watching *CSI*, or trying to cook dinner. The word of the age is "multitasking"—shorthand for the idea that I'm paying attention to very little while giving the impression that I'm intently following five things. The result is a readership that is terribly distracted and whose attention wanders the longer they have to read any one document. Jakob Nielsen, an expert on Web technology, has found that online, only 16% of readers read word-by-word; instead they skim. Once readers have learned this method, they increasingly apply it to everything they read, including hard copy.

"Once I was a scuba diver in a sea of words," Nicholas Carr, author of "Is Google Making Us Stupid?," wrote. "Now I zip along the surface like a guy on a Jet Ski."

What's more, the e-age has increased the amount we read. Judge Alex Kozinski of the U.S. Court of Appeals for the Ninth Circuit once estimated that he has to read 3,500 pages a month. The workload of a lawyer is no less. All this is the equivalent of a Tolstoy novel a week—and what we're reading, of course, isn't

Tolstoy. If you don't get to the point quickly and convincingly, chances are your readers won't be hanging around until you do.

A dim-witted reader will understand it too. Let's be honest: At least some judges and lawyers aren't terribly bright. These readers are probably not going to understand much of what you say under any circumstances. If you lead with a simple statement of your conclusion, at least they get the most important information.

So for all these reasons, lead with your conclusion. There's a saying in the military: Tell them what you're going to tell them; tell them; tell them what you just told them. The same principle applies here. If you can relate the argument in a way that hooks the reader, so much the better. That's what Andrew L. Frey and Evan Tager did in this case in Arkansas trial court:

> There is an old riddle: Which weighs more, a ton of feathers or a ton of bricks? While many find the question deceptive at first, the correct answer, that a ton is a ton regardless of what is being weighed, becomes irrefutably clear once explained. But in enacting and now defending the NR exemption, the State has managed to get the answer wrong—a ton of soybeans or chicken feed is treated as though it weighs less than a ton of baked beans or dog food.

The problem with a lot of legal writing is that it meanders for pages before quickly coming to a definitive conclusion in the closing moments. If you want to write in that fashion, so be it. If you do, however, you should cut about the first seven-eighths of everything you write and then reorganize. We passengers don't want to sit in the car while you're figuring out what to do. We just want to get to the destination as quickly as possible.

II. Organizing Your Workplace Around Eight Rules

The law, William Prosser once wrote, is "one of the principal literary professions. One might hazard the supposition that the average lawyer in the course of a lifetime does more writing than a novelist." Yet we lawyers don't usually think of ourselves as professional writers. Once we do, it helps to approach writing as other seasoned experts do, by applying the following eight maxims.

1. Remember that most writing difficulties are organizational difficulties.

"Every writer I know has trouble writing," said the novelist Joseph Heller. It's one key way we present ourselves to the world, and a certain amount of apprehension comes with the territory.

Sometimes, however, that anxiety can be paralyzing. This may seem oversimple, but if you think you have writer's block or are taking too long to write, the problem is probably that you're spending too much time writing (or trying to) and not enough time thinking.

Reflection is a key part of the composition process. Novelists don't take long daily strolls because they're all trying to walk off hangovers. They understand as professional writers that writers have to work through what they have to say, both consciously and subconsciously. Yes, lawyers are busy, but the more you try to short-circuit the process of reflection, the harder you are likely to make it for yourself.

"Writing is thinking. To write well is to think clearly," the well-known historian David McCullough has said. "That's why it's so hard."

As a onetime litigator, I understand the problem. You tell yourself, "If I can just get this committed to a draft, I'll feel so much better about myself, and I can change it later!" And it's true that some who suffer from writer's block have a fear of being judged, and getting something down does launch them. Yet you know what happens: Ten other things crop up and you don't have time to make the necessary changes. Moreover, it's human nature for writers to fall in love with their own prose, first draft or not. Computers have been wonderful boons to writing because they make it so easy to edit, but the new ease of revision has also encouraged many writers to begin drafts before they're ready—and to be less critical of their work than they should be.

I've also noticed two other odd notions circulating among attorneys. "I was taught in grammar school to use the writing process as a voyage of self-discovery, to find what I think," one lawyer once told me. That may be true in the world of fiction writing, but not in this endeavor. The legal universe is a highly competitive, fast-moving world where readers prize well-planned, concentrated bursts of information. Another said, "If I'm writing a brief, I can bill that to a client, but if I'm thinking about what I'm going to write, I can't bill that." That lawyer was wrong. Clients are paying you to think as well as to write. Do so.

2. Writing is something that most people do best alone.

"All you need is a room without any particular interruptions," the writer John Dos Passos once advised. Yet a solitary approach to composition runs against the group nature of most legal practice. Lawyers tend to work on cases in teams. They attack problems the way Ulysses Grant fought the Civil War—by throwing divisions at them.

Consultation with colleagues in the formative stages of writing and in editing can be of great use. When crunch time comes, however, your coworkers can be distracting. The more you allow yourself to be interrupted or to take calls or check e-mail, the harder you're going to find it to get started and keep going.

3. Turn off the Internet.

There's a saying that's been floating around for years now: Good writing is 3 percent inspiration and 97 percent turning off the Internet. There's a lot of truth in the adage. Yes, it helps to be able to do research immediately, but the value of instant research is far outweighed by the distractions the Web poses, which are far more alluring than those writers have faced before. Write now; look it up later. Otherwise, you'll be interrupting yourself all the time.

4. Most writers need a regular time to compose.

The process of free association that makes writing effective is very different from the act of "thinking like a lawyer." Thus, most good legal writers need to create a routine in which they establish regular periods of isolation—say, every morning from ten to twelve, when they can go to a library without phones. Writing is like exercise: The more you make it part of an everyday schedule, the easier it becomes.

"Serious writers write, inspired or not," Ralph Keyes once wrote. "Over time they discover that routine is a better friend to them than inspiration."

5. The person who does the research should do the writing.

Lawyers frequently have others do their research. It's as if two reporters were sent to the Middle East to spend weeks researching the continual political crisis there. On their return, you wouldn't debrief them and then write the article yourself; you'd ask them to present their own findings. While discreet questions can be assigned to others, the process of research is usually inseparable from the process of writing, because we use our research to determine not only what we will say but how we will say it.

It's true that research is time-consuming. For most writers, however, that expenditure of time comes with the territory. When Leo Tolstoy set out to write *War and Peace,* he could have looked at the size of the project, hired thirty researchers, and, like many senior partners, spent his days meeting with clients and colleagues. If he had done that, his final text wouldn't have been the *War and Peace* we know and love; it would have been an inferior novel. So it goes with legal documents. Writing quickly and writing well tend to be somewhat contradictory propositions.

6. Don't divide the drafting of a document among many writers.

Lawyers seem to think they can magically split the work of writing among many with no damage to the final product. It's no surprise that in the overwhelming majority of such cases, the final draft has no one style.

Of course, some people are terrific researchers, ghostwriters, and speechwriters. Theodore Sorensen worked so well with President John F. Kennedy that after a while it was often hard to discern where Sorensen stopped and Kennedy began. Yet it took years to forge that relationship and its mutual style. If law offices insist on parceling out research and encouraging ghostwriting, they should find lawyers with compatible styles and have them work together for years so they learn one another's styles and work habits.

In my travels, I've noticed a sentiment in law offices that writing should be left to associates while the partners supervise. Unfortunately, the same attitude seems to pervade the judiciary, where much of the writing is left to the clerks. This makes little sense, though I understand the pressure judges feel when they have to turn out dozens of opinions a year in complex matters. In the rest of the culture, however, people recognize that the older one gets, the better one becomes as a writer. The owners of the Globe Theatre didn't go to William Shakespeare when he turned thirty-five, make him a partner so he could spend his time meeting with rich contributors, and take him out of the playwriting business. They understood that he still had his best years ahead of him. If litigators and judges aren't writing their own briefs and opinions—which is, after all, the most important work they do—what message does that send?

Younger lawyers and clerks may not be in a position to change the way the work they do gets parceled out. If nothing else, though, they should understand that any form of literature that is composed as most legal documents are will turn out to be awful. Treat writing as a commodity rather than a craft, and the results are predictable.

7. Don't stop when you're stuck; instead stop when you don't want to.

This rule seems counterintuitive. The tendency is to stop when you're stymied, figuring that the path ahead will come to you later. But often it won't, and you've now created a formidable obstacle to beginning again. No one wants to sit in front of an empty screen, trying to figure out where to go next.

Instead, stop when you've got a full head of steam, reasonably sure of the next two or three things you want to say. Stopping may be painful, but you're now in a position the next time you sit down to begin writing. Hemingway used to stop writing in the middle of a sentence for the same reason; it gave him an easy place to begin again. You don't have to go as far as he did in creating an incentive the next time you sit down, but the example is a good one.

8. Keep a notebook and learn from other lawyers.

If writers learn by emulation, law students are taught early on to model themselves on judges. That's a mistake. The task of a judge is very different from that of a lawyer, and the differences surface in the writing of each. The job of a litigator is to persuade a judge or a group of them; the job of a judge is to decree, and to persuade a very different group of readers (lawyers, litigants, other judges) more subtly, without appearing to be persuading. The lawyer traffics in conflict, the judge in solutions. The lawyer writes for a small or even a single audience; the judge, in theory, writes for a larger one. Yes, Brandeis should be required reading for every law student. But it is Brandeis the advocate, not Brandeis the judge or law-review author, who ought to be the role model. Besides, most judges are poor writers, in part because they farm out much of what they have to write to clerks who don't know what they're doing, and in part because no one ever gives them the editorial feedback they need to improve.

As the poet once put it, a good artist borrows; a great artist steals. One of the great deficiencies of legal education—and there are many—is that most students still graduate without ever having read more than a smattering of good writing by practicing lawyers. It would be hard to find a business school professor who hated capitalism and finance, or a medical school professor who had never met a patient. Yet the elite law schools are full of professors who have never practiced law and look down on those who do.

Practicing lawyers who keep a notebook including impressive documents they have read can start to remedy that. It's easier now than ever, since smart phones can function as mininotebooks. In the same way that labor or environmental lawyers follow decisions in their specialties, legal writers ought to observe carefully what their colleagues are writing and learn to incorporate their better ideas. While you don't want to plagiarize, keeping a regular written record of phrases or approaches that others have used successfully is one of the best ways to learn how to improve your writing. Law offices, too, should provide their attorneys with examples of what they consider to be well-written briefs, memos, and even e-mails. A "house style" isn't a necessity, but it wouldn't hurt either.

Jodi Picoult and Stephen King may not be America's greatest writers, but they are productive, turning out hundreds of pages a year. If, however, you put them in the conditions under which most lawyers try to write—grabbing a few minutes on the run, with the phone constantly ringing, their days scheduled to the last minute, no role models—they wouldn't be able to get much good writing done either. The more you can try to remember the precepts outlined in this chapter, the easier you will make it for yourself as a legal writer.

CHAPTER 2

The Rules of the Road

I. The Overview: The Importance of Basic Principles, Especially in the Internet Age

II. Your High School English Teacher Knew Best: Employing the First Nine Key Rules of Legal Composition

1. Use strong verbs.

2. Eliminate legal jargon.

3. Write clearly and simply, while keeping things as short as possible.

4. Don't hedge. If you must hedge, explain why.

5. Keep your sentences to twenty-five words or less.

6. Move most subordinate clauses to the beginnings or ends of sentences.

7. Write for your readers, not for yourself.

8. Use specific imagery, not vague generalities.

9. Remember that understated prose is the best form of expression.

III. The Tenth Rule: Use Simple Language

IV. The Eleventh Rule: Use the Tools of the New Age

I. The Overview: The Importance of Basic Principles, Especially in the Internet Age

Getting organized is the first step in writing. Yet even lawyers who structure their material well often find that their prose suffers from a common set of problems. Their sentences begin to resemble the Code of Federal Regulations. They keep throwing around phrases such as *res ipsa loquitur*, which few readers can understand and even fewer can relate to.

We all know there are basic principles in learning to write anything well. Authors have devoted entire books to the subject: William Zinsser's *On Writing Well*, William Strunk and E. B. White's *The Elements of Style*, and Joseph Williams's *Style* are some of my favorites, and their tracks are all over this chapter. Legal writers should also make Bryan Garner's *A Dictionary of Modern Legal Usage* one of their primary reference books; his work is the source of some of the examples of bad legal writing (which Garner culled from other sources) used throughout this book.

It is true that the edict to make it "plain and simple"—embodied in these books and in "rules of writing" promulgated by George Orwell and others—is the product of an earlier era. Some, such as writers Adam Haslett and Stanley Fish, have recently argued that these rhetoricians have moved writing too far in the direction of simplicity, forsaking the beauty of well-crafted and more ornate prose.

They have a point, but it doesn't apply much to lawyers' writing, and does so even less to prose composed to be read on a computer at work. I've seen very few lawyers whose writing was too simple. The problem is almost always that the sentences are too long, the prose too ornate, the verbs too weak. Moreover, while elaborate prose has its place, that place is not the smart phone or computer, where readers skim as much as they read. As Brenda Wineapple wrote in the *American Scholar,* "Americans have traditionally gravitated to a plain and simple style—the down-to-earth, the real, the concrete, and the unpretentious, which are presumably the most American." To write in another fashion is to misjudge your audience.

Here, we will spend only a few pages on eleven important principles of composition as they apply specifically to your writing. Some you'll recall as you compose your initial draft. Since you are going to want to concentrate on the substance of your message as you write, however, many are probably better applied in the editing process, discussed in the next chapter.

II. Your High School English Teacher Knew Best: Employing the First Nine Key Rules of Legal Composition

Pedantic as they may appear to be, here are the first nine principles of writing that you need to remember. You may have learned them in high school English class years ago, but reading endless opinions as a lawyer tends to obliterate even the finest education. While nine rules may seem like a lot, they have special—and easy—application to legal and business writing and many apply even more in the e-age when nuance and indirection are increasingly lost on readers.

1. Use strong verbs.

Use active verbs far more than passive verbs. Take the sentence "Jane kicked the ball." "Kicked" is a verb in the active voice. Contrast that with the sentence "The ball was kicked by Jane." "Was kicked" is in the passive voice. A good writer uses the passive voice around 25 percent of the time and even less in e-mail and other related documents. Lawyers, however, tend to use it at least half the time, with law professors often coming in at close to a 90 percent clip.

One example from a typical legal memo should suffice (citations are omitted):

> Restitution on grounds of mistake is most commonly allowed when both parties are mistaken as to some fact material to the transaction. Traditionally, a unilateral mistake is grounds for recovery only if enforcement of the contract would be unconscionable, or if the other party had reason to know of the mistake. . . . All these black-letter rules are founded on the equitable principle of unjust enrichment.

Though much of the legal jargon could be eliminated as well, simply changing the verbs does this:

> Courts allow restitution on grounds of mistake only when both parties err as to some fact material to the transaction. A party can recover for a unilateral mistake only in an unconscionable contract, or if the mistake was apparent. . . . The underlying equitable principle of unjust enrichment defines these black-letter rules.

Why are lawyers so wedded to the passive voice? It's often a way of removing the writer from the action, thus appearing to be more official and impartial. Certainly judges use it for that reason since they don't want to say, "This is my judgment," but rather "This judgment was forced upon me by the precedent." The passive removes the personal, replacing it with the scholastic.

But for the rest of us (with a few exceptions), it's a lousy way to write. "All fine prose is based on the verbs carrying the sentence," wrote F. Scott Fitzgerald. If your verbs are weak, so is your prose.

Writers implicitly recognize this weakness, so if they use the passive voice often, they tend to add a number of adjectives and adverbs to compensate. That just makes matters worse, cluttering the page. A writer clinging to the passive also tends to leave out some of the main information. "This action was filed in the Southern District of New York," writes the litigator, never bothering to tell us who filed it. True, the information may be obvious from what's gone before, but you're still asking readers to put the pieces together. A few similar passive sentences and those readers give up: You're asking them to do too much work. The passive voice "sanitizes and institutionalizes [lawyers'] writing and often anesthetizes the reader," former U.S. Court of Appeals judge Patricia Wald once complained. "All views are attributable to an unknowable 'it.' "

In legal writing, you should avoid the passive voice in most cases for two additional reasons. First, think about how you give directions. When someone asks how to find a certain landmark, you tell her, "Take I-95. Get off at Exit 28. Go to the third light and make a right. Proceed two miles." Without even thinking about it, you give the directions in the active voice—"take," "get off," "go," "make," and "proceed." If you gave the directions in the passive voice (and you never would)—"I-95 should be taken. Exit 28 should be traversed"—few would find the landmark.

Legal writing is often a form of giving directions. You're telling clients what they should do or telling courts what reasoning you'd like them to apply. As with directions, if you write in the passive voice, your readers can't even begin to figure out what you're saying.

Second, the purpose of rhetoric and advertising is quite similar to that of legal writing. In each, the writer is often exhorting readers, attempting to persuade them. Yet speechwriters and writers of ad copy rarely, if ever, use the passive voice. It's "Tastes Great—Less Filling," not "It should be tasted because it is less filling." "Just Do It," commands Nike. If the slogan were "It should just be done!" it's hard to imagine anyone would buy Nike's products.

This is true of rhetoric as well. "Ask not what your country can do for you, ask what you can do for your country," said President Kennedy in his famous inaugural address, in 1961. I can't even begin to put that sentence in the passive voice. "Yes, we can," said Barack Obama in his 2008 campaign, in notable contrast to "It can be done by us." "I have a dream," said Dr. Martin Luther King, Jr., in 1963, in perhaps the most famous American speech in modern times. If King had gone to law school, he might have proclaimed, "A dream has been had by me." It's not the same.

Still, the passive voice obviously has its uses. If you want the reader to focus on the object of an action, the passive voice enables you to encourage this. ("The pedestrian was struck.") This works if we don't really care who was driving the car. And if you're a lawyer representing the "who" who did the "what" to the "whom," the passive voice is your friend. "Smith fired the gun," the prosecutor should write. "The gun was fired," aptly counters the defense attorney, implying that causation is lacking. The problem is that many of the prosecution or plaintiffs' briefs I read use the passive voice too. By doing so, these lawyers undercut their case.

Politicians speak in the passive voice all the time, in just such a defensive posture. "Mistakes were made," they'll announce, leaving the impression that someone else made them.

"[T]he Chinese Embassy was inadvertently damaged," said Bill Clinton after NATO bombed the embassy during the Balkan conflict in 1999. John Leo, a former columnist for *U.S. News & World Report*, once wrote that the passive voice is "a terrific screen to conceal choices, responsibility, and moral conflicts." If that's your goal—and it rarely should be—by all means use the passive.

Remember two other points as corollaries. First, avoid weak verbs. Verbs like "seems," "suggests," "appears," and "is" do not convey as much action as others. Occasionally we need to use these weaker verbs: "She *is* a woman" is better than "She *constitutes* a woman." Many times, though, lawyers adopt constructions in which the weak verbs can be eliminated. "It was Justice Kagan who said" can be changed to "Justice Kagan said." "He will be a participant" can be revised to "He will participate."

Second, avoid the use of the generic passive. "It is widely known," writes the lawyer, never bothering to tell us who widely knows it. Try to identify your subjects for your readers. Otherwise, there's too much room for ambiguity. As the noted Canadian justice John Laskin wrote, "[F]orget the wind up, and make the pitch."

2. Eliminate legal jargon.

Lawyers use a lot of odd words and phrases that no one else uses and few understand. Your writing should pass what I call "the McDonald's test." If you were to read the document you're drafting aloud in McDonald's, would people understand what you're saying? If not, your prose is too removed from ordinary language. Pretend that you are writing for a nonlegal audience that will not understand terms such as "caveat" and "ex parte." If you do, you'll find that your prose is clearer and that you are often using jargon as an excuse for failing to explain yourself.

Your style and choice of words should be as conversational

and contemporary as possible. That's why many writers read their work out loud when they are editing or even writing. "I read primarily to my wife, Yolanda, and I also have a friend whom I read to. I read aloud so I can hear if it's fitting together or not," the noted writer John McPhee told the *Paris Review*.

For example, some lawyers like to use a lot of ancient verbiage, such as "heretofore," "hereunder," and "said document." That sounds great for those living in London circa 1590, but such prose, even in formal documents, creates a barrier between writer and reader. You would never go to the counter in McDonald's and say, "Said milk shake—I will quaff it!" So don't write that way either, as one litigator did: "It all fully appears from the affidavit of the publisher thereof heretofore herein filed."

Lawyers also use a lot of Latin. Some of it is a convenient form of shorthand, as in the use of *habeas corpus* or *res judicata*. A lot of it is unnecessary, however. When I see *infra* and *supra*, I still end up turning the wrong way. (Why not just give the page number?) Similarly, in McDonald's, you'd never announce, "Assuming, *arguendo*, I don't get the burger but the fish filet." A bilingual debate is going on in this country, but it isn't about Latin and English any longer, a fact a judge on the Illinois Appeals Court must have forgotten when he earned a *Scribes Journal of Legal Writing* "Legaldegook Award" by writing, "*Parens patriae* cannot be *ad fundaban jurisdictionem*. The zoning question is *res inter alios acta*." (See *Mississippi Bluff Hotel v. County of Rock Island*, 420 N.E.2d 748, 751 [Ill. App. Ct. 1981].)

Finally, lawyers use a lot of odd words they would never think of using in ordinary speech. "In the instant case," they write, meaning, one supposes, that if you mix powder with milk, you get a case. Or they write, "This case is on all fours with another case." Whenever I see such a phrase, my instinct is to help the case get on its feet. If you were talking with a friend over coffee, you'd say, "This case is consistent with that case," or "It's a lot like this other case." You should write the same way.

Eliminating jargon is a particular problem for law students and paralegals (as well as prisoners arguing *pro se*), who become fascinated with the new words and concepts they are learning in their introduction to the profession. Everything they read, including the work of their professorial role models, encourages them to compose in this pretentious style. Take, for example, this typical passage from an article in the *Harvard Law Review:*

> The hermeneutic tradition suggests that historical disconti-
> nuities are so substantial that interpretivism must make inco-
> herent claims because it can achieve the necessary determinacy
> of past intentions only at the cost of an implausible claim about
> consistency of meaning across time.

I know someone else who is making incoherent claims.

An editor can't even begin to rewrite this sentence so people can understand it. Yet a lot of legal literature—both inside academia and beyond—is composed of texts, opinions, treatises, and articles written in this befuddled prose. Not only does the profession write in this incoherent style, it elevates the style to the pages of its leading law reviews.

3. Write clearly and simply, while keeping things as short as possible.

Like most writers, lawyers should convey the maximum amount of information in the fewest number of words. Unfortunately, legal writing tends to be full of clutter, no matter how eminent the writer. I once heard a story about a law graduate who went to clerk for the great Judge Jerome Frank, of the U.S. Court of Appeals for the Second Circuit. On his first day, Judge Frank gave him a fifteen-page opinion to review and edit. The clerk pored over the draft, anxious to do a good job, and found it extremely wordy and repetitive. After a week, he returned the draft to the judge, the fifteen rambling pages cut to three tight ones.

For a week he heard nothing. Finally Judge Frank stuck his head inside the clerk's office. "I really like the three pages you wrote," he said to the clerk. "Just add them to the beginning of my opinion."

In *On Writing Well*, a wonderful book all writers should read, William Zinsser pointed out:

> Consider all the prepositions that are routinely draped onto verbs that don't need any help. Head up. Free up. Face up to. We no longer head committees. We head them up. We don't face problems anymore. We face up to them when we can free up a few minutes. A small detail, you may say—not worth bothering about. It is worth bothering about. The game is won or lost on hundreds of small details.

Coming up with broad categories that encompass these small details isn't easy. Here are six.

a. Eliminate redundancies.

Lawyers tend to be repetitious, presenting the same idea continually in the hope that readers will remember. This constant repetition is one reason that legal prose is as boring as it is.

In sentence construction too, lawyers often add a lot of superfluities. "The accident occurred at twelve noon," writes the young associate. Can it be noon at any other hour? You don't need the "twelve." "She testified about her past memories," writes the litigator. Last I looked, memories were always about the past. "The armed gunman entered the bank," the prosecutor's brief announces. Someone should tell that prosecutor: All gunmen are armed—it's part of the job description. Legal writing has hundreds of similar redundancies. Eliminate them.

b. Substitute a word for a phrase.

Even if lawyers think that they are not using ancient jargon, there's a place where they probably are. When using conjunctions and prepositions, lawyers tend to use several words when one would do. As others, such as the legal scholar Robert Smith, have pointed out, substitute "because" for "due to the fact that"; "can" for "is able to"; "under" for "pursuant to"; "if" for "in the event that"; "after" for "subsequent to"; "before" for "prior to"; "previously" for "at an earlier date"; "about" for "approximately," and "too many" for "an excessive number of." The practice undoubtedly arose when barristers and solicitors hired scriveners to do their writing for them and these scriveners were paid by the word, not the hour. But that's hardly a justification for our doing the same.

c. Avoid euphemisms.

Using professional double-speak almost always adds extra words. An Interior Department press release once referred to a nest as an "owl site center." In the 1980s, the State Department stopped using the word "killing" in its human rights reports, replacing it with "unlawful or arbitrary deprivation of life."

Lawyers and government bureaucrats are not alone in this. A ticket collector on London's Heathrow Express is now part of the "onboard customer service team." As Johnson, *The Economist*'s language columnist, has noted, the airline industry is a particular offender, asking us to "deplane," put our electronic devices "in the off position," and put our seats "in the full upright and locked position." And, as *The Economist Style Guide* points out, interest-group politics have transformed the deaf into the "hearing-impaired," the elderly into "senior citizens," and the poor into "the disadvantaged."

Using this kind of double-speak can also be a form of lying, as George Orwell warned in his famous essay "Politics and the English Language." The statute dealing with suits for nuclear accidents refers to such accidents as "incidents." Politicians may think that calling a tax increase "revenue enhancement" is a way to avoid unpleasantness. The more you try to cushion the truth with weasel words, though, the harder it is to deal directly with what you're trying to address.

I once heard a story that when an exterminator was sued for spreading a chemical negligently, the term "exterminator" was evidently too direct for the attorney. Instead, the defendant was called a "rodent operative." I doubt the change in language helped one bit.

d. Eliminate unnecessary adjectives and adverbs.

If a writer's verbs are strong, he or she doesn't need as many adjectives and adverbs. So it goes for lawyers, even though they seem wedded to the notion that the more such words they use, the better. Too many adjectives and adverbs weaken writing, albeit for different reasons. "The adjective is the enemy of the noun; the adverb is the enemy of the verb," Judge John Minor Wisdom, a wonderful writer on the U.S. Court of Appeals for the Fifth Circuit, used to warn his clerks. "Adverbs are guilty until proven innocent," quipped Howard Ogden.

Take adjectives. The problem with them is that they're often ambiguous. "When the accident happened, it was a *cold* day," writes the typical legal writer. The problem with "cold" is that it means different things to different people: What's cold in Boston isn't what's cold in Palm Springs. If she had written instead, "When the accident happened, it was twenty-three degrees outside," or "Everyone was wearing down coats," you'd know the precise conditions. With adjectives, you don't.

Why are lawyers so fond of adjectives? Probably because legal standards and judges use them so much, talking about the "*reasonable* person" test in torts or the "*substantial* evidence" threshold in administrative law. Though it may sound cynical, judges use these terms precisely because they're trying to be vague. A "reasonable person" would do almost anything, which is a way of telling juries that they have wide latitude to decide these matters. As to that standard in administrative law, how much evidence is substantial? Four documents? Twenty-five? The reviewing courts invoking the standard don't know, and even if they did, they would never tell you. By using an adjective to define "evidence," they keep the standard vague enough so they can employ it as they choose and give themselves flexibility. If you're trying to be vague, use more adjectives. Usually, however, precision is the goal.

In a similar vein, policemen taught to write reports are frequently told to avoid adjectives unless they pertain to "direction, color, or amount," according to Ellen Collett in *The Writer's Chronicle.* "These are empirical adjectives," she writes. "Because they speak to precision of detail, they resist interpretation. 'The black Escalade fired 12 shots into the dwelling on 865 Inglewood Avenue' can mean only one thing."

Lawyers should avoid using too many adverbs for an additional reason. While adverbs obviously have their place—excuse me: while adverbs have their place—in the hands of lawyers they can become unnecessary tools of exaggeration and hyperbole. "The appellant's argument is totally without foundation," lawyers write, even though "without foundation" is sufficient. A brief to the U.S. Court of Appeals for the Seventh Circuit stated, "The Court boldly and enthusiastically stated that the concept of active/passive liability (indemnification) is not applicable to a trust relationship." As in all such matters, one has to question whether the judges were that bold and enthusiastic about this concept.

"Avoid false intensifiers," Justice Laskin has warned, citing "completely wrong," "absolutely," "unfounded," "very serious error," "clearly," "certainly," "it is important to note that," and "blatant violation." "These false intensifiers usually weaken rather than strengthen the force of your argument," he says.

e. Eliminate many transition words.

In their attempts to be and seem logical, lawyers add words such as "therefore," "thus," and "furthermore" to many sentences. It's a throwback to our school days. If your writing is logical, you don't need as many transition words. Whenever possible, cut them. That goes, too, for phrases such as "of course" and adverbs like "surprisingly," "predictably," "understandably," and "ironically." As Zinsser has noted, these "place a value on a sentence before the reader has a chance to read it. Readers . . . are not as dumb as the writer thinks; they must be given room to play their role in the act of writing—to discover for themselves what's surprising or predictable or understandable or ironic. They don't want that pleasure usurped."

f. Keep things short.

The major complaint I hear from judges, clients, and other lawyers about legal documents is that they're too long. "Many judges look first to see how long a document is before they read the first word," one confided in me. "They made me read twenty-five pages when they could have cut it to six," another complained, in an all-too-typical comment. Elmore Leonard, the mystery writer, once said that he has a rule he applies whenever he writes a novel. "I try to leave out the parts that people skip," he said.

That's a good rule for everyone. And it's an especially important one in the Internet age. Today there's a premium on brevity, since distracted readers tend to absorb less the longer they read—especially on a smart phone, where once readers begin to scroll at about the forty-word mark, their attention spans shrink. In a way, the task of a writer today is often akin to writing telegrams a generation or two ago, in which you were succinct because you paid for every word.

Or, better yet, writing e-mails today is more similar to texting than it is to essay-writing. *Shorter is inherently better.*

Unfortunately, lawyers love to throw in the parts other people skip—often right at the beginning, so the reader can't avoid it. For example, readers come to the second page of a brief or memo and have to confront a four-paragraph block quote. The late *New York Times* columnist and language cop William Safire characterized things like this as a MEGO—My Eyes Glaze Over. Once readers fall into that stupor, they don't snap out of it easily. Your job as a writer is to grab readers by the lapels and make them read for as long as you can.

Many judges have told me that when they confront documents, the question is not *whether* they'll read them but *how* they'll read them. If a brief hasn't gotten to the main point in a paragraph or two, the mind begins to wander.

Of course, lawyers don't want to leave out information that could aid their cause, and sometimes it's better to err on the side of caution by being overinclusive. If that's the case, at least prioritize your points and put the questionable material toward the back. It's better to make pages 15 through 30 superfluous than to mix the superfluity throughout, because then the reader has to go through all the extraneous information to get to the heart of the matter.

"There is but one art: to omit," the novelist Robert Louis Stevenson once wrote. Though in my view he could have omitted a good deal of the text in *Treasure Island*, his advice was sound.

4. Don't hedge. If you must hedge, explain why.

Lawyers can be paranoid writers, using words such as "seems," "appears," and "maybe" throughout their writing. In a profession that demands exactitude, such words have their place and are essential. Lawyers, however, overuse them. The more you qualify what you say, the less you say. "Don't be kind of bold," Zinsser once wrote. "Be bold." Or as E. B. White put it, "Be obscure clearly."

Legislative and contractual drafters, complaints drafters,

and judges have good reasons to be paranoid writers. Other lawyers read what these individuals draft with an eye toward getting out of it. The job of construction for these writers is a painstaking process of plugging holes to assure that nothing can be misconstrued.

In other types of writing, however, judges, clients, and lawyers read our prose with no such jaundiced eye. While some assertions have to be qualified—in an opinion letter, for example—most don't. "No weasel words," Judge Wisdom cautioned in the primer he gave to clerks.

Still, lawyers hedge almost reflexively. "Apparently, it seems we can win this case," says the memo from the associate. Well, can we prevail or can't we? As Clark Welton has written, part of all this is also a trend in the language toward ambiguity, as in the constant use (mostly in spoken language) of "like," or in constructions such as "I felt sort of tired."

If you do have to hedge an assertion, always follow the qualifier with a sentence or clause that explains why. That's because a hedge introduces an ambiguity that must be clarified. "Apparently, we can win this case" could mean either "I'm not sure we can win this case," or "The law is not clear that we can win this case." Is the ambiguity in the mind of the writer or in the general state of affairs? To settle things, you might write, "Doubt is raised by a Connecticut case that went the other way." That follow-up sentence clarifies the uncertainty. Doing this will also compel you to hedge less, since few writers will follow by saying, "My doubt is raised by my terrible insecurity, which causes me to qualify everything!" Forcing yourself to explain your hedges will break the reflexive habit of legal paranoia.

Remember, too, that opinions can be qualified but facts should not be. To do otherwise is to undermine your authority as a writer. "Apparently we're in New York," makes no sense— either you are or you're not. The confusion often arises not only because lawyers become accustomed to hedging *everything,* but because we live in a culture in which the line between fact and opinion has dissipated. "The Steelers will win," shouts the ESPN analyst, when what he means, of course, is that he *thinks* they'll win. If you don't know a fact, don't hedge—find it out or somehow write around it. This includes altering the rather odd practice of drafting the facts in a complaint by constantly exclaiming, "Upon information and belief." Much of the time, don't be afraid just to allege it, if your information is sound. Minus the caveat, the worst that can usually happen is that the other side will deny it.

5. Keep your sentences to twenty-five words or less.

The basic rule is this: The more complicated your information is, the shorter your sentences should be. Legal data are frequently complex, so the least you can do for readers is to shorten your sentences and make the information easier to absorb.

Legal writers are famous for their lengthy sentences. None is longer, perhaps, than this one, quoted in the *Wall Street Journal*, from a stock purchasing offer mailed by Lyondell Acquisition Corp. to holders of Arco Chemical Co.:

> The Merger Agreement further provides that, without limiting the generality of the foregoing, from the date thereof until such time as Purchaser's designees shall constitute a majority of the Board of Directors of the Company, except as expressly contemplated or permitted by the Merger Agreement or the Disclosure Letter delivered by the Company to Lyondell and Purchaser concurrently with the execution and delivery of the Merger Agreement, or to the extent that Lyondell shall otherwise consent in writing, the Company will (a) use its commercially reasonable efforts to operate and maintain its business in all material respects only in the usual, regular and ordinary manner consistent with past practice (including undertaking scheduled or necessary "turnarounds" or other maintenance

work and including offsite storage, treatment and disposal of chemical substances generated prior to such time as Purchaser's designees shall constitute a majority of the Board of Directors of the Company) and, to the extent consistent with such operation and maintenance, use commercially reasonable efforts to preserve the present business organization of its business intact, keep available the services of, and good relations with, the present employees and preserve present relationships with all persons having business dealings with its business, except in each case for such matters that, individually and in the aggregate, do not and are not reasonably likely to have a material adverse effect on the Company and its subsidiaries taken as a whole and (b) except to the extent required by clause (a) above, the Company will not, and will not permit any of its subsidiaries to: . . . (iii) amend its Certificate of Incorporation or By-Laws or other comparable organizational documents; . . . (xi) waive any material rights or claims relating to the Company's business; (xii) accelerate vesting or conversion or approve the acceleration or conversion of any shares of restricted stock, except as provided in the Merger Agreement, or grant or approve the grant of any additional shares of restricted stock, phantom stock units, or stock options under any existing plan, except as provided in the Merger Agreement, or modify the term of any performance period or the performance objective to be attained for that performance period under any existing plan; or (xiii) authorize any of, or commit or agree to any of, the foregoing actions.

Even in its abridged form here, the sentence is 376 words long and counting.

No one wants to sound like Lt. Martin Castillo on the old TV show *Miami Vice*, for whom twenty-five words was a season's worth of dialogue. But that kind of brevity isn't going to happen in the legal enterprise. While an occasional long, well-constructed sentence does have its place, shorter is better.

6. Move most subordinate clauses to the beginnings or ends of sentences.

Take a basic sentence: "Jane filed the complaint." If you were to add a clause to that sentence, you should write, "*Before leaving for the weekend,* Jane filed the complaint," or "Jane filed the complaint *before leaving for the weekend.*" What lawyers should not write, but often do, is "Jane, *before leaving for the weekend,* filed the complaint." Or, worse, "Jane filed, *before leaving for the weekend,* the complaint."

The subject, verb, and object present the main information in most sentences. The clause is additional. Putting that clause in the middle makes it harder to read the sentence. So don't do it, unless you have a clause that has to go there because, say, it defines Jane. "Jane, *who likes to walk to the courthouse,* filed the complaint." In this case, the clause can't go at the end because it won't make sense there. In these cases, it's often better to separate the clause from the rest of the sentence not by commas but by dashes, as in "Jane—*who likes to walk to the courthouse*—filed the complaint." Yes, many of us were taught in grade school not to use dashes (the comma lobby probably got to the teachers' union). But in the Internet age, dashes stop a reader more than commas do—and that's all to the good.

7. Write for your readers, not for yourself.

We write for others. "Anything that is merely written to please the author is worthless," wrote Blaise Pascal. A story I once heard illustrates this principle. A professor was teaching a photography class and asked her students to bring her their best pictures each week so she could critique them. One student brought in a picture the teacher didn't particularly like. "It's interesting," she began, "but it's taken from such a distance you don't have a focus."

The next week the student returned with the same picture. "I like most of your work," the professor said, "but I saw this picture last week, and on second glance, the color in it isn't very good either."

The following week the student returned with the same picture. "I don't understand this," the professor said. "Every week you keep returning with the same picture, even though it's not very good."

"But you don't understand," the student finally blurted out. "I had to climb a mountain for three days to snap this!"

That's all well and good. But the amount of time you spend on something doesn't translate into whether it's meaningful for your readers to hear about it. That's a mistake lawyers frequently make.

Moreover, don't feel the need to introduce yourself in sentences. "I think that this is wrong," writes the lawyer. You usually don't need to say, "I think." Of course you think it—you wrote it. "This is wrong" is enough. Similarly, avoid the temptation to begin sentences with "It is clearly the case that," or "It is interesting to note that," or "My sense is that." It's natural to want to go into a big windup like a baseball pitcher before delivering the message, but it's unnecessary. Remember, too, that as *The Economist Style Guide* advises, "If too many sentences begin Compare, Consider, Expect, Imagine, Look at, Note, Prepare for, Remember or Take, readers will think they are reading a textbook (or, indeed, a style book). This may not be the way to persuade them. . . ."

A graphic example of what not to do came in a brief filed in the U.S. Court of Appeals for the D.C. Circuit (citations omitted):

> When we launched the instant assault upon the indictment we did not do so with the intent of winning the battle but losing the war. From our angle of vision based on two decades of experience on both sides of the appellate sufficiency question, we pursued this appeal fully convinced by the facts and the law.

With all due respect, why inject yourself? Just give us the argument. Your mental processes may be fascinating to you, but they bore a reader, unless your name is James Joyce.

Lawyers should also avoid writing in a stream-of-consciousness style, taking the reader on an excursion through their planning. Both judges and lawyers do this all the time, though in the case of judges it's more justified. Take judicial writing: One way to organize an opinion is to begin with the conclusion and then go on to describe the arguments that support the result. Yet that isn't the way many judges write at all. Often they do begin with the conclusion, but they then go on to describe many of the losing arguments and how they arrived at their findings, taking the reader on a journey through the centers of their minds. You want to ask, if these are losing arguments, *why* do we have to hear about them? Clearly, however, there are jurisprudential reasons—such as assuaging the losers and avoiding appellate reversal—that force many judges to organize opinions in this fashion. Lawyers usually don't have the same excuse.

8. Use specific imagery, not vague generalities.

Because the law is a conceptual discipline, it has a number of big, difficult-to-grasp words. We're comfortable with these because of our intellectual training, but others are not. Occasionally, as Joseph Williams of the University of Chicago has written, substituting a word that evokes vivid pictures in the reader's eye can enliven legal writing. You could write, "Law students should spend less time studying and more time having fun." A more memorable sentence, though, is "Law students should spend less time with *Blackstone* and more time with *Sam Adams.*" By substituting specific examples for general concepts, the sentence comes alive.

This is what the ad copywriter David Ogilvy did when he was writing a tagline for an old celebrated print advertisement for

Rolls-Royce. Rather than saying the car was quiet, he wrote, "At sixty miles an hour, the loudest noise in this new Rolls-Royce comes from the electric clock."

Good legal writers use this technique all the time. Justice Oliver Wendell Holmes could have gone into a long dissertation about the value of First Amendment rights and how those occasionally must be compromised if exercising them will cause harm. Instead he wrote, "The most stringent protection of free speech would not protect a man in falsely shouting fire in a theater and causing panic." It's the image that makes the sentence memorable.

The key here is to use the technique sparingly—something judges frequently forget. Former Justice John Paul Stevens was a wonderful jurist, but he was having a bad day when he wrote in a concurring opinion in *Schad v. Borough of Mt. Ephraim*, 452 U.S. 61 (1981), "And even though the foliage of the First Amendment may cast protective shadows over some forms of nude dancing, its roots were germinated . . ." You also want to use appropriate metaphors. Don't write, as an Ohio lawyer did, "Pour the allegations contained in the Plaintiffs' Complaint through a legal strainer and you would be left with one sole question . . ."

9. Remember that understated prose is the best form of expression.

In a sense, all writing is a one-to-one conversation; readers read alone. You should pretend you're talking to a person across a table in a quiet room. Queen Victoria apparently preferred conversing with Benjamin Disraeli to conversing with William Gladstone. Gladstone, she said, addressed her as if he were talking to a crowd in a stadium; Disraeli talked to her one-to-one. Too many lawyers sound like Gladstone, lecturing their audiences in a pompous style.

The best briefs are models of simple clarity and restraint, even when the circumstances seem to demand otherwise. In contrast, many litigators—especially, let's face it, many male litigators—are graduates of what I call the Rex Ryan School of Written Advocacy. These writers think that the more they overstate their points—attacking the personality of the other side, adding adverbs, and otherwise engaging in hyperbole—the more effective they are as advocates. Unfortunately, the only conclusion most readers draw from such prose is that these writers are as egomaniacal as they seem. To take but one example (citations omitted):

> The Attorney General repeats lamentations echoed earlier and often about the Attorney General's inability to prepare and to litigate the case. The Attorney General calls his asserted inabilities a lack of due process. As a consequence, the Attorney General asks the Department to enter a decision denying the . . . recovery in its entirety and on the merits.
>
> We submit that this apologia for the Attorney General's failure to have proved his case should be rejected. The proposed remedy, e.g., a denial of recovery on the merits without regard to the contents of the record, is so blatantly unlawful, and so blatantly contrary to plain statutory and constitutional requirements, that to hear such an act advocated by the chief law enforcement officer of the Commonwealth is truly grounds for pause.

The tribunal is probably still pausing. In other instances, lawyers ask rhetorical questions. "Can anyone doubt that this is wrong?" writes the attorney, inadvertently implying that if the judge does doubt it, the case is over already. It reminds me of a professor I once had at Yale Law School, who was said to be able to construct a straw-man argument and still manage to lose to the straw man.

Orwell once wrote that "the inflated style is a kind of euphemism. A mass of Latin words falls upon the facts like soft snow, blurring the outlines and covering up all the details. The great enemy of clear language is insincerity." If this condition afflicts your prose, become an ESPN analyst or work out your aggressions elsewhere. The more you turn up the heat rhetorically, the more you weaken your arguments.

III. The Tenth Rule: Use Simple Language

The nine rules already outlined are important to creating good writing. But here is a tenth rule, which goes beyond them: Use simple language. Your choice of words will make or break your composition.

Like the language of most conceptual disciplines, the law is top-heavy with big words. The *Scribes Journal of Legal Writing* once quoted this paragraph from a brief:

> It would be hebetudinous and obtuse to fail to be cognizant of the adverse consequences of a ruling in this case. However, a decision by a court should not be infected with pusillanimity and timidity. The karma of this case must not be aleatory or adventitious, but a pellucid and transpicuous analysis of the law and facts.

Most attorneys don't write this badly, but all lawyers should strive to use simpler speech. "Clearness is secured by using the words that are current and ordinary," wrote Aristotle. To be sure, a careful writer always strives for precision above all else. That's why legal writers should always keep a dictionary and a thesaurus handy. "You ought never to use an unfamiliar word unless you've had to search for it to express a delicate shade," F. Scott Fitzgerald wrote.

Still, simple words—many of which came into the English language from Anglo-Saxon—tend to convey meaning more strongly than words that came into the language later from French. Words derived from Latin tend to be conceptual words and are often "lugubriously ambiguous" and sleep-inducing. If your sentences are full of multisyllabic Latin-based words, you're courting trouble, particularly in an Internet age, in which you need your readers to get what you're saying even if they're distracted.

Part of this is because in the e-age, shorter is better. But shorter words also move audiences more. The average length of a word in English is only five letters. What's more, look at any memorable line from a speech or an advertisement (forms of rhetoric similar to legal writing) and you'll notice that almost all the words are simple, direct, and two syllables or less:

Give me liberty or give me death.
I have a dream.
These are the times that try men's souls.
Friends, Romans, countrymen, lend me your ears.

Similarly, when you're skating and fall through the ice, you don't yell, "Assist!" or "Aid!" You call "Help!" There's a lesson in that. "Assist" and "aid" come from French-Latin roots; "help" is derived from Old English.

Most lawyers think there is no way they can discern the origin of most words in the language. Yet we tend to know these things intuitively. Take the famous phrase from Winston Churchill's speech to the British people in 1940, urging them to fight on against the Nazis. As Robert MacNeil, Robert Mc-Crum, and William Cran point out in their book, *The Story of English*, Churchill, like most effective speakers, relied on words of Old English origin, with one exception. I'll bet you can spot the anomaly:

We shall fight on the beaches; we shall fight on the landing grounds; we shall fight in the fields and in the streets, we shall fight in the hills; we shall never surrender.

The odd word is "surrender," which sounds and looks different from the others. Churchill probably chose it, rather than the more consistent "give up," because the French had surrendered, and he was trying to draw a subtle distinction for his listeners as to how the British might act differently. The point for our purposes, however, is simply that it's easier to spot words of Norman origin than you might think. A thesaurus can help. So, too, can "Thrs" on the Ironic Sans website, or anything similar. Designed for Twitter users so they can shorten their words, it can help you find shorter synonyms for longer, often Latin-based words.

The language of the law tends to be overloaded with French words because in the formative periods of key disciplines such as procedure, criminal law, and property, much of the legal discourse took place in French. Even today, lawyers use so many French-sounding words—"plaintiff," "defendant," "robbery," "burglary," "jury," "indictment"—that they frequently sound like they were born in Paris. A lot of Latin also became embedded in legal language during this period because Latin was the official language of scholarship and academia. Many of these old legal terms of French and Latin origin cannot be replaced, which makes it all the more important that you counteract them by striving for simplicity with the words you can change.

In his blog Legalwriting.net, Wayne Schiess cited a study by a former student, Sean Flammer, on the effectiveness of simple language. Schiess wrote:

> The author asked judges to choose which of two versions of a legal argument they considered more persuasive. Half the judges chose between a traditionally worded (legalese) argu-

ment and a simpler, plainer (plain English) version. The other half chose between the legalese version and a version that used first person, contractions, and so on (informal). The study collected responses from trial and appellate judges in state and federal court and sorted results by those criteria and by age, experience, sex, and geographical setting (rural or urban).

Some results:

On average, judges considered the plain English version more persuasive than the legalese version 66% to 34%. Federal appellate judges chose the plain English version 77% to 23%.

On average, judges considered the informal version more persuasive than the legalese version 58% to 42%. Female judges chose the informal version 83% to 17%, and rural judges actually chose the legalese version over the informal version 55% to 45%.

In *Knauff v. Shaughnessy*, 338 U.S. 537 (1949), Justice Robert Jackson showed how to mix the large words with the smaller ones in one of the more eloquent dissents ever written:

> Now this American citizen is told he cannot bring his wife to the United States but he will not be told why. He must abandon his bride to live in his own country or forsake his country to live with his bride.
>
> So he went to court and sought a writ of habeas corpus, which we never tire of citing to Europe as the unanswerable evidence that our free country permits no arbitrary official detention. And the government tells the Court that not even a court can find out why the girl is excluded. But it says we must find that Congress authorized this treatment of war brides and, even if we cannot get any reasons for it, we must say it is legal; security requires it.
>
> Security is like liberty in that many are the crimes committed in its name.

A few other historical developments have also contributed to the complexity of legal writing. With the rise of commercial activity and the litigation that arose as a result, the eighteenth and nineteenth centuries were formative periods for legal prose.

As we've seen, during this period, many legal writers were paid by the word. It was in their interest to make the writing as cluttered as possible. What's more, then, as now, the workers and scriveners who assisted lawyers in their drafting often found them arrogant and out of touch. As Charles Dickens captured in *Bleak House,* legal assistants frequently drafted documents with an eye toward satirizing their bosses. Phrases such as "Oyez, oyez, oyez" and "Now comes the plaintiff" might have been delivered with a wink and a nudge. Finally, these assistants who aided lawyers were certainly not illiterate, but they weren't highly educated either.

As attorneys continue to perpetuate these styles, they're often imitating the language of semiliterate scribes who were being paid by the word and subtly sending up the law. It's not a role model I would follow.

What's more, the importance of writing in the legal profession is fairly new. For much of our history, lawyers didn't file briefs in the Supreme Court. Even though there were fewer justices, it was too much trouble to write those briefs by hand. What lawyers did instead was to file a short table of cases that made up the basis of the argument and then argue orally in the court, sometimes for hours. (This is still the practice in English courts and throughout Europe.) By modern standards, lawyers did little writing, and what little they did, they dictated to their scriveners.

The rise of the importance of writing in the legal profession came only with improvements in office automation. It's no coincidence that the Federal Rules of Civil Procedure were revised in the late 1930s to encourage more written discovery, because the price of typewriters had dropped precipitously during the

deflation of the Depression. It's only in the last several generations that lawyers have made writing the principal means of
their essential communication.

Legal education, however, is always slow to keep up with
the real world. Even today, almost all law courses use the case
method, studying judicial opinions rather than briefs or other
writings by practicing lawyers. A century ago, reading opinions
made sense, since little else was written down for law students
to read and study. You would think that in the subsequent century, some professors might have come up with the idea that
their students could learn more by examining the documents
they would soon have to write—briefs, memos, contracts, and
even e-mail—while growing to appreciate the role lawyers have
in the decision-making process. No such luck, however.

The oral nature of much early legal discourse also explains a
lot of the problems lawyers have with their writing now. Being
wordy, using run-on sentences, and asking rhetorical questions
are far less egregious faults for speakers than for writers. That,
after all, is why they're called *rhetorical* questions. As lawyers
have carried these habits of oral communication into writing,
however, they've made their writing worse. Reading is different
from listening. Understanding the roots of legal prose can help
lawyers learn where their problems lie.

IV. The Eleventh Rule: Use the Tools of the New Age

In the Internet age, readers read with far less absorption than
they once did. What's more, their expectations have changed,
thanks to the visual packaging that surrounds the texts they
read online.

Unsurprisingly, lawyers have once again been slow to
adapt—writing their memos in the same fashion they did a

generation ago and writing e-mail as if it were just a letter sent electronically. It's not; it's a new form of communication.

In this new age, clients are increasingly complaining about the communications they receive from their lawyers. Though we're still in the very early days of electronic litigation, expect to hear these laments repeated soon by judges as the rules change to encourage—and even require—electronic filings.

Here are the two most common complaints:

The materials they receive aren't useful. From what I hear and see, the legal reasoning within many memos and briefs is sound. The problem is that the documents are organized so poorly that they are not really useful. When I had a court hearing, I would often ask more junior lawyers to give me a memo on whether, say, I should object if a particular piece of evidence were introduced. In typical legal style, the lawyers would give me a nice fifteen-page single-spaced analysis. Beyond the fact that I hardly needed fifteen pages on the subject (and who has time to read that now anyway), the memo wasn't functional. If the matter came up, I couldn't ask the judge for a recess while I reread the document. I needed to be able to employ it on a moment's notice.

Most documents are still packaged much the same way lawyers packaged them a generation ago or even before. *How writing is formatted, however, is key to its value.* A single-spaced essay may have made some sense in the days when these documents were hand- or typewritten. But in the age of the computer and smart phone? No way.

Think about the ways in which MapQuest (or Google Maps) and Wikipedia organize information. First, the maps:

- They use the second person, which in turn, moves the writer in the direction of writing simpler prose because we sound more conversational when we use the second person;

- They provide visual illustrations;
- They are written as a numbered list, not an essay.

That last point is key. Throughout our academic careers, we're socialized into always writing essays, whether for an exam or paper. Briefs, memos, and even opinions today are simply different takes on the essay format.

But an essay is often one of the least effective ways to convey information. Were MapQuest to provide an essay on how to get to the train station, we'd likely get lost and wreck the car on the way as we tried to figure out what to do.

Worse, essay writers tend to be terribly overinclusive. We spend time describing the sights, or the cars in the other lane. Yes, lawyers might think that giving their directions in a list format is too laconic. But it gives your readers all they really care about. Using complete sentences to show us the way takes unnecessary space and clutters the page.

Of course, the Web's propensity for making things into lists can go too far. Mike Lacher at *McSweeney's* spoofed the practice in a short hit entitled "Great Literature Retitled To Boost Website Traffic."

7 Awesome Ways Barnyard Animals Are Like Communism

The 11 Stupidest Things Phonies Do To Ruin The World

8 Surprising Ways West Egg Is Exemplary Of The Hollowness Of The American Dream

6 Shockingly Evil Things The Turn-Of-The-Century Meatpacking Industry Doesn't Want You To Know

5 Insane Ways London Could Become a Dystopia (And How It's Not That Far From Reality)

1 Weird Thing Caddy Smells Like

Or, look at the way Wikipedia presents material:

- It uses different fonts and color, and puts things in boxes.
- It leads with the conclusion and then provides a written table of contents or a list that does the same.
- It uses links.
- It provides a bibliography with links.

All of these are tools lawyers should use in their memos to clients and one another. A memo that places its summary in a box up front and then uses different fonts—putting case discussions in smaller type (or even a list)—is far easier to follow. (Case discussions and quotes can even be dropped altogether if a link can provide a guide to the case itself.) Links in the table of contents enable readers to skip the parts of the memo they don't want to read.

If it's any inspiration, Christine Falcicchio and Dan Wolfe have documented how a number of judges like hyperlinked briefs. A Wisconsin judge told them, "I love [hyperlinked briefs]," and the best aspect "is its portability. . . . I took the CD home with me and did not have to drag any boxes with me. . . . I also liked the hyperlink feature . . . it allowed me to check the accuracy of the information cited in the brief . . . I was really impressed with it and showed it to several judges in the courthouse." A Texas arbitrator said, "The [hyperlinked brief] makes review of the brief easier, and the easier you make something, the more likely people are to see what you want them to see and to do what you want them to do."

As to font, the U.S. Court of Appeals for the Seventh Circuit has issued a guide that reads:

Typographic decisions should be made for a purpose. The *Times* of London chose the typeface Times New Roman to serve an audience looking for a quick read. Lawyers don't want their audience to read fast and throw the document away; they want to maximize retention. Achieving that goal requires a different approach—different typefaces, different column widths, different writing conventions.

Alex Madrigal of *The Atlantic* has reported that fifteen of the top twenty retailers in the Fortune 500 use Helvetica, a decision that may inform the way you package some of your material outside of court.

The materials they receive don't focus on what is of interest to them. Most of the time, lawyers are dealing with practical problems in the real world that demand concrete answers. Our readers want to know *what* they have to do and *how* we suggest they do it. *Why* they should is, of course, of interest to judges, and we are mesmerized by the "why" because it's the focus of our legal education and the core skill of legal research. Yet that's of little use to clients and of less use to judges than you might think, for reasons we'll talk about in Chapter 4.

"You asked me whether you can be sued for that leak in your backyard," lawyers begin, and then they go on to describe in excruciating detail all the research they did. Yet a recounting of research is of little use to clients, especially up front. It's as if you went to a doctor and told him you're worried about your cholesterol. "We'll run a blood test," says the doctor. "Come back next week and I'll tell you what you should do." You return the following week. "What should I do?" you ask the doctor. "Let me tell you how we did the test," he replies, "thinking like a lawyer," as he begins a ten-minute recitation of lab procedures. You don't care how the test was done; you want to know the results and what to do. The same goes for clients reading your legal recommendations.

To deal with these issues, it may help you to employ Power-Point as a writing tool. As a speaking aid, it's ridiculously overused. But it can be useful for writers. First, it forces you before you begin to focus on the principal points you want to make.

Second, it enables you to think more visually about how you might want to present your information in writing.

Many lawyers fear that if they adopt the eleven rules outlined in this chapter, their prose will become so straightforward that they won't sound like themselves, or they will look simplistic or foolish. Yet a complex personal style hides more of an author than it reveals. "Style results more from what a person is than what he knows," wrote E. B. White. As to fears of oversimplification, they seldom prove true for lawyers, who forget that the greatest written prose is seldom complex. Aldous Huxley, who began his literary career as an ad writer, once concluded that

> any trace of literariness in an advertisement is fatal to its success. Advertisement writers may not be lyrical, or obscure, or in any way esoteric. They must be universally intelligible. A good advertisement has this in common with drama and oratory, that it must be immediately comprehensible and directly moving.

Just listen to Justice Holmes, as he began his explanation of the common law:

> The object of this book is to present a general view of the Common Law. To accomplish this task, other tools are needed besides logic. It is something to show that the consistency of a system requires a particular result, but it is not all. The life of the law has not been logic; it has been experience.

If such a simple, eloquent style worked for him more than a hundred years ago, it will work for you too.

CHAPTER 3

The Mechanics of Editing

I. The Overview: Lawyer, Edit Thyself

II. The Five Rules of Self-Editing

1. Print your text before editing.

2. The more time you put between drafting a document and self-editing it, the better the edit will be.

3. Try to read the document out loud as you edit.

4. Apply many of the rules discussed in Chapter 2 in the self-editing process.

5. Check for typographical errors.

III. An Objective Eye Can't Hurt: The Seven Rules for Providing Effective Outside Editing

1. Separate the substantive edit from the copy edit.

2. Always be polite.

3. Make writers aware of alternatives.

4. When more than one editor works on a document, have a single editor convey all the criticism to the writer.

5. Remove jargon from the document.

6. With important documents, use a fact-checker.

7. Remember that the goal of editors is to make writers sound better but still sound like themselves.

I. The Overview: Lawyer, Edit Thyself

There is no great writing," said Justice Louis Brandeis, "only great rewriting." But most lawyers underestimate the value of editing. All writers, whether they're Margaret Atwood or the solicitor general, can benefit from a good editor. When writers produce a document, they know what they're trying to say, so they frequently read what they've composed with an eye toward what they think it is saying rather than what it actually does. Moreover, as mentioned previously, all writers have a tendency to fall in love with their own prose. An editor provides fresh, needed criticism.

In an ideal world, an objective person provides this editing. That's why all law offices or divisions should set up some kind of formal editing process in the fashion described in this chapter. If one doesn't exist, try teaming with friends and associates you trust to give you honest feedback. If you are in practice alone, you might want to consider occasionally hiring another lawyer, or even a writing professional, to review important filings.

Finding an editor is especially important for judges, who need the feedback from someone with the authority or stature to make needed changes stick. While it's true that for ethical reasons judges cannot show drafts to noncourt personnel, they could begin hiring editors on their staffs. The lack of editing is one key reason that so much judicial writing is lengthy and unfocused, not to mention boring. Of course, no one on the outside ever tells a judge that he or she cannot write—at least, no one who wants to win another case in that court. Think of the riddle that Jacob Stein, a Washington lawyer, liked to say applied to judges. Question: What do you get when you cross a parrot and a wild lion? Answer: I don't know, but you'd better be nice to it.

Even before an outside editor enters the picture, however—or because one never will—lawyers should be self-editing all their prose. Once lawyers get the hang of editing themselves, they can usually cover a double-spaced page in about two minutes. It's worth the time.

II. The Five Rules of Self-Editing

When self-editing, lawyers need to keep five rules in mind.

1. Print your text before editing.

By editing on the computer screen, you are bound to miss something, since people read more carelessly on screen than they do on paper. Edit a hard copy and then apply the changes online.

2. The more time you put between drafting a document and self-editing it, the better the edit will be.

If you reserve a decent interval between drafting and editing, you will read what you've drafted more as a first-time reader would. I know many lawyers write everything at the last minute, but doing so deprives you of one of the best tools you have for improvement. If at all possible, try to finish all drafts at least twenty-four hours before they are due, so you can review them. If that isn't possible, even a clean half-hour between drafting and editing helps.

3. Try to read the document out loud as you edit.

We've already talked about the value of reciting your prose as you create to capture the right feel. It's even more important to do the same thing when you edit your writing. First, doing so slows you down so you can capture mistakes more easily. More important, prose that doesn't sound like something you would say—remember our McDonald's test—is something you likely shouldn't write either. That's why novelists such as John Irving read their work aloud before publishing.

This tells us something important about English as a language. If you ask French readers who their greatest writer is, you'll get answers such as Victor Hugo, Gustave Flaubert, and Honore de Balzac. Do the same with Russians and you hear about Pushkin and Tolstoy. Ask the same question to almost any English speaker and the answer is Shakespeare. But Shakespeare is different from the other luminaries. They were writers, creating material to be read. Shakespeare's works were created to be heard and seen; he didn't even write down most of the plays attributed to him.

That is telling. In its purest form, English is a spoken language, not a written one. It's one reason why we don't have "high English" and "low English" nearly to the extent other languages do—with stricter standards for written speech compared to the spoken version. It's also why puns and alliteration work even in written English; the assumption is that our readers can *hear* the language they read.

4. Apply many of the rules discussed in Chapter 2 in the self-editing process.

You can do this by taking three steps. First, look at your verbs and ask if you can strengthen any of them. Second, look at your sentences and see if you can shorten any, or move clauses to the beginning or end. Finally, cut words. For example, if you write on a computer, you can catch many adverbs by running "ly" through your "Find" search.

William Zinsser once described the process of editing as changing every page to a paragraph, every paragraph to a sentence, every sentence to a phrase, every phrase to a word, and then cutting the extra words. In self-editing, you are constantly honing your message. As the writer Isaac Bashevis Singer put it in an earlier era, "The wastepaper basket is the writer's best friend."

5. Check for typographical errors.

When you look for typos or grammatical and spelling errors, don't rely on your computer spell-checker. It is bound to miss things, particularly when you've used a word improperly rather than misspelled it. The *Scribes Journal of Legal Writing* used to collect misprints and came up with a few doozies. There was a court filing addressed to the "Horable U.S. District Judge." And the brief signed "Rectfully submitted." And the sentence in an appellate brief that read, "In the index to this brief, the Court will find an extensive copulation of authorities on the subject."

I often hear students worry that they're being obsessive about self-editing, constantly changing and rearranging their prose until the last minute. That's actually a virtue. The greatest writers are more than a bit neurotic, as they anguish over each word and comma. Writing is a labor-intensive task.

III. An Objective Eye Can't Hurt: The Seven Rules for Providing Effective Outside Editing

If you take the five steps outlined in the previous section with everything you write, you will improve your prose a great deal. With important documents, though, such as a crucial submission to a client or a major brief, editing by others is essential. No matter how well you self-edit, you will miss changes that should be made.

Unfortunately, many lawyers or law students whose work is edited discover that the criticism they get is so confused and contradictory, it ends up hurting their writing more than it helps. Editing is an art, and you should try to find an editor who knows that art. Remember, too, to be constructive when you edit others. Those who review the work of lawyers should remember the following seven rules.

1. Separate the substantive edit from the copy edit.

A frequent complaint from legal editors (usually partners) is that they have to spend far too much time editing the work of associates—often rewriting the work from scratch. One has some sympathy, but a large part of the problem is that these editors aren't making a necessary distinction between substantive editing and copyediting. Were they to do that—and take steps within the office to distinguish between the two—they'd save a lot of time and the associates would receive better editing.

With substantive editing—say refashioning the arguments or memo recommendations so they make better sense, or putting the points in the correct order, or leading with a distinct conclusion—legal editors would be better off not starting their task confronting a fully written draft. Rather, they should ask the writer to submit an outline of principal points first—detailing the key first paragraph and a brief explanation of how each point will be laid out. "When you think you're ready to start writing, write a blurb," the novelist Len Deighton once advised. "[I]t is essential to have a description of 500 to 1,000 words. This blurb should remain in view while you are writing. It will keep you from wandering off into detours."

Still, this précis needn't be an essay. Often a PowerPoint can accomplish this, since it forces writers to think in basic terms about what they're going to say and how they're going to say it. In a sense, this initial process is like approving an architect's plan before he or she begins to build. Better to catch the major mistakes at a stage before construction.

Once the editor signs off on this plan—and it can be as detailed as required—writing the document should be straightforward. At that point, all that's often needed editorially is a copy edit, which can be supplied, really, by anyone qualified to do so. This copy edit corrects for grammar, sentence structure, usage, and the like.

At that point, the finished document goes back to the writer. Unless the copy editor has somehow changed the legal analysis, writers should have little to do at that point. In the long run, this will save time. And writers should have better documents too.

2. Always be polite.

Writers take criticism of their prose the way they react to disapproval of their clothes or hair. It doesn't sit well. "An editor should tell the author his writing is better than it is," T. S. Eliot once observed. "Not a lot better, a little better." To paraphrase W. B. Yeats, "Tread softly, because you tread on my prose."

Far too many legal editors are maladroit in their critiques. Think of the example of Angelo Dundee, the trainer of former boxing great Muhammad Ali. If Dundee offered a suggestion ("Start throwing the jab"), Ali would frequently do the opposite, just to show who was boss. So if Dundee wanted Ali to throw the jab, he learned to say, "Muhammad, I really like the way you've been using the jab." Then Ali would take the "suggestion." Dundee knew his pupil, which is why he had one key attribute of a good editor.

3. Make writers aware of alternatives.

Because writers have difficulty seeing that there is more than one way to express a thought, much of the editing they receive is too vague to be useful. Telling lawyers "This needs to be more argumentative" does nothing for them unless you show them specifically what you mean. That doesn't mean that editors must rewrite the document, but they do have to illustrate in a sentence or two the criticisms they pass on.

Remember again that there are two types of feedback. The line-by-line edit along the lines we discussed in Chapter 2— examining sentence structure, verbs, and extra words—can be provided by a copy editor at the end. Unless the editor has changed the meaning of the prose, the suggestions or corrections will stand.

"Substantive editors" should focus only on, well, substance. They can make several comments at the end of a document about improving the piece as a whole, but these should be specific. These suggestions should also be limited in number; if editors give a writer a dozen ideas to incorporate, the writer will hardly remember the suggestions. With comments, editors should concentrate on the big picture. A scattershot approach doesn't work any better with editing than it does in making arguments.

4. When more than one editor works on a document, have a single editor convey all the criticism to the writer.

If your office has created a setup in which more than one editor reviews a document, it always helps if all criticism is filtered to the writer through a single editor. Editing is a subjective process, and the comments of one editor are bound to conflict at times with those of another. You cannot put writers in the untenable position of having to resolve contradictions themselves. That often leads to poor writing and even poorer office politics.

5. Remove jargon from the document.

Lawyers don't just use jargon such as Latin phrases and old words. Over time, they also tend to sound like what they do.

Tax lawyers start sounding like the tax code. Social Security lawyers begin to resemble the regulations of their field. Prosecutors start sounding like policemen, informing friends that they've got to go "move their motor vehicle."

A good editor removes the jargon, especially when the audience is not composed of specialists. A tax brief for a local tax board or the federal tax court in Washington should be written in a different style from a brief dealing with the same points filed in a state or federal court of general jurisdiction, which is not staffed by tax specialists.

This is a particular problem for plaintiffs' lawyers or legal service attorneys, who end up minimizing the harm to their clients by couching it in jargon. The jargonesque language of bureaucracy and professionals is designed to make them function better by minimizing pain. That makes sense: Physicians use lingo ("suturing" for "stitching," etc.) because acting with less emotion supposedly allows them to do a better and more professional job.

But plaintiffs' or legal services attorneys who do the same are often doing their clients a disservice. Their task is to detail the pain or hurt in human terms—not lessen it.

6. With important documents, use a fact-checker.

Yes, the Web has opened up vast sources of information. That's the good news. The bad news is that a lot of it is inaccurate. Using a fact checker for important court documents and other writing in which accuracy is important is never a bad idea. A writer who is sloppy factually is eventually found out and loses credibility—not only for that document but for others in the future.

7. Remember that the goal of editors is to make writers sound better but still sound like themselves.

Many legal editors think the point of editing is to make writers sound just the way they would themselves. That's wrong. If you want something written precisely the way you would, you should draft it.

Obviously, an editor has to do many things—clean up the prose, for instance, or move a point that needs emphasis to the front of a document. Yet legal editors are often heavy-handed. "[Ezra Pound] was a marvelous critic because he didn't try to turn you into an imitation of himself," T. S. Eliot once said. "He tried to see what you were trying to do."

Mary Norris, a copy editor at *The New Yorker*, once said that a copy editor needs to have self-doubt. "It's always good before changing something," she said, "to stop and wonder if this is a mistake or if the writer did this for a reason."

If lawyers are overly imperious in their editing, that is partly because of the extent to which they encourage ghostwriting in their practices, where the whole point is to get one writer to sound just like another. Associates frequently draft documents that partners then review and sign.

For the most part, that's a disturbing trend. It's difficult to be an effective ghostwriter, because it involves both learning someone else's style and subordinating your own style to that way of writing. It's especially difficult to be a ghostwriter for someone a writer doesn't like, yet lawyers ask others to do it all the time. This is an invitation to undertake a schizophrenic form of writing, which if nothing else further explains why legal prose is often as bad as it is.

PART II

The Fundamentals of Argument for All Lawyers

CHAPTER 4

The Art of Argument

I. The Overview: Make Persuasive Arguments by
Outlining the Thesis, Researching It Later

II. The Four Principles of Advertising
Lawyers Should Know

1. Before you begin writing, ask yourself, "What's the big idea?"

2. Devise a one- or two-sentence slogan that embodies your position in the matter.

3. Make it interesting.

4. Study the product and the industry you're "advertising." The more you know about them, the more you're likely to come up with good ideas for selling them.

III. The Three Beginning Principles
of Argument Writing

1. Facts often make the argument; arguments don't often make the facts.

2. Be accurate.

3. Don't overargue.

I. The Overview: Make Persuasive Arguments by Outlining the Thesis, Researching It Later

Argument is the core of legal writing. Even if you're not a litigator, you're usually engaged in the process of trying to convince someone of something—a client to take an action or other lawyers to do the same. Yet when I originally set out to write this book, I discovered something I didn't expect. I interviewed a number of judges, and asked some, "What is the main thing that has surprised you about the submissions you read?" Almost all groaned about their length, as we discussed in Chapter 2. But a number also complained about how unpersuasive these advocacy documents were. One told me, "Often I read the appellant's brief and say to myself, 'Well, if that's the way you feel, I may have to rule for the other side.' And then I read the other brief and I'm perplexed. Both sides have managed to steer me away from their position."

This is puzzling, given that lawyers usually think of themselves as persuasive. But there are a number of reasons for it. As we discussed earlier, we come out of an analytic, academic tradition—not a persuasive one. That academic method encourages us to back into our conclusions—rarely an effective method of persuasion.

There is also a jurisprudential reason for that lack of persuasiveness. Let's pretend you're debating your views on capital punishment with a friend. You're likely to begin by making arguments based on the ethics of the penalty, whether it's applied fairly, and whether it deters crime. In a lighter vein, if you're discussing what movie to go see this weekend, you're likely to make arguments based on reviews, what mood you're in, or which theater is closest to your house.

You're unlikely to say to your friend, "Let's go see *Casablanca*, because that's the movie we saw last week and I think we ought to see the same film every time we hit the theaters." And you're probably never going to say, "Let's keep the death penalty, because that's what we've always done before." Arguments based on precedent aren't terribly persuasive in our culture. We live in a society obsessed with the current. If you go up to someone on the street and cite precedent, they're apt to cry, "It's time for a change!" and demand something new.

Lawyers, however, rely on precedent too much, both in litigation and in other areas of practice. Of course, if you dispense with precedent entirely, your briefs will read much better but you won't win many more cases. But we all know that case law can be pliable; enough is coming out every year that a judge can probably use it to prove that the sun rises in the west. Moreover, in litigation, if a case is really going to be decided by the precedent, you don't need my advice or anyone else's on how to construct the argument. The winners and losers are clear.

The problem is that most matters fall somewhere in between. One side has its set of precedents, the other side its cases, and judges or others must choose. This is not a mathematical exercise, where a judge adds up each side's citations and announces, "The plaintiff wins, nineteen to seventeen!" Instead, what judges do initially, as we all do when we read arguments, is intuitively lean toward a particular position. Supreme Court Justice William O. Douglas once wrote:

Chief Justice Hughes made a statement to me which at the time was shattering but which over the years turned out to be true: "Justice Douglas, you must remember one thing. At the constitutional level where we work, ninety percent of any decision is emotional. The rational part of us supplies the reasons for supporting our predilections."

Even outside the lofty domains of the Supreme Court, the intuitive attraction of an argument is paramount. All prior case law really does is tell judges that if they rule for you, they won't get reversed, because others have done something similar. In most instances, precedent is not the theory that proves your case; it is the evidence that supports your theory.

So any time you compose an argument, which means virtually all types of legal writing save the formal drafting of contracts and the like or opinion letters, my advice would be to do enough research first to get a general sense of the law. No matter how complex the matter, this research should never take more than an hour or so. Then put all your research aside and ask yourself, if I had to explain to a judge, another lawyer, or a client why we should win without resorting to any precedent or law, what would I say? In laymen's terms, why are we right? Then write those reasons down. By the way, make sure those reasons rely on good common sense, not some high-minded policy rationale you learned in law school.

It takes a fair amount of work. "The first step of copywriting is to brainstorm," wrote David Droga, an ad executive, in the *Wall Street Journal*. "What are we trying to say? What specific mood are we trying to evoke? We toss around images, key phrases, associations. We throw down dozens of half-baked ideas in sweaty notebooks. It's painful."

After taking these initial steps, go back and do the rest of your research. Obviously, if you discover new arguments supported by a lot of precedent, you are going to want to insert them. Similarly, if you wrote down arguments that aren't supported by any case law, you're going to want to eliminate them. Certainly you don't want to twist what you find in research to fit a misconceived theory that can lead you to lose a case you might have won.

Far more than you may have envisioned, however, the case law will tend to support your original rationales. That makes sense: Cases stand for principles. It's important for you to begin with these principles and then find the case law, rather than to work in the usual manner of finding the case law and moving backward to find the rules.

Outline the argument, research it later. Both lawyers and law students often spend so much time developing their supporting research that they forget that the core of most arguments is rather simple. When I was a beginning litigator, I would often spread research all over the office in an attempt to distill fifty pages down to one. It was a waste of time: I would have been far better off trying to begin with one page and working in the other direction.

In any complex or lengthy matter, use the same method. Many authors facing a 500-page book project begin with a paragraph synthesis, which they then expand to several pages. Once they have their core, they divide what they will need to research into the sections they require to explain the thesis— sometimes twenty or more. Once the author has these sections, every piece of research is placed into a section. Sure, these change as the project is researched. But the alternative is to try to take thousands of tidbits at the end and organize them. It's virtually impossible.

II. The Four Principles of Advertising Lawyers Should Know

Studying the rhetoric of persuasion is not something lawyers commonly do. Yet all of us can learn from effective advocates, and some of the most able in American culture work in the advertising industry. Writing arguments in that context is clearly different from writing as a legal advocate. Advertising, after all, often rests on puffing ("The best money can buy") or on a meaningless expression of implied claims ("To be sexy, wear this cologne").

If you keep those caveats in mind, however, there are similarities, and some of the principles ad copywriters live by can be helpful to legal writers. Here are four.

1. Before you begin writing, ask yourself, "What's the big idea?"

Before writing copy, most ad writers make themselves describe in a sentence or two the main idea they're trying to get across. It's what the advertising theorist Rosser Reeves once called "the unique selling proposition"; it's what Harvard Law School professor David Rosenberg has called "the core of your case." Lawyers should do this too.

Too many advocates, writing in the paranoid fashion I described earlier, are afraid to choose an argument to emphasize, with the logical result that they end up emphasizing none. Take the old slogan of Miller Lite Beer: "Tastes great, less filling." That gives us two simple and memorable reasons to buy the beer. If your average lawyer had drafted that slogan, it probably would read something like "Miller Beer—tastes great, less filling, comes in an easy-opening can, you can find it anywhere, it's cheaper than Bud," et cetera, et cetera. The result would be that you couldn't remember any reasons to buy the brand.

When I taught my seminar at Harvard Law School, I used

an overnight exercise to illustrate my point. I used to give each student four or five well-written briefs from federal court. "Take these home," I would tell them, "and pretend you're a judge with a limited amount of time to spend on each." The next day when they came back, I would ask, "Which argument did you find most convincing in the third case?" Inevitably, the students could hardly remember the third case, much less what its arguments were. The problem wasn't that the briefs weren't well crafted; they were. But they weren't nearly as focused as they needed to be. In today's world, very few readers complain that they're not given enough information; the lament is that the writer has given them too much.

Say a judge is sitting in chambers and a colleague asks what your case is about. The judge describes the case in one sentence. Then the colleague asks who should win. The judge responds with another sentence, maybe two. Your whole brief is an attempt to control the substance of those two or three sentences. You should go through every section, every page, even each paragraph of your filing and ask yourself, "How does this relate to the main idea I'm trying to get across?" If it doesn't, you shouldn't necessarily leave the point out, but you should greatly reduce the attention you give it and you should probably move it to the back.

Too many advocates treat the process of briefing as if they were a waiter at a cocktail party. They carry around a platter of hors d'oeuvres and ask judges or their readers if they'd like one. That's not advocacy. Your job is to *tell* readers which one to select. You don't want to waive arguments, but if you're presenting five to a court, the main one should make up roughly two thirds of your brief, the second about one fifth, and the other three the remaining eighth or tenth. Otherwise your argument lacks the focus it needs to be memorable and convincing. Don't make judges or clients spend a lot of time on trivial arguments.

Toward the end of the voluminous briefs filed by both sides at various stages in the historic school integration case *Brown v. Board of Education of Topeka*, 347 U.S. 483 (1954), the lawyers for the NAACP Legal Defense Fund (which included the future Justice Thurgood Marshall) focused on their "big idea" when they wrote:

> These infant appellants are asserting the most important secular claims that can be put forward by children, the claim to their full measure of the chance to learn and grow, and the inseparably connected but even more important claim to be treated as entire citizens of the society into which they have been born. We have discovered no case in which such rights, once established, have been postponed by a cautious calculation of conveniences. The nuisance cases, the sewage cases, the cases of the overhanging cornices, need not be distinguished. They distinguish themselves.

2. Devise a one- or two-sentence slogan that embodies your position in the matter.

Once you've got your core idea down to a few sentences, the goal is to see if you can make it into a kind of slogan, sound bite, or refrain. Advertisers aren't dumb, and neither are poets: They use a refrain because it makes their message memorable.

The same principle works in advocacy writing as well. Just ask Justice Antonin Scalia. In a dissent in *Rankin v. McPherson*, 483 U.S. 378 (1987), he began, "I agree with the proposition, felicitously put by Constable Rankin's counsel, that no law enforcement agency is required by the First Amendment to permit one of its employees to 'ride with the cops and cheer for the robbers.' "

In their Supreme Court brief in *Hawaii Housing Authority v. Midkiff*, 467 U.S. 229 (1984), Harvard Law School professor

Laurence Tribe and his co-counsel begin their statement of the case with a similar slogan-like sentence: "The issue in this case is whether the United States Constitution freezes our fiftieth state into its feudal past."

In the famous Pentagon Papers case, *New York Times Co. v. United States*, 403 U.S. 713 (1971), the *New York Times* and the *Washington Post* went to the Supreme Court to preserve their right to publish the papers. The Nixon administration opposed these efforts on grounds of national security and sought a prior restraint to prevent publication. Alexander Bickel, the Yale Law School professor representing the *Times*, began his brief by describing how a prior restraint violates the spirit of the First Amendment. If speech is unlawful, he argued, punish it criminally after the fact, don't censor it. He wrote, "A prior restraint therefore stops more speech, more effectively. A criminal statute *chills*. The prior restraint *freezes*" (emphasis added).

Bickel won his case narrowly, and that memorable phrase or slogan helped him win it. Forcing yourself to come up with a two-sentence slogan in a case helps you find the big idea we discussed in point 1. And it does so in a way that the reader will be apt to remember. It's probably a terrible idea to use the O. J. Simpson criminal trial in the 1990s as a good example of anything, but Johnnie Cochran and Barry Scheck used "slogans" to great advantage in their jury arguments. Long after the trial was over, the jurors were telling the press, "If it doesn't fit, you must acquit."

Two additional notes about writing legal slogans: First, your slogan has to explain *why*. Some ad slogans in the real world do this: An old *New York Times* slogan, "All the News That's Fit to Print," told the reader the reason he or she should read the paper.

But in today's ad world a lot of great slogans don't give us a rational explanation. "Just Do It" may be the most well-known ad line of the age, but you could hardly stand up in the Supreme Court and say, "Reverse Miranda—Just do it." Memorable? Yes. But in our world, that's hardly enough.

Second, memorable taglines in speeches, poetry, songs, and ads tend to have similar attributes. They're usually pithy. Often they use alliteration (Dr. King's "not by the color of their skin but by the content of their character" or Justice Cardozo's "[t]he cry of distress is the call to rescue"). They tend to rely on strong verbs, and are grounded in specifics or images, not concepts. Repetition can add a sense of rhythm. ("To be or not to be.") As we've noted, they rely almost exclusively on short words that came into the language from Anglo-Saxon. In their book *Made to Stick*, the Heaths (Dan and Chip) identify six factors that make ideas "stick":

a. Simplicity
b. Unexpectedness
c. Concreteness
d. Credibility
e. Emotions
f. Stories

Rely on these in trying to come up with your aphorism and you'll be on the right track.

3. Make it interesting.

As they say on Madison Avenue, "You can't bore a reader into buying a product, you can only interest him or her in buying it." The same holds true for legal arguments. Sure, judges and others have to read what you write, but there's nothing that dictates *how* they read it. I know a lot of your material seems boring. Yet as William Zinsser has said, you don't have to want to spend a year at Walden Pond to become engrossed in how someone else did.

How do you make the written argument interesting? The most obvious way is through the facts. As shocking as it may seem to first-year law students, the law is almost always boring, especially to judges. After all, anything you tell the court about the law has probably been said hundreds of times. "In communications," the ad theorist Bill Bernbach once said, "familiarity builds apathy." Under the system of precedent, we must use stale arguments that have been used before. Novelty is a loser. Your facts, however, are new, and it's there you have a chance to weave a narrative that can draw in the reader. "We judges want to know the facts, the real-life conditions, the actual practices underlying a legal challenge," former federal judge Patricia Wald has written. Use that opportunity. In the overwhelming number of cases, once judges have read your facts, their minds are made up because they know from experience what rules to apply.

4. Study the product and the industry you're "advertising." The more you know about them, the more you're likely to come up with good ideas for selling them.

This rule applies to legal writers as well. Legal research has its place. Yet factual research can frequently be more important to an advocate. No matter how much legal research you do, you're unlikely to come up with anything new. Even if you do, under the system of precedent, a judge will probably ignore it. "I've got a brand-new theory about Title VII" is not something that you usually tell a court, and for good reason. Instead, we lawyers argue by stressing how old our ideas are: "Your Honor, you've heard about this theory of Title VII in numerous cases we've cited in our brief." We practice in a system that rarely rewards creativity in legal research. And familiarity breeds apathy.

Factual research is different. Anything new that you discover you can potentially use. Moreover, the newness of the information makes it likelier that the judge will pay attention to it. Skillful advocates use the discovery process to obtain the kinds of facts or descriptions they want to employ in their statements of fact and then find a way to get them into a record. Being a good advocate is a lot like being a good detective or journalist: You're searching as much as listening.

In his wonderful book *On Advertising*, David Ogilvy wrote:

> When we advertise Shell, we give the consumer facts, many of which other petrol marketers could give, but don't. When we advertise KLM Royal Dutch Airlines we tell travelers about safety precautions which all airlines take, but fail to mention in their advertisements. When I was a door-to-door salesman, I discovered that the more information I gave about my product, the more I sold.

Thus, in a tort case in which you're trying to establish the severity of injuries your client suffered, you want to find the right kind of detail to make your point memorable. Don't just list the maladies. Research and describe them. What is an average day like for the client? What is it like when she tries to take a step? What could she do before that she can't do now? Good factual research and probing investigative questioning in discovery will provide the answers, with the Internet often making such research easier than before.

In "Vignettes from a Narrative Primer," Philip N. Meyer describes how in a 2000 Supreme Court case, *Williams v. Taylor*, 529 U.S. 362 (2000), the defendant's lawyers refused simply to label their client's childhood as "traumatic"—as lawyers often do. Instead, they took the time to go through the juvenile records, finding the graphic report of a social worker who wrote (the names have been changed):

> Doreen and Moses [the parents] were sitting on the front porch and were in such a drunken state, it was almost impossible to get them up. They staggered into the house to where the chil-

dren were asleep. Dolores, age 1, and Moses Jr., age 3, were asleep on the sofa. There was an odor of alcohol on the breath of Moses Jr.... Peter had just awakened and was very sick. He said he was hungry and had been drinking whiskey. Leo was completely passed out and never could be awakened. He did not have on any clothes.... The home was a complete wreck.... There were several places on the floor where someone had had a bowel movement. Urine was standing in several places in the bedrooms. There were dirty dishes scattered over the kitchen, and it was impossible to step any place on the kitchen floor where there was no trash.... The children were all dirty and none of them had on under-pants. Moses and Doreen were so intoxicated, they could not find any clothes for the children, nor were they able to put the clothes on them. There was stuffed pickle scattered on the floor in the front bedroom....

Like a good ad, a good legal argument is often grounded in factual specifics, repeated in a slogan-like rhythm. In the introductory summary to his celebrated brief in *Gideon v. Wainwright*, 372 U.S. 335 (1963), the case that established the right to counsel in criminal cases, future Justice Abe Fortas begins with a general recitation that quickly became memorable for its particularity:

An accused person cannot effectively defend himself. The assistance of counsel is necessary to "due process" and to a fair trial. Without counsel, the accused cannot possibly evaluate the lawfulness of his arrest, the validity of the indictment or information, whether preliminary motions should be filed, whether a search or seizure has been lawful, whether a "confession" is admissible, etc. He cannot determine whether he is responsible for the crime as charged or a lesser offense. He cannot discuss the possibilities of pleading to a lesser offense. He cannot evaluate the grand or petit jury. At the trial he cannot interpose objections to evidence or cross-examining witnesses, etc. He is at a loss in the sentencing procedure.

III. The Three Beginning Principles of Argument Writing

In any kind of advocacy writing, litigation or otherwise, there are three initial rules to keep in mind.

1. Facts often make the argument; arguments don't often make the facts.

The facts tend to be far more important to many arguments than most lawyers and law students think. Certainly law school gives us the impression that facts are interchangeable; law professors hand out canned facts and concentrate on "the law" to the exclusion of almost anything else. As New York University Law School professor Anthony Amsterdam wrote:

> When I was in law school, I spent virtually all of my time learning analytic techniques for predicting or arguing what was the legal result, or what should be the legal result, in a given fact situation. Since I got out of law school, I have spent virtually all of my time dealing with situations in which the facts were not given, in which there were options as to what fact situation should be created—situations in which I had a choice whether to present evidence on certain aspects of the facts in litigation or to leave the record silent on those aspects.

The facts are important for several reasons. First, most arguments commonly made in our culture are factually based. If we want to argue why one team will win a game rather than another, we focus on the known attributes of each. Second, facts come at the beginning of a brief or argument, and as we've already learned, first impressions are strong. Third, the facts are a way to appeal to a judge's or reader's feelings. That is hardly an illegitimate form of persuasion, as long as you're also making a logical, legal argument later in the brief. "The real importance of the facts," wrote Frederick Wiener in his classic *Briefing and Arguing Federal Appeals*, "is that courts want to do substantial justice and that they are sensitive to the 'equities.'"

Finally, judges and other legal readers are far more dependent on your rendering of the facts than they are on your version of the law. Face it: Judges consider themselves the experts in law. No matter what you tell them about it, they're going to take your interpretation with about fifteen grains of salt. In contrast, your facts are new and best known to you; your ability to be persuasive with them is far greater. Give judges the facts in a case and they can make up their minds. Give them the law and they still need to know the facts.

Moreover, what makes the jobs of judges interesting on a day-to-day basis are the facts in your cases, not the doctrines. When judges go home at night, they don't announce to their partners, "I had an interesting 10(b)(5) case today, involving a securities action, brought pursuant to the U.S. Code"—at least, not if they want to stay in that particular relationship. They tell stories composed of your facts. It's not that different from the *New Yorker* cartoon in which a judge announces, "Court will adjourn until ten o'clock tomorrow morning. I want to see what my wife makes of all this."

In addition, as litigation gets increasingly complex, the facts assume greater importance. Take any administrative law case. How much can you say about "arbitrary and capricious"? It's all been related before. You can tell a court a lot, however, about the facts—how the agency tested the standard, how it issued its regulations, or how the standard affected people's health. In fact, almost any administrative case turns on the facts and how you relate them.

The same holds true for most statutory or regulatory matters, including tax. We can read the laws or the code ourselves. But what did your clients do and why did they do it? Relate your facts compellingly and your argument will tend to take care of itself.

To be sure, in some matters you are better off stressing the law, not the facts. The question is one of emphasis. Every lawyer has a story to tell, even if it's not a great story in literary terms. It goes back to the old maxim "If you've got the facts, pound the facts. If you've got the law, pound the law. If you've got neither, pound the table."

2. Be accurate.

Most lawyers pay lip service to this rule by going through five cite checks before they file their papers. Cite checks are fine as far as they go. But judges and others also expect lawyers to tell the truth—about the facts of their case, the cases they have cited, and the positions they represent. Lawyers who play fast and loose with the facts and the law will be discovered by a conscientious judge. And when they are, it's usually the end of the case.

Why do lawyers stretch the truth? It comes from the locker-room mentality we discussed earlier, and a feeling that the legal process is a game in which skillful players can manipulate the rules to win all the time. That's a mistaken notion. Under the discovery rules, a lawsuit is essentially an effort to present each side's case as fairly and vigorously as possible so the court can make an equitable decision. While your job is to present your case effectively, you must realize that for every winner, there is at least one loser. The problem for many lawyers is that they have never learned how to lose gracefully.

3. Don't overargue.

Any argument, like a novel or symphony, must modulate in tone to be effective. Every point does not have to be the essential point, and every contention is not of equal value.

Some advocates insist that every sentence of a brief must make a point forcefully, or at least reveal which position the advocate is defending. These are the same people who consider Led Zeppelin the greatest rock band that ever existed and Tchaikovsky's 1812 Overture the model of classical music. A written argument is far more effective when it tells the reader honestly about a case, sometimes even conceding that some contentions are weaker than others. "I like, to the point of being unduly swayed by, a brief that contains not one pejorative adjective or innuendo concerning one's opponent or the trial judge," the late Judge Frank Coffin once wrote. Or, as La Rochefoucauld wrote, "We confess little faults in order to suggest that we have no big ones." Do the same here.

CHAPTER 5

The Role of Narrative in Argument

I. The Overview:
Storytelling Is an Essential Skill for All Lawyers

II. The Story

III. The Six Rules of Strong Narrative

1. Think of yourself as a storyteller.

2. Write about people.

3. Remember that plot is overrated in the telling of a story.

4. Create "word pictures" that make the story come alive.

5. The more specific the details, the better.

6. Use realistic dialogue that reveals character.

I. The Overview: Storytelling Is an Essential Skill for All Lawyers

Over the past decade or so, arguments have been circulating that because of the influence of computers and the ever-growing video culture, audiences put a smaller premium on the value of traditional narrative—especially if they're Generation Xers or younger. No doubt the role of narrative changes from medium to medium. But the power of stories seems to be a constant—from the *Iliad* and *Odyssey* to the Bible, and on through all the films and shows and even video games that comprise electronic culture. After all, the most wildly successful artifact of modern popular culture, *Star Wars*, is light on character but heavy on linear plot. Didn't the whole thing begin with the line "Once upon a time, in a galaxy far, far away . . ."?

It may well be that the more jangled, discordant, and impersonal communication becomes, the more important the power of narrative is, since it is one of the few universal forms of expression. This is true of legal discourse as well. Though storytelling is an art rarely taught in law school, it is an essential skill for a legal writer. As we have already discussed, most briefs revolve around the facts. In technical writing, as we shall learn, audiences often try to organize the complex material around the details, which can be made into a narrative. Even in memos, the ability to tell a good story can be indispensable.

"Like fiction, legal cases aim for verisimilitude, which is not quite the same as the truth," Elizabeth Gumport wrote in the UK's *Guardian*, in a review of *Iphigenia in Forest Hills* by Janet Malcolm. And, as Malcolm wrote herself, "If any profession (apart from the novelist's) is in the business of making things up, it is the profession of the trial lawyer." An overstatement perhaps, but the point is well taken.

In this chapter, we will examine what makes good narrative writing. To do that, we will first read a short article from the *New York Times*. While reading the story, try to analyze it as a critic or an artist might. How does the writer, Michael Winerip, lay out his tale? What makes this piece compelling reading? The answers will provide clues that will enable you, as a lawyer, to improve your writing. If you want, you can even read it aloud.

II. The Story

Bangor, Me.—It was a year ago when Zach Woodward, a junior at Bangor High School, asked his mom if Brian Raymond could move in with them. Once again, Brian had no place to live. Brian Raymond and Zach Woodward had been best buddies since third grade and stayed close, even when it became clear that something was terribly wrong at Brian's house; even when Zach, a popular boy, was ribbed by other friends for hanging out with Brian. "What do you always have to bring Brian for?" they'd ask.

"Mutt and Jeff" is what Zach's father called them. Zach is 5 foot 4 inches and 130 pounds; Brian, 6 foot 4 inches and 230 pounds. As to why they're friends, Zach says, "He's so big, he protects me," though it isn't true. Of the two, Zach is the athlete, a tennis and hockey player built like a concrete plug. Brian is more a gentle giant, a bit of a computer geek.

"For a while people felt I was addicted to my computer,"

Brian says. Zach's mother thinks the reason they're so close is that ever since they were little they were two boys who loved books.

Sophomore year, when Brian's mother entered the local mental hospital, he began living on his own in apartments, with friends, in a room at someone's house. About 600,000 teenagers between the ages of 15 and 19 are listed by the Census Bureau as heads of household and of those, 80,000, like Brian Raymond, live on their own.

To pay his way, Brian worked after school at Service Merchandise, a department store, and started a computer repair business. His guidance counselor, Jim McNamara, would ask if he was eating; Brian would assure him that he was, though there were many nights when there was no food in the apartment.

Brian is not a boy to complain, so it took a while for Mr. McNamara to figure out how hard his life was. Looking now at Brian's transcript, he can see that 10th grade was the low point. Brian had always been a math and science whiz. "He got a C in Algebra II," Mr. McNamara says. "That should never have been."

When Zach asked his mother about Brian's moving in, Bridget Woodward said, "I have to talk with your dad"—Mark Woodward, the editor of *The Bangor Daily News*—even though she knew it would fall mainly on her. Mrs. Woodward, an aide in the local office of Senator Susan Collins, is finicky about her home, and kept mentioning the extra laundry, the food, and how they would fit everyone's beverages in one refrigerator. But what she was thinking was, "Do I want all this responsibility?"

Zach was hopeful: "Mom didn't say no. She said she had to think about it." The truth was, Mrs. Woodward liked Brian. She was impressed that a boy with so hard a life had such nice manners. She remembered how on summer mornings when he was little, before all the Woodwards were awake, he was at the house calling for Zach. She told him not to come by until 10, and after that, you could set the clock by it: summer mornings at 10, Brian at the door.

In the end, Mrs. Woodward said yes. And if she had not? "I don't know," Brian says. "Kind of what I've been doing is going along and hoping it works out. I never had too many options."

It is hard to know why life's weight sinks some children while others, like Brian Raymond, keep bobbing up. Part of Brian's good fortune is that good people have helped at the worst moments: the Woodwards; Mr. McNamara; his girlfriend's family the Irelands, who took him in for short stays, made sure he had food and clothes and gifts on his birthday; Gerry Palmer, a businessman who helped Brian start his computer repair service, and Irv Krupke, a teacher who let him use the computers in drafting class whenever Brian had a free period.

But there is more to it. People seemed willing to do so much in part because Brian rarely asked. "He's very soft spoken, doesn't push himself on somebody," Mr. McNamara says. "People respond."

While Bangor is a small, blue-collar city of 34,000, few here know Brian's story. When a reporter arrived from New York to spend a day at the high school, a secretary said, "Which Brian Raymond do you want?" (Turns out that there's a freshman Brian Raymond, too.)

Brian knew how to blend in. "If you look at Brian," Mr. McNamara says, "you don't see a kid who seems to come from the depths of poverty. He keeps himself clean, dresses well, knows how to get along with people and what he needs."

His advanced-placement computer teacher, Stephanie Lord, says the only hint she had that something was amiss was when she sent home progress reports to be signed by parents and Brian's came back with a waiver from the principal.

Which is not to say he's perfect. "He is a teenaged boy," Ms.

Lord says. He drinks Diet Pepsi at 8 a.m., talks too much in class with Brian Webber (Deanna Jones, the English teacher, is constantly yelling, "Brians!") and can be lazy if the subject doesn't appeal to him. "I don't think he's even read the last two books," Mrs. Jones says.

He hasn't. "I like reading," he says, "it's just the 'Epic of Gilgamesh' and stuff like that doesn't really interest me." While most top students took an S.A.T. prep course, Brian did not. "I didn't want to spend the money," he says. "I figured that I would do well enough." He did: of a possible 800 he scored 690 in math and 730 verbal.

His mother was a factory worker, his father managed a truck stop, and though the father was manic-depressive, "for a while," Brian says, "it went under and no one even saw it." By sixth grade, it was plain. In a manic phase, he says, his father spent all the rent money; in a depressed phase, he sat in the living-room chair all day. "Since he tried to commit suicide, he was not the same," Brian says. "The whole family had to go to counseling. My counselor said my defense mechanism was to separate myself from the rest of the family."

Brian spent hours alone in his room. "I had my computer. That was it."

After his parents divorced, his mother had a breakdown and was also hospitalized. When she was released, he says, "things were fine for a while, but then Mom left to live with a boyfriend." Brian and his younger sister, who had serious problems and is now in foster care, were home alone for weeks at a time.

According to school records: "The quality of his family life deteriorated drastically.... His mother, who was living with a male friend rather than at home, would call to check up on Brian and his sister. They received ... inadequate financial support from her. There were days without food.... Brian's sister ... and many of her friends would come to the house to party and spend the night.... This situation became intolerable for Brian.

His one joy during sophomore year was Erika Ireland. They met in middle school, where they both were in gifted classes, but as Brian says: "I didn't pay much attention to her. She was real quiet. I talk a lot."

In 10th grade, they had the same English class. This time when Brian talked, Erika talked back. "One day," he says, "Erika said she's seen me walking home from school and I ought to stop by her house sometime." He did, that day.

"I was walking down the hill by my house," Erika says, "and he came up behind me singing loudly." It was Brian's way of saying hello. That night, Erika's mom insisted on driving him home. Brian had her drop him in front of the Woodwards'. It took the Irelands months to piece together the truth. "I didn't want to scare them off," Brian says now. "They have a normal situation."

In his junior year, Brian's guidance counselor told him that he could get a legal-aid lawyer and become emancipated from his family. "Brian went there by himself," Mr. McNamara says. "He was that determined." On Jan. 23, 1997, Brian's petition for emancipation was granted.

These days, Brian's biggest problem is senioritis. And while he's still known as a computer guy—he wrote the program Mr. Krupke uses for all his drafting classes—he's known for other stuff too, like being Erika's boyfriend.

Brian has been accepted to several engineering programs, including the one at the University of Maine in Orono and the Rochester Institute of Technology in New York. Erika will go to Orono and thinks Brian should, too. "It makes a lot more sense than Rochester," she says. "Rochester's a 12-hour drive. Half the people he fixes computers for are in Orono—it'll be a strong base for his business."

Brian is not sure. He has been all over cyberspace but never in an airplane and is tempted by a faraway place. "Every day Erika and I fight about it," he says. "I don't know."

Even Mrs. Woodward admits that Brian has fit in nicely at their home. They converted a small study for his room and bought a second refrigerator, so there is plenty of space for everyone's beverages.

It is the most home Brian has known. "Those places I rented," he says, "I just had a fridge and had to stay in the room. Here, I can sit down, watch TV. It's more like I live here; it's kind of cool."

Mornings at the Woodwards' are hectic. Mr. Woodward's rushing off to the newspaper, Mrs. Woodward to the Federal Building. The boys are always late and eat their pancakes standing at the kitchen counter. One pancake is plenty for Zach; Brian eats four.

Mr. Woodward once asked his wife why she bothered cooking pancakes every morning instead of letting them grab cereal. His wife told him those boys would remember those pancakes the rest of their lives.

III. The Six Rules of Strong Narrative

What makes Winerip's piece tick? For starters, the author follows most of the rules we have outlined so far, from using strong verbs to cutting out clutter. His style is understated and conversational. Here are six other suggestions that arise from the way he and other effective narrators write, many of which may be relevant in argument writing, depending on the matter at hand.

1. Think of yourself as a storyteller.

Audiences relate to stories in ways they don't relate to more analytical recitals. What gave Ronald Reagan much of his strength as a speaker was his ability as a superb storyteller—he was so good that audiences didn't mind that he occasionally fiddled with the facts. (This is not recommended in legal writing!)

Instead of giving the typical political speech criticizing welfare, Reagan would tell a story (apocryphal or not) about a welfare mother who misused her benefits. In a somewhat similar vein, according to the Bible, Christ rarely lectured people, announcing precepts the way a lawyer might. Instead he told stories, or parables, and the audience intuitively responded to what he said.

These lessons apply to you as well. On one level, a lawsuit is simply a clash of competing stories. If you tell your story better than the lawyer for the other side, you won't always win, but you will have a far better chance of prevailing. "Every lawsuit is a story," Chief Justice Roberts once said in an interview. He went on:

> I don't care if it's about a dry contract interpretation; you've got two people who want to accomplish something, and they're coming together—that's a story. And you've got to tell a good story.

In the course of a good story, audiences will listen to almost anything, as long as you don't stray too far from the narrative. That's why intellectual property lawyers can often get across the uniqueness of a new product—not through a boring analysis of the components of an invention, but by giving us the story of how and why the inventor came up with the innovation. If, out of the blue, Michael Winerip started lecturing us on how children in many states live alone, we wouldn't pay attention. In the course of a good story, however, the reader hangs on every word.

"When you have a product that's just like another product, there are any number of ways to compete," Barbara Shaw, a professor of marketing at Rutgers, has written about the advertising world. "The stupid way is to lower prices. The smart way is to change the value of the product by telling a story about it."

2. Write about people.

All good stories revolve around individuals. "Never present ideas except in terms of temperaments and characters," André Gide once said. In the Winerip story, the author describes the issue of children living alone in terms of Brian Raymond and his relationship with his friend Zach Woodward. Many other characters populate the story, from the members of Brian's and Zach's families to Brian's teacher, to his girlfriend. Again, it's one of the basic traits of humanity that people like to hear stories about others rather than lengthy conceptual dissertations. Often a critic will say disparagingly of an article, "It's a human interest piece," but we are, after all, writing for other humans. Better that than a zebra interest piece.

The admonition to write about people is so obvious that it seems scarcely worth mentioning. Yet it's a principle that lawyers forget all the time. That's because lawyers are weaned on an odd form of narrative—the judicial opinion. The opinion too is a story, but a peculiar one. Like all stories, it has a plot, with a beginning, a middle, and a conclusion. However, an opinion's plot does not follow Aristotle's definition of either tragedy or comedy. Instead, an opinion tells its readers about rules. Indifferent to the usual elements of storytelling, it tends to relegate its characters to minor roles. What happened to Mrs. Palsgraf, the plaintiff in Justice Cardozo's infamous opinion in *Palsgraf v. Long Island R.R.*, 162 N.E. 99 (N.Y. 1928), which all law students study in first-year torts class? We're too busy talking about foreseeability even to notice. What of Tompkins, the unfortunate plaintiff in that stalwart case from first-year civil procedure class, *Erie R. Co. v. Tompkins*, 304 U.S. 64 (1938)? We're more concerned with figuring out what happened to *Swift v. Tyson*, 16 Pet. 1 (1842), than with what happened to the people.

Judges have a reason for writing this way. The more they focus on individuals, the more subjective their writing becomes. And the more subjective their opinions are, the less objective the rules they are trying to create and enforce can be. Judges have a professional reason to turn people into objects, often using labels like "promisor" and "tortfeasor" to help them do so.

You, however, are not a judge, and the more you write like one, the less anyone—including a judge—is going to care about what you say. No one would ever want to read a novel titled *A Day in the Life of the Reasonable Man*. Nor is there going to be a huge audience for a miniseries called *The Holder in Due Course: The Sequel*. Even if you represent a corporation or an organization in your practice, these entities are made up of people. Most of the time you want to humanize your clients, if only by giving them names other than "plaintiff" and "defendant," or better yet, putting us in their shoes. Jim McElhaney, the venerable legal academic, once told the story of a Maryland lawyer who kept calling the defendant by his first name, Bobby. When the jury came back, the foreman announced, "We find Bobby not guilty."

"Basically fiction is people," the science fiction author Theodore Sturgeon once said. "You can't write fiction about ideas."

To be sure, there are exceptions. A lawyer for the defendant in a product-defect suit in which the plaintiff has been injured or killed may well want to talk only about "the plaintiff" and "the defendant" and keep things as dry as possible. But lawyers tend to overdo the impersonality. In his contribution to a book on advertising, *The Copywriter's Guide*, Robert Chase gave this advice: "The direct mail copywriter must learn to like people—all kinds of people. He must learn to understand them, to be amused by them, to sympathize with them. He must know what motivates them; what they want to be, do, and own."

Argument writing in a legal context is somewhat different from copywriting. But in its focus on the individual, it is much the same.

"Don't write about Man," E. B. White advised. "Write about a man." His advice is well taken.

3. Remember that plot is overrated in the telling of a story.
Many legal writers have become "Dan Brownicized." They think that the best way to tell a story is to have multiple plot twists, including a cliffhanger at the end.

That's wrong, if not for Brown, then for you. Most great novels have rather inconsequential plots, and often it's clear from the first page what is about to transpire. It's how you get there that counts. "All happy families are alike. Each unhappy family is unhappy in its own fashion," Tolstoy began *Anna Karenina*. Even at that point, you know that things are probably not going to go swimmingly for the Karenina clan. Yet you don't throw the novel out because Tolstoy has given away the ending.

The same holds true with the Winerip story. By the end of the first few paragraphs, the reader already knows that things will work out for Brian and the Woodwards. That doesn't matter: It's *how* that happens that draws us in—it's our involvement with the characters that counts.

In a brief to a judge or a letter to a client, the reader is going to know the conclusion long before you get to explain the facts. No matter: You can still make the story compelling. You don't have to repeat the "point" of a story at the end for the reader to understand it, either. "The editors I had at *The New Yorker* quietly helped me in peculiar, small ways," the writer Irwin Shaw once said. "One thing they taught me was the value of cutting out the last paragraph of stories, something I pass down as a tip to all writers. The last paragraph, in which you tell what the story is about, is almost always best left out."

4. Create "word pictures" that make the story come alive.
Throughout his story, Winerip skillfully uses detail to bring us into the story, focusing on detail rather than concepts. The metaphor for whether the Woodward house will become too crowded by Brian's presence is a crowded refrigerator that we can picture. The story ends with a memorable image of the boys

in the kitchen eating pancakes. There's frequent dialogue—an aural picture, so to speak.

Creating these "word pictures" is one of the hardest things for any writer to do, but it is what separates the great writers from the also-rans. Anyone can tell a story with people in it, up to a point. The power to make that story jump off the page, however, is more difficult, if only because it requires three skills. First, you must have the ability to paint the picture—to use words skillfully to create the right image. That means you must have an eye for the right kind of detail, since writers can't empty their notebooks and put everything they see into a story. When Hemingway was asked how a writer can train himself to develop this power of observation, he replied:

> Watch what happens today. If we get into a fish, see exactly what it is that everyone does. If you get a kick out of it while he is jumping, remember back until you see exactly what the action was that gave you the emotion. Whether it was the rising of the line from the water and the way it tightened like a fiddle string until drops started from it, or the way he smashed and threw water when he jumped. Remember what the noises were and what was said. Find what gave you the emotion; what the action was that gave you the excitement. Then write it down, making it clear so the reader will see it too and have the same feeling that you had. . . .

This skill that Hemingway describes doesn't come easily to most lawyers. After all, we're trained to look at the world much as judges do—to seek the overarching principle rather than the particular.

Look at it this way: If you take the prototypical legal book—a hornbook or treatise like "Prosser on Torts"—what interests the lawyers? Usually, it's the rules in the text dealing with such topics as negligence, false imprisonment, and strict liability.

What would interest a creative writer, however, is the material in the footnotes—the stories, the people, and the details. Your legal training will come in handy when you are writing about rules, but as a storyteller, you need to look at the world through the opposite end of the telescope. You're trying to capture a certain innocence of outlook, like that of a child or of someone who travels and sees a place for the first time. A good creative writer grounds the general in the specific, not the other way around.

Second, inexperienced writers often think that the best way to use detail is to describe people. That's incorrect. Detail is much better used to capture place. Yes, you're writing about people, but readers don't mind being given only a few details about an individual, since the ambiguity actually makes it easier for them to put themselves into the character. There's very little physical description of Zach and Brian and none for the other characters. Yet my guess is that you have an image of Mrs. Woodward in mind as you read the story, despite the lack of description.

The same principle holds true in literature. In F. Scott Fitzgerald's *The Great Gatsby*, the author does give us some key details about the characters, describing Jay Gatsby's shirts and Daisy Buchanan's marvelous laugh, which has "the sound of money." Most of his description, however, is reserved for Gatsby's mansion and the atmosphere of the party. Like almost all great writers, Fitzgerald puts us in the shoes of the characters without telling us too much about how they look.

Third, readers tend to remember those specifics that activate the senses. A good writer looks for descriptions that tell readers what they would see, hear, or feel physically. "There is nothing in the intellect that is not first in the senses," said Aristotle. Or as Anton Chekhov put it, "Don't tell me the moon is shining; show me the glint of light on broken glass."

In his book *Revising Fiction*, David Madden compared two

similar passages written by Raymond Chandler, describing a greenhouse where a character waited. In the first, in a short story called "The Curtain," Chandler wrote:

The air steamed. The walls and ceiling of the glass house dripped. In the half light enormous tropical plants spread their blooms and branches all over the place, and the smell of them was almost as overpowering as the smell of boiling alcohol.

When Chandler rewrote and improved the same scene for his novel *The Big Sleep*, he wrote:

The air was thick, wet, steamy and laced with the cloying smell of tropical orchids in bloom. The glass walls and roof were heavily misted and big drops of moisture splashed down on the plants. The light had an unreal greenish color, like light filtered through an aquarium tank. The plants filled the place, a forest of them, with nasty meaty leaves and stalks like the newly washed fingers of dead men. They smelled as overpowering as boiling alcohol under a blanket.

True, this would hardly be an appropriate style for a brief (unless you're writing some kind of brief noir). Yet the passage shows how physical details can be used to evoke a scene. *Show* your readers what to think; don't *tell* them. And even a brief noir may not be that inappropriate, at least if Chief Justice Roberts is an example to follow. He began a dissent from a denial of review in *Pennsylvania v. Dunlap*, 555 U.S. (2008), like this:

North Philly, May 4, 2001. Officer Sean Devlin, Narcotics Strike Force, was working the morning shift. Undercover surveillance. The neighborhood? Tough as a three dollar steak. Devlin knew. Five years on the beat, nine months with the Strike Force. He'd made fifteen, twenty drug busts in the neighborhood.

Devlin spotted him: a lone man on the corner. Another approached. Quick exchange of words. Cash handed over; small objects handed back. Each man then quickly on his own way. Devlin knew the guy wasn't buying bus tokens. He radioed a description and Officer Stein picked up the buyer. Sure enough: three bags of crack in the guy's pocket. Head downtown and book him. Just another day at the office.

"Avoid the abstract," the novelist V. S. Naipaul has advised. "Always go for the concrete."

5. The more specific the details, the better.

General factual descriptions weaken your prose. Notice how many statistical details Winerip gives us, such as the population of Bangor (24,000), the number of teenagers listed as heads of household (about 60,000), and Brian's SAT scores.

There's a lesson in that. Readers remember specific bits of information more than generalities, even if they seem harder to recall. Moreover, the specificity shows readers that the writer is in control and has taken the trouble to determine the facts. Writers who say that someone buying a car spent "thousands of dollars" are implicitly telling readers they couldn't be troubled to find out what really happened. That's a bad impression to leave with your audience.

However, as California federal judge Andrew Guilford has reminded readers, "Don't include nonessential dates," since the reader will try to remember them, crowding out other information.

6. Use realistic dialogue that reveals character.

We'll discuss in our section on affidavits how to write good dialogue. For now, it's worth noting how much dialogue this story has and, equally important, how the dialogue captures the characters. Note how Brian sounds like a teenager—"Here I can sit down, watch TV. It's more like I live here; it's kind of cool." Even the quotes from the school records add a note of realism to the story.

The power to create a compelling narrative is one that lawyers use constantly in their practices. Of course, they usually can't write exactly like Michael Winerip, because the circumstances or rules prevent them from exercising as much creative freedom. Yet the ideas that inform good storytelling are similar.

The main place these skills come to the fore is in writing facts in litigation. It is to this topic that we now turn.

PART III

Writing in Litigation

CHAPTER 6

Writing the Facts

I. The Overview: You Can't Write Your Facts Until
You Know Your Arguments

II. The Fifteen Rules of Writing Facts in Litigation

1. Always include a fact section.

2. Always distinguish between your statement of facts and
your statement of the case.

3. In your first paragraph of the fact section, tell your readers
what you're going to tell them.

4. After the initial paragraph, lead with your strongest facts;
don't feel compelled to tell your story chronologically.

5. Deal with the facts against you.

6. Don't argue in your fact section.

7. Show, don't tell.

8. Use quotations to make your story come alive.

9. Each fact in your story must be there for a purpose.

10. Deal with your best facts only once in the fact statement.

11. You can occasionally write about things that are not in the
record, as long as you call attention to that fact.

12. In a story without much plot, don't be afraid to use topic
headings.

13. Give judges only those facts they need to decide the issues in the brief or memorandum you are currently filing and divide them as necessary.

14. If you're in a jurisdiction where you must number your facts, write the narrative first, then do the numbering.

15. Avoid putting new facts in your argument section.

I. The Overview: You Can't Write Your Facts Until You Know Your Arguments

A good story makes any argument come alive. In his book *Briefing and Arguing Federal Appeals*, Frederick Wiener quoted the petitioners' brief in what could have been a dry case dealing with the interaction between a federal grazing law and a state statute regulating abandoned horses. Yet this brief in *Hatahley v. United States*, 351 U.S. 173 (1956), makes compelling reading through the facts (citations omitted and names changed):

> The animals were rounded up on the range and were either driven or hauled in trucks to a Government-owned or -controlled corral 45 miles away. Horses which could not be so handled were shot and killed by the Government's agents on the spot. The remainder were accorded brutal treatment: the horses were so jammed together in the trucks that some died as a result, and in one instance, the leg of a horse that inconveniently protruded through the truck body was sawed off by a federal employee, one Fred R. Lee. Later, the animals were taken in trucks to Provo, Utah, a distance of 350 miles, where they were sold to a glue factory and horse meat plants for about $1700—at around 3 cents a pound—no part of which was received by petitioners.

As noted in the last chapter, writing the facts in both trial and appellate litigation should be like telling a story. Because the narrative in litigation is based on a record and focused on specific legal issues, however, a writer constructs it differently from the usual story. I often hear lawyers say, "I'm going to write the facts and get them out of the way and then figure out what to say in the argument." This is the wrong way to construct a legal story. Lawyers can't write their facts unless they know their arguments, because without the arguments, they don't know what story to tell.

Therefore, the first task that litigators have to accomplish to tell their story well is to figure out specifically what their legal arguments are going to be and what's in the legal record. You don't need to draft the argument section first, but you should outline it in a page or two. Then study the record so you know what facts you can use. Remember what I said in Chapter 4: Like an investigative reporter, good litigators will already have gotten into the record, through discovery or other means, those facts and details they may need to construct a commanding narrative.

Once you've absorbed the record, you should put it aside and ask yourself three questions:

1. What's the story I want to tell?
2. What do I want readers to think after they've read my facts?
3. What facts relating to my issues will they find most compelling?

Having answered these questions, try writing a draft of the facts, remaining true to the record without looking at it. Which side you're on will determine not only what story you tell but how you tell it.

When you've finished this draft, look at the record and make sure there is support for every fact you've used. (Many jurisdictions require you to cite the source in the record for every fact.) Any assertions that can't be supported by the record should be cut. It's still important to start with your story and work back to the record, though, rather than the other way around. Too many litigators get so involved in the details of the record that they lose the thread of their story.

II. The Fifteen Rules of Writing Facts in Litigation

Along with the suggestions that follow, keep in mind all the points we established in the previous chapter: use detail, focus on people (while not actually describing them too much), and occasionally use imagery.

Here, then, are fifteen rules (short, don't worry) to remember in writing facts in litigation. (Many also apply to advocacy writing in general.)

1. Always include a fact section.

Many briefs or memoranda in support of motions contain no statement of facts. This is a mistake. No matter how short or trivial the facts are, it is your job to set them out for the court separately from your legal arguments.

I often see briefs in which the lawyers write, "We accept the plaintiff's view of the facts." I often wonder why they don't just accept the plaintiff's view of the law too, so everyone can go home early. Even in the rare case when both sides agree on a stipulated set of facts, you should always give the court your version, if only because the judge may have a question about the facts while reading your brief. You don't want judges looking at the other side's filing when they should be looking at yours.

2. Always distinguish between your statement of facts and your statement of the case.

The rules of most courts require both a procedural history (the story of what happened to your client after this became a legal matter) and a fact statement (the story that gave rise to the cause of action). Most judges, however, pay little attention to the boring procedural history, unless a procedural issue is at hand.

I would advise against combining these two sections in most cases, even if your local rules allow you to do so. The statement of facts is usually the most important part of your brief, and if you begin it with a tedious procedural recitation, the reader's attention will drift. By putting each in its own section (or subsection), you let the reader know what to skim, and you can begin your significant facts on a strong footing.

3. In your first paragraph of the fact section, tell your readers what you're going to tell them.

A summary paragraph is almost always essential, as it provides a context for the facts to come. Jacob Stein and his associates did this well in a Supreme Court case, *Richardson-Merrell, Inc. v. Koller*, 472 U.S. 424 (1985) (some names changed):

> This is a suit by an infant child and her parents, the Kollers, against petitioner, Richardson-Merrell, Inc., alleging that the child was born without arms and legs because of Mrs. Koller's ingestion during pregnancy of petitioner's product, the drug Bendectin. In February 1983, nearly three years after the suit was brought, and shortly before trial was to begin, petitioner moved to disqualify the Kollers' primary counsel, Messrs. Phillips and Simpson, alleging two discrete acts of misconduct. The trial was postponed indefinitely, and for the next eleven months the case changed from an inquiry into petitioner's alleged wrong to a massive inquiry into the conduct of Phillips and Simpson.

Or take the appellants' statement of facts in *Schieber v. City of Philadelphia*, 320 F.3d 409 (3d Cir. 2003), authored principally by Jane Istvan, who went on to co-author an article on brief writing with Sarah Ricks, "Effective Brief Writing Despite High Volume Practice," that every lawyer should read. According to Ricks and Istvan, "The theme of the brief was that the crime victim had no constitutional right to be rescued from the violence inflicted by the criminal, a private actor, because no state actor had personally put the victim in danger or prevented the victim from being rescued by private parties." (Footnotes omitted.)

Following our rule, the brief opens with the key fact supporting their case—that a private person, not a government actor, committed the crime:

> In the early morning hours of May 7, 1998, a private individual with no connection to municipal government raped and murdered Shannon Schieber in her Center City Philadelphia apartment.

4. After the initial paragraph, lead with your strongest facts; don't feel compelled to tell your story chronologically.

Like judges, almost all litigators relate their facts chronologically, beginning with the event that happened first in a historical sequence and proceeding forward to the present.

This is probably the worst mistake most litigators make in their writing. Modern novels, short stories, and movies rarely begin with what happened first. Instead, they start with an important event that leaves a strong impression. Then the narrative proceeds, with the author filling in the earlier facts as background as the plot moves along.

The only two groups left who tell stories chronologically—at least in American culture—are lawyers and six-year-olds. When my older son was a pre-schooler, he'd come home and

I'd ask him what happened during the day. "Well, first I went to my locker and I saw Ms. Jones and she said, 'Hi,' and I said, 'Hi, Ms. Jones,' and then I hung up my coat and went into the classroom," and he would proceed to tell us about the whole day, in chronological order (and often in real time).

But by the time he was eight or so, we'd ask him the same question, and he'd say, "I had shop today," even if that wasn't what had transpired first. In other words, he had already learned that in our culture, we don't tell stories "in order" anymore but, in ESPN style, we go to the highlight reel first, talk about that, and then at some point pick up an account in some kind of order (maybe chronological, maybe not) to account for the rest of the day.

Yes, stories were once told chronologically and some biographies still are. But the introduction of movies in the early twentieth century shattered our notions of chronological time. Thanks to fast cutting, we became accustomed to the notion that stories can be told a variety of ways and that if someone walks into a room and walks out a second later with a beard, time has passed. (Before, when time passed, calendar pages might be torn off, as in *Casablanca*.)

There's a reason why experimental novelists such as Virginia Woolf and James Joyce played with our notions of time in similar ways in the early part of the twentieth century. They had all been exposed to movies (and also to the relativistic notions of Albert Einstein), and so they were among the first to understand that storytelling had irrevocably changed. Today, of course, we take these notions for granted. Unless, of course, you're a lawyer (or six years old).

Sure, judges still choose to tell their stories from the beginning because they're trying to tell an "objective" story. Yet objectivity of that sort is an elusive goal in any other form of storytelling, because a narrative is always filtered through the mind of an author.

The Japanese filmmaker Akira Kurosawa made just this

point in his famous 1950 film *Rashomon*, which tells about the killing of a man whose wife was raped by a highway bandit. Kurosawa tells the story from several viewpoints, including the woman's, the bandit's, and the husband's soul's. In each case the story proceeds differently, because the teller has experienced the same set of facts differently.

Litigation writing is similar, which is why lawyers should lead with their best facts that relate to the issue at hand. *Who* you are determines *what* you consider important. Imagine the Three Bears are going to sue Goldilocks for trespass, and you are writing the facts in a brief for each side. Begin by asking yourself three questions, each of which requires a one-sentence answer:

1. Given my client, what do I want to argue?
2. What's the story I want to tell to support that argument?
3. Given that argument, where is the best place for me to begin my story?

If you represent the bears, you want to focus on the violation of their home. That means the best place to start your story is probably the moment the bears arrive home. You might begin by describing in exquisite detail how the furniture was broken, how the expensive porridge was eaten, and so on through all the damage in the house.

If you represent Goldilocks, you should tell your story differently. You want to concentrate on what it's like to be a small girl lost in the woods. You might begin your story with Goldilocks in that forest, and only after you've etched that scene in our memories do you begin moving her to the house.

In a similar fashion, consider an age discrimination case. Most of the time, plaintiffs begin with a boring chronological recitation of how old the plaintiff is, how long she's worked for this company, and so on. Far better in most cases to go right to the heart of the matter and describe the discrimination she encountered when she turned sixty-five.

If you're on the other side and your argument is that she was treated this way not because of her age but because she was acting erratically, you want to focus first on the details of that—say, how she insisted on answering the phone in ancient Greek and so on.

Yes, as with our Goldilocks example, these two versions of the same story begin in different places. That should not confuse a judge, however, because we have all become accustomed to the idea that stories can start almost anywhere, depending on the perspective of the author. A judge would also not be distressed by the fact that neither story begins "at the beginning," since very few narratives do. I have heard a few judges say that they prefer having the facts set out chronologically because it makes it easier for them to write their opinions. Your task, however, is not to help judges write opinions but to win your cases (except in the jurisdictions where local rules require you to set out those facts in chronological order).

Note, however, that in writing complaints or in listing facts for a different purpose (to show which ones are undisputed, for example, in a summary judgment motion), using a chronological approach is fine.

Otherwise, lead with your best facts, no matter when they occurred in the course of a controversy. Here's how an effective appellate brief in a criminal case began (the names have been changed):

> It is undisputed that Jesse Lowry was singled out for an undercover, warrantless entry into his home solely on the basis of a vague, stale, and unsubstantiated rumor. This rumor began to interest the Jonestown police in the fall of 1984 . . .

Not writing chronologically will have the added benefit of forcing lawyers not to begin each paragraph with a date—"On

September 23, 2011, the plaintiff got into his car," and so on. You don't want to include dates that you don't want readers to remember. And, if dates are of interest, it's often far better to include a timeline or chart than to do so in written fashion.

An alternative is to begin your facts by setting a context for your story, placing it within a larger, often historical, struggle. A good example of this strategy comes from a brief filed in the U.S. Court of Appeals for the D.C. Circuit by the attorneys at Shea and Gardner for the Peabody Coal Company in *In Re Permanent Surface Mining Regulation Litigation*, 653 F.2d 514 (D.C. Cir. 1981) (*en banc*). The facts begin with this recitation:

> There are coal reserves in 37 states. In 1976, there were 6,161 operating mines. Of these 3,739 were surface mines, accounting for 57 per cent of the 679 million tons of coal produced.
>
> Most of the surface coal mines are small, typically located in the eastern United States. Others, typically in the western states, are very large. Surface coal production in 1976 was distributed according to mine size as follows . . .

No, there isn't much plot there, yet this opening does an excellent job of setting the scene in a way favorable to this appellant's interests. By the time you've finished these two initial paragraphs, you know that the industry includes a lot of small businesses and that these lawyers are on top of their material. There are worse ways to proceed.

Another group of plaintiffs who set up their facts well in the beginning was a group of environmental organizations that sued the government in the 1980s to stop a plan for selling public land to reduce the federal deficit. These plaintiffs began their facts in a brief opposing a motion to dismiss, by trying to tell a story of how the government disposes of land (citations and footnotes omitted):

Throughout American history, the federal government has owned vast amounts of land, particularly in the western United States. These lands, once acquired, were held by the United States for a number of reasons.

Because uses for land and the government's needs change, sometimes the federal government must dispose of land it no longer needs. Although several agencies have the authority to sell surplus land, the General Services Administration ["GSA"] and the Bureau of Land Management ["BLM"] are the agencies charged with disposing of most surplus land. . . .

Before the Reagan administration took office, the amount of land disposed of each year under both statutes was relatively small compared to the government's holdings. For example, receipts for GSA sales of surplus real property were about $60 million a year.

But in 1982, the defendants dramatically changed both the policies and programs of the federal government concerning disposal of public lands. This change consisted of a massive program, carried out by several agencies whose actions were closely intertwined. These agencies already have begun to carry out the goals of the program. An examination of events in the past year illustrates how this program has taken shape.

Yet another terrific example of the technique came in a 2007 appellate brief for the U.S. Court of Appeals for Fifth Circuit, filed on behalf of defendant Jeffrey Skilling by former Solicitor General Walter Dellinger and other lawyers:

STATEMENT OF FACTS I. SEPARATING
FACT FROM FICTION

Popular myth shrouds Enron and its collapse. Any fair understanding of this case, and Skilling's arguments on appeal, first requires shedding its lore.

Debunking Myth No. 1. This case is not about Enron's bankruptcy, and never was. Skilling resigned months before scandal and bankruptcy befell the company, when—even according to government witnesses—the prospect of bankruptcy was inconceivable. The Task Force acknowledged this in closing:

"This case is not about what caused the bankruptcy of Enron. You don't have to worry about that. You don't have to think about that during your deliberations. It's not about what caused the bankruptcy." [citations omitted]

There's an old story about a couple who come upon a man on his hands and knees under a streetlight. "What are you doing?" they ask.

"I'm searching for a contact lens I lost," he says.

The couple begin looking, and gradually about six or eight other people join them. They all look for fifteen minutes without success.

"This is odd," the woman says finally. "We've looked everywhere. Where did you drop the lens?"

The man points behind his shoulder. "I dropped it in that dark alley back there."

"Then why are we looking here?" the woman says.

He points up. "Because this is where the light is," he answers.

Judges can only look where you throw the light. Make sure that initially it's on the facts you want them to remember the most. This is the tactic that lawyers at Mayer Brown used in a product liability case in which they were representing the company against a quadriplegic—clearly a sympathetic plaintiff if there ever was one. Here is what they wrote near the beginning (citations omitted and names changed):

On March 11, 1989, plaintiff Devin McBride, a vehicle mechanic in the Army, stationed at Fort Carson, Colorado, accompanied some Army friends to ride a three-wheeled off-road all-terrain vehicle ("ATV") on a mountain near Pike's Peak. The particular vehicle that McBride rode that day, a 1982 ATC 200, was designed by defendant Honda Motor Co. It was sold by defendant American Honda Motor Co. to a dealer in Colorado, who in 1982 sold it to its first owner. The ATV ultimately went through seven owners, at one point being in such a state of disrepair that it sold for only $25. By the time it reached its seventh owner, McBride's friend Melanie Major, the ATV no longer had its owner's manual and remained in a severe state of disrepair. Among other things, the left brake lever was broken, rendering the front brake inoperable; the rear brakes were badly out of adjustment and, as a result, barely functioned; and, for one reason or another, the vehicle pulled noticeably from its intended course, causing the rider to need to make adjustments to compensate.

Although McBride had never before ridden an ATV, and indeed did not know anything about ATVs, he ignored the specific warnings on the vehicle to wear a helmet and to read the owner's manual. According to his own testimony, "[a]ll I'm thinking about is going for a ride. I'm not thinking about, you know, an owner's manual or anything like that."

5. Deal with the facts against you.

Better the court should hear bad news from you than from your adversary. It's even worse if judges discover the news on their own and think you were trying to cover it up. The cover-up is almost always worse than the crime.

In his book, Wiener illustrated what can happen when an advocate fails to address bad facts. This excerpt was taken from a respondent's brief (the names have been changed and citations have been omitted):

We have documented the United States Attorney's argument on the defense of extortion with record references, not only in order that it might be considered against the context of the evidence in the case, but also because the Smiths' brief falls considerably short of reflecting all the pertinent facts.

(1) The Smiths start by saying that Milton Smith and Morris Smith voluntarily enlisted in the Air Corps. They fail to state that Sam Smith had them volunteer for the Air Corps in order to avoid having them drafted and assigned to the infantry.

(2) The Smiths admit that their concern, the Paris Thread Corporation, paid the Berg Company for the uniforms furnished to Jones and other officers of the First Bomber Command. They fail to state that, at Sam Smith's request, the Berg Company's books were later altered to show that the officers themselves paid for the uniforms.

How should litigators deal with unfavorable information? Don't lead with a bad fact, unless it's the key fact in a case and judges will be able to think of little else until you've addressed it. Instead, do some of the things I have urged you *not* to do when writing well. For example, take the bad fact and put it in a clause in the middle of a long sentence or even paragraph, where the reader is more apt to disregard it. This is what Jane Istvan and the other appellant lawyers did in the *Schieber v. City of Philadelphia* brief we talked about earlier. According to Istvan and Sarah Ricks, "the Statement of Facts . . . attempts to neutralize an unfavorable fact—that another neighbor did not think the witness who called 911 had equivocated on the source of the noise . . . by [placing it in] . . . the middle of a paragraph, sandwiched between two favorable facts":

On May 7, 1998, between approximately 12:00 a.m. and 1:15 a.m., Ms. Schieber's next door neighbors, Leah Basickes and

Parmatma Greeley, heard a noise. Greeley thought the sound came from the direction of Shannon Schieber's apartment, but Basickes disagreed and made it "very clear" that the noise came from outside. [Citations omitted.]

Another option for deemphasizing a fact is to use the passive voice to deemphasize action. Sherman didn't open the door; "The door was opened." This implies that Sherman had little to do with it.

This is the technique Harvard Law School professor Alan Dershowitz and other lawyers used in their brief in *Tison and Tison v. Arizona*, 481 U.S. 137 (1987), a Supreme Court appeal challenging the death sentence of two brothers. When describing part of the crime in the facts, the lawyers wrote (record citations omitted): "Both automobiles were driven down a dirt road off the highway. The family was then placed by the side of the road, and the Tisons' possessions were placed in the Mazda. The Lincoln was then driven fifty to seventy-five yards further into the desert."

Finally, you might apply Novacain to a situation by giving it little detail. A writer who wants us to remember a situation will describe it in all its glory. The Big Corporation didn't just fire Clark; it carried his furniture into the hall and then changed the lock on his office, so when he showed up for work he couldn't open the door. The defendant describing that situation might simply say, "Clark was dismissed." With no color, there's little to attract our attention.

Another way to deal with unfavorable facts is to place them toward the end of your fact section. In our Goldilocks example, after the lawyers for the Three Bears have described all the damage they found when they came home, they should mention that Goldilocks was lost in the woods first. By doing so at the end, they deemphasize that fact, or at least put it in some kind of context. Similarly, after the attorneys for Goldilocks have told us all about her being lost in the woods, they can turn to the damage she caused in a paragraph or two.

These techniques work because the best arguments are those that convince us without our being aware that we've been persuaded. No judge looks at a brief and says, "You used the passive voice—you're trying to pull the wool over my eyes!" Yet that's precisely why these techniques succeed. It's not your job to lay out the unfavorable facts in a way that draws attention. (That's your adversary's job.) As long as the unfavorable facts are in the fact section and they are accurate, you've met your professional responsibility.

A final way to deal with bad facts is to confront them head-on. This is what a Washington lawyer did in a case before the United States Court of Appeals for the Federal Circuit, *Meehan v. United States Postal Service*, 718 F.2d 1069 (Fed. Cir. 1983). In his statement of facts, this lawyer, who was defending the appellant, wrote (citations omitted and names changed):

> Told there was no work, Barnes testified, the employee's voice got "a little louder than normal"; he got "extremely upset" and hit the desk. And he said "I only want to work here until December and then I'm going to Florida anyway. And I'm going to take one of the motherfuckers out before I go."

The lawyer followed with this footnote:

> The term "motherfucker" is not essential to the construction of the charged words as a threat to kill, and it will be mentioned again only when necessary to note an inconsistency between two witnesses.
>
> It may be noted, however, that obscene as it is, it is now street talk for a (not necessarily disliked) male person. The term is defined variously as an "exclamation of anger," "insult; derogatory name; bastard" and a "positive complimentary name for a

friend" (E. E. Landy, *The Underground Dictionary*, 135, Simon & Schuster, N.Y., 1971); as "any despicable person or thing," "a superb person or thing," and "a male buddy or chum" and as "a term used between males" (The English Language Institute of America, *A Dictionary of Contemporary and Colloquial Usage*, cc-20, 1972); "any male; the connotation is not necessarily negative" (C. Major, *Dictionary of Afro-American Slang*, 82, International Publishers, 1970).

The term is no longer underground. Counsel recently heard it in a well-regarded current movie, *An Officer and a Gentleman*, and read it, albeit in censored form, in a magazine article entitled "Inside the Post," by Robert Pack, as having been spoken in anger by the head of a major corporation. *Washingtonian*, December 1982, vol. 18, No. 3, 144, 147.

Conceding what is true, or that evidence conflicts, actually enhances your credibility.

6. Don't argue in your fact section.

Arguments are for the argument section; your fact section strives to deal with facts. The most obvious way in which litigators violate this rule is by lying or exaggerating. Not only is this unethical, it's stupid, since judges who get the impression that you're playing fast and loose with the facts don't believe anything you say. As David Ogilvy once advised, tell the truth, but make the truth interesting.

As noted earlier, you can use your first few sentences to set out the thesis of your story with a slant: "This is a case about a group of oil companies that set out to drill for oil in the North Atlantic without getting the required permits." At that point, however, you can no longer categorize your facts but should simply relate them.

Beyond exaggeration and outright lying, there are subtler

ways in which litigators violate this rule, often inadvertently. Keep the following points in mind:

a. Don't make legal conclusions in your facts.

Statements like "The other car had the last clear chance to avoid the accident" or even "They were operating the machine negligently" are not facts. Those are your legal conclusions, which make up the argument. In the fact section, you can describe in great detail what the other car was doing to give it the last clear chance, but you shouldn't draw the legal conclusion itself until the argument section.

b. Adjectives and adverbs are usually not facts.

Adjectives are opinions about facts and therefore generally don't belong in a fact section. When you write, "It was a rough ride," rough is not a fact. If someone testified that it was "rough," you can quote him. Beyond that, however, your job is to describe the actual, observable facts that might lead an observer to conclude it was rough: "The occupants bounced out of their seats every thirty seconds," or "One bump was so hard that a seat belt broke." Those are facts and they're also a better way to describe what happened.

c. You cannot ascribe feelings or mental states to people in a fact section.

"She felt bad about the accident," the inexperienced litigator writes. How can anyone know that? If the woman said she felt bad, you can quote her. As any student of Freud understands, however, people frequently don't tell the truth about how they feel, and sometimes they don't even know. You can write, "She had tears streaming down her face," because that's a fact we can observe. "She felt sad" is not capable of observation. The irony, of course, is that if you write about tears streaming down her face, readers will conclude on their own that she's sad, so you don't need to say it.

7. Show, don't tell.

In litigation writing, as in creative writing, the more descriptive your prose is, the better it is. I once gave a course in Miami that a number of former criminal defense lawyers attended. One told me about a case in which his client had allegedly committed a series of burglaries in the area. The lawyer was filing a motion arguing that his client was mentally incompetent to stand trial. In the first sentence of the fact section, he wrote, "On the morning of the burglaries in question, my client tried to eat a live cat for breakfast."

From that point on, the reader is already leaning strongly to a finding of mental incapacity. This writer knew that if you simply quote your experts while the other lawyers quote theirs, the reader becomes confused. Experts *tell us* what to think. If you *show us* first and let us draw the conclusions for ourselves, you tend to be far more persuasive.

As you write, you need to think of yourself as a cinematographer or, better yet, a playwright. What would you show on stage or on the screen to dramatize your scene? This will move you in the direction of showing, since it will force you to rely on characters, rather than concepts, and what these characters do, rather than what they think. Shakespeare's *Hamlet* is a work of genius for a number of reasons. But a key one is that Shakespeare creates a compelling drama about a mental state—how someone can't make up his mind. How he manages to do this is a lesson for all narrative writers.

In his book *Writing Persuasive Briefs*, Girvan Peck provided an excellent example of how to ground even conceptual facts in specifics. This passage came from the government's brief in the antitrust case *United States v. United States Gypsum Company*, 438 U.S. 422 (1978) (citations omitted and names changed):

In 1962 Stephen Michaels, chairman of the board of United States Gypsum (USG), authorized in writing a select group of pricing officials to participate in the discussion and exchange of prices and terms and conditions of sale with USG's competitors. He allowed inquiry into the entire "competitive situation in a market." Michaels recognized that such exchanges would have to be reciprocal (*ibid.*):

> It is often advisable to answer such inquiries [from competitors], because otherwise the competitor may be misinformed as to our prices and policies and answering the inquiry may avoid consequences unfavorable to the Company.

The "unfavorable" consequences that the defendants sought to avoid were lower prices and nonadherence to published terms and conditions of sale. Deviations often were reported on forms used by the defendants' field sales forces to request authority to meet competition. If a "deviation"—whether or not it actually existed—led to lower prices or better conditions of sale by any major competitor, the "deviation" would spread. . . .

The more competitive activity there was in a market, the more the defendants exchanged information in an attempt to abate that competition.

8. Use quotations to make your story come alive.

There are many things as litigators we can't do. We can't make things up. We can rarely, if ever, be funny. We have to remain focused on the issues at hand. But one thing we can do, because we're surrounded by them, is use quotes. Yet rare is the brief or argument that does.

That's a huge mistake. Narrative writers use quotations frequently both because they reveal character and we hear them—they activate our senses. As in our *New York Times* story, quotations can be effective, because they make the characters come alive. We *hear* the pleas of witnesses and parties.

Abe Fortas helped secure the right to counsel in criminal cases by effectively quoting the court proceedings below in *Gideon v. Wainwright*, 372 U.S. 335 (1963) (citations and footnotes omitted):

> At the commencement of the trial, Petitioner informed the trial judge that he was "not ready" because "I have no counsel." Petitioner expressly requested that counsel be appointed to assist him at the trial, but that request was denied by the trial court. The colloquy is as follows:
>
> "The Defendant: Your Honor, I said: I request this Court to appoint Counsel to represent me in this trial.
>
> "The Court: Mr. Gideon, I am sorry, but I cannot appoint Counsel to represent you in this case. Under the laws of the State of Florida, the only time the Court can appoint Counsel to represent a Defendant is when that person is charged with a capital offense. I am sorry, but I will have to deny your request to appoint Counsel to defend you in this case.
>
> "The Defendant: The United States Supreme Court says I am entitled to be represented by Counsel.
>
> "The Court: (Addressing the Reporter) Let the record show that the Defendant has asked the Court to appoint Counsel to represent him in this trial and the Court denied the request, and informed the Defendant that the only time the Court could appoint Counsel to represent a Defendant was in cases where the Defendant was charged with a capital offense. The Defendant stated to the Court that the United States Supreme Court said he was entitled to it."

By adding a few quotations, Fortas took what appeared to be a rather mundane legal matter and gave it the drama it deserved.

"Dialogue brings a novel to life. It is possible to compose fiction without it, just as Georges Perec was able to write an entire book without using the vowel "e," but one had better be a genius to affect such forms of composition," the novelist Frederic Raphael once wrote.

9. Each fact in your story must be there for a purpose.

First-time readers of a story don't know what's important and what isn't, so they treat everything with equal importance. If you start injecting into your statement of facts a number of details that don't have much to do with your basic premise, you start to confuse your readers and may lose them. I often ask litigators why they have put a certain detail into their facts, and they reply, "It's for effect." They never consider the follow-up question: "Why that effect?" The facts you include should be relevant to your legal contentions.

In his book, Wiener quoted a brief in which the statement of facts read:

> Frank O. and Andrew E. Wilson, doing business under the trade name of Lone Star Oil Company, a partnership, own and operate a chain of seven retail gasoline filling stations in the City of ———, Texas. And, they also own the real estate on prominent business corners of the City of ———, upon which they have erected magnificent structures and equipment to house their businesses.

No matter how lovely those buildings were, they had nothing to do with the issue at hand. They shouldn't have been mentioned.

Anton Chekhov, the great Russian author, once said that if there's a gun onstage in the first act, it had better go off in a later act. Otherwise, the audience is paying attention to a prop that is ultimately distracting them. This principle holds true in litigation writing even more than it does in creative writing. You should be able to go over every detail in your facts and justify how each relates to a larger legal point you're trying to establish.

If not, you have to question strongly why you've put it in the story. "Dullness won't sell your product, but neither will irrelevant brilliance," Bill Bernbach, the ad guru, has said. A few key details directly on point create a far stronger impression than a wave of irrelevant descriptions, no matter how colorful. In fact, the more colorful they are, the more memorable they are, which is a detriment if the facts aren't relevant.

10. Deal with your best facts only once in the fact statement.

Inexperienced litigators think that the best way to drive their most compelling facts home is to repeat them several times. That's wrong. If you describe a situation compellingly once in the facts, repeating them in this section only lessens the impact.

The late Irving Younger, a wonderful legal scholar and litigator, used to tell a story that illustrated this point. It concerned a famous New York case involving the Triangle Shirtwaist Company fire in 1911, the worst factory fire in New York history, which killed 146 workers. (The owners were tried for manslaughter and were acquitted when the jury could not establish whether they had ordered that the doors be locked. A civil suit brought later by twenty-three victims resulted in payments of $75 to each of the families.) Early in the trial, a woman who had survived the fire testified. Breaking down several times, she related to a hushed courtroom what it had been like as her friends and fellow workers were overcome by smoke and tried to escape through doors and windows.

Younger would ask his students, "If you're the lawyer on the other side, what do you do now?" What the lawyer did, in so many words, was to acknowledge the horror of the situation, and then quietly ask the woman to tell her story again and again. Part of the reason he did that, as Younger told it, was to show that her testimony had been rehearsed and memorized. By repeating her story over and over, however, the woman also drained the emotion from it. As she retold her tale, she was less emotional, and the reaction of listeners was less visceral too.

A similar thing happened in the infamous first Rodney King California assault case in the early 1990s. The first dozen or so times people saw the videotape of King being beaten by police, it was horrifying. Once the tape had been repeatedly played, however, or broken down into slow-motion instant replay, it could not have the same galvanizing effect on its audience.

If anything, your opponents are going to want to repeat your key facts in their fact sections to diminish them. Don't do it to yourself. If judges have heard a story five thousand times, they're less likely to pay attention to it the five thousand and first. Remember: Familiarity breeds apathy.

11. You can occasionally write about things that are not in the record, as long as you call attention to that fact.

Lawyers are so intent on writing about what did happen that they forget that what didn't happen (but could have) can occasionally be revealing. Let's say an auto accident case has a very detailed police report that goes on for pages, describing everything from the pavement to the leaves on the trees by the road. Despite such specificity, however, there is no mention of skid marks. A lawyer can certainly note in the fact section that despite such a detailed report, no mention of skid marks appears, and then go on to develop the implications of this point in the argument section.

Sherlock Holmes used the same technique in the famous story "Silver Blaze," written by Arthur Conan Doyle:

"Is there any point to which you wish to draw my attention?" asked the Inspector.

"To the curious incident of the dog in the night-time," replied Holmes.

"But the dog did nothing in the night-time."

"That was the curious incident," responded Holmes.

The dog should have barked at an intruder. What didn't happen—but should have happened—told Holmes the truth.

If you use this technique, make sure you use it sparingly and carefully. It's an old trick of trial lawyers to try to get a jury to focus on what the client didn't do, in the hope that jurors will forget what the client really did do. There's a word, however, for the kind of literature that focuses continually on what didn't happen; it's called fiction. Most of the time in litigation writing, your job is to focus on the facts that did happen.

12. In a story without much plot, don't be afraid to use topic headings.

This happens frequently. Suppose you have a contract or Uniform Commercial Code (UCC) case that lacks a well-defined narrative. In such cases, you should divide the facts into sections to highlight the essentials a judge should remember. If you put the language of the contract in one section, the warranty in another, and, say, a list of complaints about the car in another, you've at least presented your key facts in a clear way that a judge is likely to remember. This is what Laurence Tribe and his co-counsel in the Supreme Court case of *Hawaii Housing Authority v. Midkiff*, 467 U.S. 229 (1984), did when they divided their facts into sections:

A. Why the Hawaii Land Reform Act Was Passed.

B. How the Hawaii Land Reform Act Works.

C. Contemporaneous State Proceedings Under the Act.

D. The Federal Proceedings Below.

Or, in a motion arguing for personal jurisdiction or change of venue, you might want to number your facts. This highlights for the judge the factors that support your argument.

Similarly, if you're a criminal defense lawyer arguing that both the search and seizure and the lineup were unconstitutional, you're not going to be able to link those in one smooth narrative. Better to break your facts into two sections—facts surrounding the search and facts encompassing the lineup. This isn't the way a short story writer would do it most of the time. But for our purposes it works, just as someone writing the facts in a contract case needs to focus almost exclusively on two things—what the contract says and what the parties did or didn't do.

Another group of writers who dealt well with technical facts is University of Texas Law professor Charles Alan Wright and the others who wrote the appellants' brief in *San Antonio Independent School District v. Rodriguez*, 411 U.S. 1 (1973). In this case, the appellants were challenging a lower-court ruling that found a Texas law for financing education unconstitutional. After briefly setting out the dynamics of the case in one paragraph, the appellants wrote (citations and footnotes omitted):

Although the details of the Texas system for financing public education are fairly complex, the general plan can be fairly readily described. It is of the sort known to educators as a "foundation plan." In essence, it is a combination of ad valorem taxes levied by school districts with a state contribution that is intended to assure that every child in the state has at least a minimum foundation education. The state contribution is calculated in a fashion that has a mildly equalizing effect.

The heart of the Texas system is the Minimum Foundation Program. Under that program more than a billion dollars a year is provided to cover the costs of salaries of professional personnel, school maintenance, and transportation. Eighty percent of the amount to which a school district is entitled under the Minimum Foundation Program is paid by the state from general revenue. The balance of the cost of the minimum program comes from the school districts under the Local Fund Assignment. An economic index is used so that each county's contribution to the Local Fund Assignment approximates that county's percentage of statewide taxpaying ability. Within each county the portion of the Local Fund Assignment that each school district is expected to contribute is the percentage of the county's assignment that the value of the property in the school district is of the value of all of the property in the county. Thus, while the state contributes, on an overall basis, 80 percent of the cost of the Minimum Foundation Program, in some districts that lack the ability to raise substantial funds by local effort the state contribution is in excess of 98 percent of the cost of the Minimum Foundation Program, while in districts with greater ability to pay the state contribution is less than 80 percent.

Each district is then free to supplement the minimum program with additional funds raised by local ad valorem taxes. In combination, the Texas plan assures every child in the state of a certain minimum level of education on a nondiscriminatory basis but allows each local school district to provide educational benefits above the minimum to the extent that the district wants and can afford them.

This isn't the most fascinating of topics, but the brief takes an exceedingly complex legislative framework and in three paragraphs makes it understandable for the reader in ways other lawyers should emulate.

13. Give judges only those facts they need to decide the issues in the brief or memorandum you are currently filing and divide them as necessary.

This is a concentrated form of writing. At the beginning, as we've noted, you want to summarize in a sentence or two the facts surrounding the whole controversy.

After that, however, give judges only the facts that are pertinent to the motion or issue at hand, following our "Chekhov rule" yet again. If you are arguing to compel production of a document in discovery, after the initial summary sentence write about only the facts that relate to this issue.

14. If you're in a jurisdiction where you must number your facts, write the narrative first, then do the numbering.

In some places such as Canada, litigators are required to number their facts. Fair enough, but if you do that as you're writing, you'll find it exceedingly difficult to create a good story. You'll write the narrative more as a list, and you'll find it much easier to fall into the trap of telling the story chronologically, often leading each sentence with a date.

In these cases, try instead to write the story as we've outlined and put in the numbering last. This should keep you on the right path. Note, however, that in locales where you must number the undisputed facts for a summary judgment motion, you're far less concerned with telling a story. In those cases (and with complaints, as we'll see later), don't worry about using chronology or numbering as you write.

15. Avoid putting new facts in your argument section.

It is repetitive to state many facts twice, first in the fact section and then in the argument. It's necessary, however, because a judge won't take factual assertions as true if they're made for the first time in the argument section. Try to put all your necessary facts in the fact section to establish their veracity. Then return to the few you need to use in the argument section.

Writing the facts takes more creativity than litigators commonly imagine. Always remember, though, that the winner in litigation is not the lawyer who tells the best story; it is the lawyer who tells the best story that is supported by a strong legal argument. If a widow is suing the federal government over the death of her husband in a military exercise, her facts may seem terribly eloquent. In contrast, if the government's defense is sovereign immunity, its facts are going to seem quite boring; its story is simply that the soldier worked for the government. Still, if that's a strong legal defense, the government has told the right story.

Even if the other side's facts seem particularly moving or compelling, your job is not to knock down your opponent's story but to tell your own. As we will learn in the next chapter, the lawyer who turns a lawsuit into a debate usually wins the debate but loses the lawsuit.

CHAPTER 7

Writing Arguments

I. The Overview: Remembering the Six Initial Precepts of Legal Argument

1. The lower you are in a court system, the shorter your submissions should be.

2. In most cases, concentrate on winning the case, not on helping the judge write the opinion.

3. Since a lawsuit is not a debate, don't make responding to the other side the focus of your argument.

4. Keep your style understated and avoid military and sports metaphors.

5. Keep your filings as short as possible, regardless of venue.

6. In the coming years, keep in mind the advantages of the electronic age.

II. The Sixteen Rules of Writing Arguments

1. Lead with your best argument, though you must deal with procedural issues first.

2. Use the "CRAC" method of argument: Conclusion, Rule, Analysis, Cases.

3. Use the case law effectively.

4. Package your citations so they are at the ends of sentences and the ends of paragraphs.

5. Avoid the tendency to respond too aggressively.

6. Never label or characterize your opponents.

7. Take a clear stand that can be summarized in two sentences.

8. Be careful when you make arguments in the alternative.

9. Limit the use of footnotes.

10. Start a new section every four pages or so.

11. Always view your case from the judge's perspective.

12. Avoid humor and displays of literary acumen.

13. Use history as much as you can.

14. In complex or unusual cases, tell the judge what you're doing and why you're doing it.

15. Do not use the future tense.

16. Don't save anything for the final paragraph.

III. Writing the Introduction and Headings

1. Always include an introduction of a page or less.

2. Make your headings specific and persuasive.

IV. Work Habits for Litigators

1. No briefs should be written by a committee.

2. Writers should do most of their own research.

3. Be careful of Web research.

4. In office litigation divisions, separate the writers from the speakers.

5. Always try to read a good brief in your substantive area before writing one.

I. The Overview: Remembering the Six Initial Precepts of Legal Argument

A strong argument is at the core of any case. And when writing arguments in any context, always remember the principles from advertising discussed in Chapter 4:

Outline the argument; research it later.
Focus on the big idea.
Try to come up with a memorable phrase that embodies your position.

Remember, too, that in law school we focus on one style of litigation argument—argument in the Supreme Court. That's terrific if you end up being solicitor general, but the truth is that given the general direction of the legal profession, some of us are likelier to end up as defendants in the Supreme Court than as lawyers there.

In other words, litigation styles are quite different in the less rarefied atmospheres of the nation's trial courts. Obviously, styles and rules can vary according to jurisdiction and the type of court, so *always check your local rules before filing*. That said, here are six initial precepts that should guide your litigation writing.

1. The lower you are in a court system, the shorter your submissions should be.

From time to time, an advocate may need to file a lengthy brief in a lower court. In administrative proceedings, advocates often must assemble voluminous documents to make a proper record. In general, however, trial judges are running courtrooms and have less time to read than appellate judges do. Don't waste it.

2. In most cases, concentrate on winning the case, not on helping the judge write the opinion.

A brief serves two purposes: helping the judge decide who should win, and helping that judge write an opinion justifying the result. In school, we spend an inordinate amount of time examining the second factor—the role of the opinion in the result. In part that's because we spend our years in law school studying opinions, and in part it's because we study mostly Supreme Court cases, where the question of how the justices reached a particular result is often of primary importance.

In the real world, it's different. Your client is not going to be happy if you say, "I've got good news and bad news. The good news is that thanks to you, ripeness law in this circuit will never be the same. The bad news is that you lost." Winning is usually what matters.

These two goals—winning and helping the judge draft the opinion—are often at odds with each other. Advocates attempting to focus on the opinion, perhaps because they're filing an *amicus* brief or have clients interested in the development of precedent in an area, are going to write a different kind of brief from the usual one. They're going to be more scholarly and less focused, giving more explanatory information than usual and using footnotes. Ditto for briefs in the highest courts: A recent study by Pamela C. Corley, a political scientist at Vanderbilt, used antiplagiarism software to ascertain that about 10% of the prose in majority Supreme Court opinions in 2005 came from the briefs.

Thus, before you start writing any brief, you should ask yourself, how much am I concerned with the opinion, as opposed to the result? The answer will dictate the way you approach drafting the brief.

In several seminars I've attended, I've heard judges tell lawyers to file briefs that judges can just plug into their opinions. Don't follow this advice, because it reveals a misunderstanding of the role of lawyers. Judicial opinions have a unique style, which is inappropriate for advocates. Judges' writing is read with far more scrutiny than ordinary prose, and this dictates a labored, self-conscious approach. Judges write about principles, not people. All that is fine for the judiciary, given its job. If you do the same, however, you will undercut the effectiveness of your advocacy.

3. Since a lawsuit is not a debate, don't make responding to the other side the focus of your argument.

As we have learned, a lawsuit is a clash of stories that, in the best-litigated cases, are like two ships passing in the fog in the night. Don't drive your ship into others. The more attention you pay to answering the allegations of the other side, the less you will devote to making your own case. Your primary job is to explain why you should win. Even if you make the perfect rebuttal, you're only back to square one.

This principle applies to virtually any type of argument. Even if you are eloquently answering each of your opponent's charges in a political campaign, you're still debating an agenda set by that opponent.

Usually it is responding parties who allow their opponents to define the debate in court and weaken their chances. That's why defendants and appellees should usually draft their reply before they see anything from the other side; otherwise, they will tend to frame the issues in a way their opponents have selected. A story used to be told in the solicitor general's office about Frederick Wiener, a litigator there and author of *Briefing and Arguing Federal Appeals*. "Why aren't you working on the brief?" he'd ask lawyers. "We're the appellees," they would answer, "and we haven't heard from the other side." "What's the problem?" Wiener would retort. "We don't have a case?" Of course you do, and you usually know what you're going to argue long before you read anything from the opposition. Sure, you can modify your draft once you've seen what the other side has filed, and you do want to answer the other side's main contentions toward the end of your brief. To achieve proper focus, however, it's better to start drafting early than late.

Of course, in some cases litigators have to respond point by point to what the other side has raised—for example, if your opponents have filed a motion to dismiss your complaint, or if they are arguing that the court has jurisdiction over a particular defendant. The whole debate is conducted on the moving party's terms. Such situations are unavoidable because of the way courts have set the standards in a few areas. And, of course, when appellants file reply briefs, they should be responding to the other side's arguments.

In most other instances, however, don't turn your positive arguments into rebuttals. One good way to avoid this is to use an occasional footnote to respond to a minor point, rather than responding in the body of the text.

4. Keep your style understated and avoid military and sports metaphors.

As we discussed in Chapter 2, you don't want to be a graduate of the Rex Ryan School of Written Advocacy. Consider a story about two orators in ancient Greece, Aeschines and Demosthenes, who were debating the merits of Philip of Macedon, a general who was threatening their country. When Aeschines, a supporter of Philip, had finished, the people commented, "How well he speaks." When his opponent, Demosthenes, sat down, they said, "Let us march against Philip." You want to write briefs the way Demosthenes spoke. As advertising guru Bill Bernbach once put it, "Our job is to sell our client's merchandise . . . not ourselves. Our job is to kill the cleverness that makes us shine instead of the product."

This dictates a low-key style in which you convince a judge in a restrained fashion. Judges aren't interested in resolving abstract arguments and debates; their job is to do justice and find "the truth." Legal argument is a very odd form of rhetoric. After all, the more you call attention to the fact that you're advocating, the more you lose credibility in the eyes of a court. In a sense, you want to position yourself as a credible member of a colloquium—seeking answers, just like the judge.

Able litigators make clear arguments quietly, in contrast to many litigators who scream out an analysis in a way likely to be ignored. You don't want to use words such as "obviously," or phrases like "this court must," or even "should." An example of what not to do comes from this one impossibly long sentence in an appellate brief from an Oklahoma criminal case several decades ago:

We must respectfully submit it would be a travesty of justice, a rape upon the fundamental principles of law and in violation of every decision that has been rendered by this Honorable Court, and an injustice that all the spices of Arabia could not cure, and would disgrace and bankrupt an honest citizen, an honest merchant and a blameless family and would not tend to enforce the law, but would cause hatred and disrespect to the law of our State and Nation and there would be great injustice inflicted or could be inflicted upon a citizen of our state, and without extending this argument, which could be for many hours, but with an abiding confidence in the wisdom of this Court, we consign the future hopes, the tears of the loved ones and the laws of our nation to the bosom of this Court.

Part of the problem is that in the United States, New York is still the unofficial capital of commerce—and thus the law. And in New York, it's a cultural style to be "in your face," so to speak. It's like the old joke: "How do you recite the alphabet in New Jersey? F***g A, F*** B, F*** C," and so forth. Even in Gotham and its environs, however, in a courtroom, understatement is king.

In contrast, defusing objections by acknowledging them and even conceding an occasional minor point adds to your credibility. A wonderful example of an eloquent concession comes not from a brief but from a concurring opinion by Supreme Court justice Robert Jackson in *McGrath v. Kristensen*, 340 U.S. 162 (1950). In this passage, Jackson tried to explain why he was now ruling in direct contradiction to something he had written when he had served as attorney general (citations omitted):

> I concur in the judgment and opinion of the Court. But since it is contrary to an opinion which, as Attorney General, I rendered in 1940, I owe some word of explanation. I am entitled to say of that opinion what any discriminating reader must think of it—that it was as foggy as the statute the Attorney General was asked to interpret. . . .
>
> It would be charitable to assume that neither the nominal addressees nor the nominal author of the opinion read it. That, I do not doubt, explains Mr. Stimson's acceptance of an answer so inadequate to his questions. But no such confession and avoidance can excuse the then Attorney General.
>
> Precedent, however, is not lacking for ways by which a judge may recede from a prior opinion that has proven untenable and perhaps misled others. See Chief Justice Taney, recanting views

he had pressed upon the Court as Attorney General of Maryland in *Brown v. State of Maryland*. Baron Bramwell extricated himself from a somewhat similar embarrassment by saying, "The matter does not appear to me now as it appears to have appeared to me then." *Andrew v. Styrap*. And Mr. Justice Story, accounting for his contradiction of his own former opinion, quite properly put the matter: "My own error, however, can furnish no ground for its being adopted by this Court. . . ." *United States v. Gooding*. Perhaps Dr. Johnson really went to the heart of the matter when he explained a blunder in his dictionary— "Ignorance, sir, ignorance." But an escape less self-deprecating was taken by Lord Westbury, who, it is said, rebuffed a barrister's reliance upon an earlier opinion of his Lordship: "I can only say that I am amazed that a man of my intelligence should have been guilty of giving such an opinion." If there are other ways of gracefully and good-naturedly surrendering former views to a better-considered position, I invoke them all.

It's a subtle distinction, but you want judges to say, "That's a strong case," not "That's a strong brief." The latter statement implies that what you wrote tried to influence judges unduly; they will resist that as part of their institutional skepticism. A judge is far more apt to accept what looks like a helpful, credible suggestion than a diatribe.

That's one reason you want to avoid military and sports metaphors and expressions. Avoid using words such as "battle," "war," and expressions such as a "level playing field," "move the goalposts," "hold the fort," and "par for the course."

5. Keep your filings as short as possible, regardless of venue.

As we've noted, one of the most frequent complaints one hears from judges is that the material they receive is too long.

"I have yet to put down a brief and say, 'I wish that had been longer,'" Chief Justice Roberts has said, and he is hardly alone. "I've never read a brief that I couldn't put down in the middle. It is not the best part of the job," Justice Anthony Kennedy told the *ABA Journal*.

One problem may be that they and their colleagues are hardly setting a good example. The *Wall Street Journal* noted that the pathbreaking *Brown v. Board of Education* opinion in the 1950s came in at under four thousand words. When the Supreme Court revisited a similar issue in 2007 in *Parents Involved v. Seattle*, the word count was around 47,000. In fact, the median length of decisions has more than doubled in the last fifty years.

"I believe that anything can be cut to three hundred words," the great writing teacher William Zinsser has advised. Maybe not in court, but that's your model.

6. In the coming years, keep in mind the advantages of the electronic age.

We are still in the early days of the Internet revolution and electronic filing is not being widely used yet. Most courts have strict rules about fonts and the like. But someday soon, electronic filing will proliferate, changing the way we cite and use cases because we'll be able to hyperlink. In the meantime, there are ways we can use some of the lessons of the Internet age to improve our court filings.

In Chapter 2, we discussed how to package your material to make it more compelling, using the lessons of MapQuest, Google Maps, and Wikipedia. Even today, graphics can help a brief with a timeline, a bar graph, or even a list of characters in a case in which there are a number of entities to keep track of. I would be far more wary of photos—unless *seeing* something is key to a case. Judge Richard Posner of the U.S. Court of Appeals for the Seventh Circuit once told this story:

Many years ago I was on the panel that heard an appeal in a trademark dispute between the Indianapolis Colts and the Baltimore CFL Colts. The briefs described the trademarked products (such as hats and T-shirts) but did not include pictures. At the oral argument, one of the judges (OK, I confess—it was I) asked the lawyer for the Indianapolis Colts whether he had any of the products with him. He was a little startled but went to his briefcase and pulled a pair of hats, one an Indianapolis Colt hat and the other a Baltimore CFL Colt hat. The hats looked identical. He won his case at that moment. He was lucky that he was asked that question. He would not have needed luck had he included a photograph in his brief.

II. The Sixteen Rules of Writing Arguments

How, then, should you put these principles into play in a brief or memorandum of law? The following rules should help.

1. Lead with your best argument, though you must deal with procedural issues first.

Since any advocate wants to set the terms of a debate, you don't want to follow your adversary's outline of issues. Rather, lead with your strongest argument, generally following with your second strongest, and so on. This is particularly true for those who are filing a responding brief. As Supreme Court Justice Ruth Ginsburg once advised, "Respondents or appellees do well to lead from strength, telling their side of a case affirmatively, instead of in a series of 'not so's' keyed to appellant's presentation and provoking the court to wonder: 'Doth this appellee protest too much?' "

A strong start is essential, often presented in an introduction which the judge reads before anything else. Professors Charles Fried and Kathleen Sullivan did this in their "Summary of Argument" in the Supreme Court flag-burning case *United States v. Eichman*, 496 U.S. 310 (1990). Fried and Sullivan successfully attacked the 1989 Federal Flag Act, which prohibited knowing defacement of the American flag as unconstitutional. They began the section by saying (citations omitted):

> The flag is nothing but a symbol. It is only sometimes government property. It is not part of some regulatory scheme—like the draft card in *United States v. O'Brien*, or Little Bird of the Snow's social security number in *Bowen v. Toy*. A symbol is only a form of communication. It communicates emotions, ideas, or attitudes. Communicating is what symbols do. And if something is only a symbol, it does nothing else than communicate. The strong emotions displayed in the dissent in *Texas v. Johnson* and in the debates on this Act were all concerned with the meaning and power of a symbol, of an insubstantiated idea.
>
> Burning the flag in the circumstances charged here was also nothing but a symbol. It too was an act of communication and only an act of communication. The crime charged here was not the destruction of another's property. It was not an interference with a government regulatory program. It was not an intrusion on the physical space or tranquility of others. It was not a nuisance or an act of environmental pollution. It was a statement.

Because judges want to deal with procedural issues before they get to the substance, you must do the same. There is nothing to prevent you, however, from dealing with the procedural issues quickly and then returning to them at the back of the brief. For example, any judge who has been on the bench more than a week knows the standards for summary judgment. If you have such a case, you should briefly discuss those standards at the beginning of the argument section of your brief. However, a short paragraph is often enough, and you can postpone a further discussion until the end. By dealing with the procedural issues quickly, you lead judges to the key substantive arguments you want them to read (and they want to consider) as soon as possible.

Similarly, lawyers defending the government in cases challenging administrative or agency action know they have a favorable standard of review working in their favor. Nonetheless, they frequently spend so much time stressing that standard at the outset that the reader is left wondering why they seem to want to avoid discussing the substance. In many cases, government lawyers would be well advised to deal with the procedural standard of review quickly and then go on to argue why the government did the right thing, no matter what standard applies.

Lawyers love to argue procedure—the terms of the debate. In the end, though, most cases are decided on their substantive merits. Don't get so mesmerized discussing the parameters of the argument that you neglect the argument itself.

2. Use the "CRAC" method of argument: Conclusion, Rule, Analysis, Cases.

As we've discussed, most lawyers back into their conclusions. They present the issue, then go on to discuss the rules, and finally present the essence of their argument. Yet this is not the way most people argue in the real world, and with good reason: It's terribly unconvincing.

As we've seen, when we argue outside the courtroom, we tend to give our conclusions first and then follow with a brief analysis that includes the evidence to support the conclusions. Legal argument should be similar: You should give your conclusion (C); then a brief statement of your rule to support the conclusion and tell us why you should win (R); then your detailed analysis of the facts (A); and finally your cases (C).

In his *amicus* brief on behalf of the respondent in *Atascadero State Hospital v. Scanlon*, 473 U.S. 234 (1985), a case involving complicated issues of Eleventh Amendment immunity and an interpretation of the then recently passed Rehabilitation Act, Harvard Law School professor David Shapiro began his argument in a similar straightforward fashion (footnotes omitted):

> Under existing precedent, a state may claim Eleventh Amendment immunity from private suit in a federal court even if the suit is brought by a citizen of that state, and even if the basis of jurisdiction is that the action arises under federal law. *See, e.g., Hans v. Louisiana*, 134 U.S. 1 (1890); *Edelman v. Jordan*, 415 U.S. 651 (1974). But this Court has recognized the power of Congress, when acting under Section 5 of the Fourteenth Amendment, to abrogate that immunity in order to implement the Amendment's requirements. *See Fitzpatrick v. Bitzer*, 427 U.S. 445 (1976). Moreover, the Court has upheld congressional action subjecting a state to suit as part of the exercise of other powers delegated to Congress, at least when the conduct of the state can fairly be said to constitute consent. *See, e.g., Parden v. Terminal Railway*, 377 U.S. 184 (1964).
>
> Congress, in the relevant sections of the Rehabilitation Act, has effectively exercised this power to abrogate Eleventh Amendment immunity.

It is difficult to find a better example of a complex case reduced to its essentials.

In almost all legal arguments, the extensive discussion of cases should come toward the back, unless a case is so central or new that you must discuss it first, or you are dealing with a very case-specific area of the law, such as criminal procedure. If a clear favorable precedent controls your matter, by all means invoke it early. In the vast majority of cases, however, the precedent isn't so clear, so it's important to establish a core rationale first. This rationale will often emanate initially from the facts of your case, not from the precedents you use to support the argument.

3. Use the case law effectively.

Many lawyers make ineffective arguments because they spend way too much time analyzing the case law. Whenever possible, argue propositions, then cases. Then, as you use your cases, keep the following presumptions in mind:

a. Avoid long descriptions of law.

A brief is not an exam. Your job is not to show judges how much you know about a particular subject. Rather, it is to give them only that information they need to support the result you are seeking. In general, the more you analyze a precedent, the less you tend to make effective arguments. A supporter of the death penalty would hardly be served by interrupting a strong argument about deterrence with a detailed, academic discussion of how the Bible treats capital punishment. Unless you are dealing with new or complex areas of the law, be succinct.

b. You rarely want to analyze a case for more than a sentence.

Whenever you cite a case, you have to explain *why* you did so. Such an explanation, however, need be only a phrase, a clause, or a parenthetical. Key or controlling cases must be discussed or distinguished in some detail, but the intricacies of other cases are of little interest to judges. They are intrigued by the broad holdings of the cases you cite and, of course, the details of your case.

However, pointing out a detail that distinguishes your case from the precedent can be useful.

In addition, always be clear with a judge about what's dicta from prior cases and what's the holding. Never use a phrase such as "The authorities are evenly divided." They rarely are.

c. Avoid asking the court to overrule precedent.

Trial judges must follow the law of the jurisdiction, and so must appellate panels not acting *en banc*. If you ask them to do something else, you will lose.

In some once-in-a-lifetime cases, lawyers will decide that their best shot is to try to change an existing precedent. If that's your strategy, be straightforward about it, as Irving Younger was in his brief in *Desist v. United States*, 384 F.2d 889 (2nd Cir. 1967):

> We are aware that our argument would require the overruling of *Goldman v. United States*, 316 U.S. 129 (1942) and *On Lee v. United States*, 343 U.S. 747 (1952)....
>
> Until the Supreme Court overrules *Goldman* and *On Lee*, it would be futile to argue here what has been foreclosed there. And so we shall not, except to point out that the electronic eavesdropping in this case was carried out despite the lack of a statute authorizing such activity, and thus with no prior judicial supervision whatsoever.

d. Short quotes from opinions are better than long quotes, but no quotes are frequently better than short ones.

Short block quotes are fine. Any quote longer than two or three sentences in litigation, however, begins to become distracting. If you must quote something at length, try to put the quote in an appendix or a footnote and use something shorter in the text.

The basic rule of quotation in ordinary writing is this: You quote someone if the quotation speaks directly to the point, or if the author said something far more eloquently than you could. Judges are generally poor writers for some reasons beyond their control; crafting a majority opinion bears some of the liabilities of writing legislation, since you're creating "law." That's why dissents are often more eloquent.

Thus, you only have to worry most of the time about the first reason. When arguing for the *New York Times* in the Pentagon Papers case, *New York Times Co. v. United States*, 403 U.S. 713 (1971), Alexander Bickel began his argument with just such a quote when he wrote:

> This case lies, as is obvious, at the core of First Amendment concern, namely, the interest in "uninhibited, robust and wide-open" debate with respect to public affairs. *New York Times Co. v. Sullivan*, 376 U.S. 254, 270 (1964). This Court said just the other day, in *Rosenbloom v. Metromedia, Inc.* . . . .

Note the reference to "just the other day." Politely quoting a court's own words back to it is never a bad idea.

Even in cases when you want to quote a court, though, you are occasionally better off paraphrasing the holding than quoting it, since you can take that holding and put it in your own words. Lawyers frequently tell me that they're afraid to paraphrase because judges will think they're lying. There's an easy solution to that: Don't lie; paraphrase accurately. If you do, you have nothing to worry about.

e. Don't overload your argument with citations.

Many lawyers include too many case citations in their filings. No matter how much research you do, you don't have to include everything you found in your brief.

Using string cites is fine, but in most instances include no more than three cases in your string. I've yet to meet the judge who looks at the fifth case cited in a long string and exclaims, "I love that case! You win!"

There are two exceptions to this rule. If you're trying to show how a number of other jurisdictions have endorsed the rule you're invoking, cite the other locales. And in federal court, a number of circuits are known to have expertise in particular matters because they handle a lot of cases in those areas. Thus, in an administrative case, you might cite something from the D.C. Circuit, just as you might look to the Second and Third Circuits for expertise on securities law; to the Fifth and Eleventh Circuits for civil rights law; or to the Ninth and Tenth Circuits for public lands or environmental law.

f. Adapt your citations to the court in which you are arguing.

Law students are usually given the admonition on the first day of classes to stay within their jurisdictions when citing cases. That hasn't stopped a lot of lawyers from ignoring it, however. Legal practice is localized. If you are arguing in a Missouri court, the judges there don't care about the holdings of courts in New Hampshire, unless you have nothing from Missouri to offer.

Lawyers often add extra citations from around the country because they've done the research and figure it can't hurt. But it can damage your argument considerably. If Missouri judges see a Missouri cite and a New Hampshire cite for a proposition, they don't necessarily conclude that the advocate is a good researcher. Instead, they often conclude that the Missouri case is not really as strong as it looks, because the advocate has seen fit to look elsewhere for support.

4. Package your citations so they are at the ends of sentences and the ends of paragraphs.

Lawyers don't tend to realize how disruptive citations are to the flow of an argument. If we were watching *Grey's Anatomy* and every fifteen seconds there was a reference—"This episode of *Grey's Anatomy* owes a lot to an episode of *ER*, which actually came from something that appeared on *Marcus Welby*," viewers would change the channel within seconds.

Of course, we have to use cites; they come with the territory.

But there are ways to use them that make them far less disruptive, since even judges tend to skim over them. First, move cites to the end of the sentence. That means (and all these cites are imaginary ones):

"In *Jones v. Fisher*, 946 F. 2d 235 (3rd Cir. 1985), the Court held that all children must bring shovels to the playground,"

should be recast so that it reads:

"In 1985, the Third Circuit held that all children must bring shovels to the playground." *See Jones v. Fisher*, 946 F. 2d 235 (3rd Cir. 1985)."

This has the effect of recasting the sentence so the information can be read without getting derailed by the cite.

Second, even a long cite at the end of a sentence will tend to send readers into a stupor, causing them to miss part, if not all, of the next sentence. Therefore, any time a longer cite with a parenthetical or a string of cases ends a sentence, begin a new paragraph with the next sentence. That means:

"In a 1985 Third Circuit Court of Appeals decision, that court held that all children must bring shovels to the playground." *See Jones v. Fisher*, 946 F. 2d 235 (3rd Cir. 1985); *see also Maxwell v. Doherty*, 832 F. 2d 454 (6th Cir. 1982) (holding that the shovels must be less than a pound). In other similar cases, . . .

should be recast so that it reads:

"In a 1985 Third Circuit Court of Appeals decision, that court held that all children must bring shovels to the playground." *See Jones v. Fisher*, 946 F. 2d 235 (3rd Cir. 1985); *see also Maxwell v.*

Doherty, 832 F. 2d 454 (6th Cir. 1982) (holding that the shovels must be less than a pound).

In other similar cases, . . .

This helps the reader not to miss the information at the beginning of the next sentence.

There are some who argue that a better method is to put all the citations into footnotes. Perhaps, but the problem with that method is that the writer ends up with many pages with two lines of text and a string of footnotes. Few enjoy reading in this fashion. Better to use our method.

5. Avoid the tendency to respond too aggressively.

You should not answer each allegation and argument raised by the other side. Your job is to address the principal issues the other side raises, and then only in a way that supports arguments you have already made. Before you begin writing, ask yourself what's wrong with the other side's conclusion and write down your answer in a sentence or two. That answer should be incorporated somewhere in the argument. Remember, however, that the more you repeat an argument to answer it, the more you often end up bolstering it.

It's usually not helpful to take your opponents' arguments and talk about all the dire things that will happen if the court rules against you. Judges see such a style of overargument in the briefs they read far too often, and they usually dismiss it, as I'm sure they did in response to this filing from a respondent, cited in the *Scribes Journal of Legal Writing*:

To adopt Petitioner's argument that it should be allowed to rely upon information not given, which was not asked for, would result in bad policy and negatively affect the ability of the Comptroller's Office to answer any taxability question because of a fear that possible questions which could be raised by someone like Petitioner, but aren't, will not be answered, and result in claims like the one before us today.

6. Never label or characterize your opponents.

A lawsuit should be a clash of ideas, not personalities. The more you belittle your opponents or comment on their ethical and moral inadequacies, the more you degrade yourself in the eyes of the court. You rarely, if ever, want to mention your adversaries.

Even comments such as "The appellant's reliance on these cases is misplaced" are an attempt to move the discussion away from ideas. You have no idea whether the other side's reliance on those cases was misplaced or not. If you have to challenge the other side's argument, do so straightforwardly by saying, "The cases cited by the appellant do not apply in this matter." Or follow the example of Jacob Stein and his associates, who wrote in the beginning of a Supreme Court brief in *Richardson-Merrell, Inc. v. Koller*, 472 U.S. 424 (1985) (footnotes omitted):

> From the record thus amassed the material facts emerged essentially undisputed. Petitioner's statement distorts that record, and thus we are compelled to set forth the facts in a comprehensive manner.

Don't follow this example from a federal appellate brief:

> With all due respect for my colleague, I have to tell this court that it's been told an incredible fairy tale, packed with lies and misrepresentations.

Attack the position, not the person.

7. Take a clear stand that can be summarized in two sentences.

Simplicity is your friend. Judges are looking for ways to reduce cases to their basics. If you can do this in a way favorable to your side, you are doing your clients a favor. True, we lawyers have to play the hands we're dealt. Yet it's undeniable that attorneys who present a complicated argument to judges are at a rhetorical disadvantage. As Ninth Circuit judge Alex Kozinski once put it, "Simple arguments are winning arguments; convoluted arguments are sleeping pills on paper."

Though you should always be careful about attacking the opposing side, this Washington lawyer for the Golden West Baseball Company was able to walk the tightrope. He did his client a favor when he began the facts in his brief in *King and King v. Golden West Baseball Company*, 19 F.3d 27 (9th Cir. 1994), saying, "Appellant's counsel has done a masterful job of attempting to create a complicated morass out of a simple, straightforward, factual and legal case."

Other great advocates attempt to do much the same thing. When Alexander Bickel was arguing in the Supreme Court on behalf of the *New York Times* in the Pentagon Papers case, he wrote one heading that read simply, "ON THE FACTS OF THIS CASE, THE GOVERNMENT CANNOT PREVAIL WITHOUT A STATUTORY BASIS. NONE EXISTS." A justice reading that heading knows quickly how and what to decide. If a statutory basis exists, Bickel loses. If not, he prevails on this point.

8. Be careful when you make arguments in the alternative.

For reasons of clarity, among others, you should be reluctant to make too many arguments in the alternative. First, these arguments can confuse a judge by making your case more complicated. There is something unsettling about lawyers who argue that no matter how we analyze matters, they must win. Arguments in the alternative can blur the clear lines between sides, making strong contentions less distinct.

Arguments in the alternative can weaken your principal case in another way. Think of it in terms of our earlier example with advertising: If you run a terrific series of ads for Miller Lite—selling the beer because it tastes great and is less filling—you don't want to turn around the next month and suggest to audiences, in the alternative, that if the beer tastes bad, they should still buy it because it's cheap. Arguments in the alternative often contradict what we just told the judge several pages ago was an airtight argument.

You may have to make such arguments occasionally. Making them does, however, carry a cost, and if you do so, you should let the reader know that the alternative argument is not the principal theme or contention of your brief.

9. Limit the use of footnotes.

Litigators should use footnotes sparingly. They are useful in research, and thus in memos, indicating to readers what sources you have used and where related materials can be found. In briefs, however, you rarely need to tell readers these things, since you are already using citations to support your assertions.

Two generations ago footnotes were rarely used in briefs, just as three generations ago they were scarcely seen in judicial opinions. Over time, however, judges began hiring law clerks who, sadly, were schooled in the culture of footnotes bred in our nation's finest law schools. As these clerks began drafting opinions, judges—much to their detriment—began incorporating footnotes into their writing. Lawyers inevitably began copying them.

This is a terrible trend. Good writers want to retain control of their material, telling readers what they should read. But how do readers deal with footnotes? Do they read all, some, or none? Do they read them as they go along, or do they go back? I have no idea, and neither do you, since the approach to footnotes among readers is hardly uniform. That means that writers who use them lose control of their material.

Having said that, there are a few good uses for occasional footnotes. Specifically,

a. If you're responding to a minor contention of the other side's;

b. If you have a long quote you don't need to put into the text;

c. When long string citations really are needed;

d. When an alternative argument should be preserved but not emphasized;

e. If you have a minor point that you feel you need to include in the brief but don't care whether the judge remembers it or not, and

f. If you're writing a brief in which you're focusing as much on the opinion judges will write as on the result they will reach. Footnotes enable you to talk to judges (or their clerks, if they have them) about how to approach the drafting of the opinion and the development of precedent.

When you use footnotes, try to put them at the ends of sections, or at least at the ends of paragraphs and sentences. That way they are not too disruptive. However, except in unusual circumstances, do not use footnotes to cite cases or to the record, unless your local rules encourage you to do so. As we noted earlier, the recommendation here is not to use footnotes to cite cases except in memos.

10. Start a new section every four pages or so.

Readers need a chance to consolidate what they have read. Give them a chance to do so by breaking your argument into frequent sections. As you do, remember that you need to use basic divisions—I, II, III—occasionally with a Subsection—(A) or (B). If you break up the argument into too many subarguments, you only confuse the reader. The more basic your sections are, the better.

11. Always view your case from the judge's perspective.

There is an inevitable clash of roles in litigation. Even for lawyers who appear in court all the time, writing a brief is a big deal. That's not so, however, for the judges who read them. No matter how earthshaking your case seems to you, it is just one of many to them, yet another day at the office.

Avoid the temptation to hype the importance of your subject matter. If your case is significant, that will readily become apparent to your judicial readers. What's striking about so many of the great briefs filed over the past half-century is how understated they were.

In addition, think about the constraints on judges and how they are likely to view your arguments, and adjust your style accordingly. For example, if you are arguing for a preliminary injunction, the standards are virtually the same everywhere— likelihood of success on the merits; irreparable harm; a balancing of the equities, and a weighing of the public interest. A judicial determination will vary from case to case. Often, however, the standard that concerns judges the most in such matters deals with irreparable harm, because if the controversy is going to disappear tomorrow, the judge is more likely to act to preserve the status quo for trial.

Given that fact, litigators should usually address irreparable harm first, since it's the standard uppermost in the judicial reader's mind. Yet few do. Instead, they are content to deal with the standards as courts have announced them, leading with likelihood of success.

Similarly, we all know that the stated standards for a change of venue are uniform and vague—dealing with the convenience of the parties and the interests of justice, among others. Yet a good advocate also knows that judges are apt to ship off cases they don't want to hear and keep the ones that look interesting. A case that an advocate successfully presents as tedious and time-consuming is likelier to get moved in most courts, just as that same case will tend to remain if the lawyer opposing the motion makes it look manageable and enticing.

Always think of your judicial readers. When asking courts to rule in your favor, remember that judges need to know specifically what a victory entails. "More cases are decided wrongly by judges because they don't understand the underlying problem than because they read cases badly," Judge Patricia Wald has said.

12. Avoid humor and displays of literary acumen.

To paraphrase G. K. Chesterton, a good brief tells us the truth about its hero, but a bad brief tells us the truth about its author. An argument isn't about you: It's about the principles the court should adopt and your client. The more you call attention to yourself as a writer, the less effective you tend to be as an advocate. Your prose should be conversational but workmanlike, understandable without being flashy. "Read over your compositions," Samuel Johnson once advised, "and when you meet a passage which you think is particularly fine, strike it out."

Those who ignore this rule do so at their own peril. Take former U.S. Court of Appeals judge Abner Mikva, who got a little carried away when he wrote in *Community for Creative Non-Violence v. Watt*, 703 F.2d 586 (D.C. Cir. 1983) (*en banc*):

> The Mall and Lafayette Park are special places in the stock-pile of American fora. They are at the very heart of the nation's capital where ideas are to be expressed and grievances are to be redressed. Thus, the focus of this case is the symbolic locus of the First Amendment.

An admonition to avoid flowery language has several ramifications for the litigator. First, unless you or your conduct is at issue, don't mention yourself through such phrases as "I think," "I feel," or "It seems to me." Second, it's hard enough to be funny when speaking; it's nearly impossible to be humorous in writing. Don't even try. Almost all attempts at litigation humor fall flat, leaving readers to ponder what the writer meant by telling such an awful joke. As David Ogilvy once put it, people don't buy from clowns. Besides, most good attempts at humor contain more than a bit of self-deprecation, and lawyers tend to be poor at that.

Nor should you quote literary figures. A knowledge of William Shakespeare is nice, but the only Shakespeares your judicial readers care about are the ones, if any, currently serving on the local appellate bench, whose edicts they are compelled to follow.

13. Use history as much as you can.

Readers generally like history. What's more, even though interpretations of the past can differ, many readers tend to treat historical narratives as fact. While legislative history can be deadly, albeit necessary, other historical explanations are anything but. Tell judges the circumstances that led to the passage of key statutes or movements that affect the law in your case. The celebrated "Brandeis brief," filed in *Muller v. Oregon*, 208 U.S. 412 (1908), used a number of reports on labor conditions to make a compelling case that state statutes limiting the hours of working women were constitutional. After reviewing the statutes of other states that had acted similarly to Oregon, Brandeis organized a ninety-five-page section entitled "The World's Experience upon which the Legislation Limiting the Hours of Labor from Women Is Based." He divided this section into subsections, with titles such as "The Dangers of Long Hours" and "Laundries."

Historical overviews can often be done in the fact section, not in the argument, adding to their persuasiveness and the appearance of objectivity. In their Supreme Court brief in *Hawaii Housing Authority v. Midkiff*, 467 U.S. 229 (1984), Laurence Tribe and his co-counsel included a brief history of the Hawaii Land Reform Act at the beginning of their facts. You don't want to give a court unnecessary material, but to quote Justice Holmes, sometimes a page of history is worth a volume of logic.

14. In complex or unusual cases, tell the judge what you're doing and why you're doing it.

If you were explaining your argument orally to a judge, from time to time you would provide background. "I'm going to spend the next five minutes giving you the legislative history of NEPA," you might say. "This might seem odd at first, but unless you know that history, it's difficult to follow the next stage of our argument."

For some reason, litigators are afraid to do the same in their writing. Don't be. Providing a context is a boon to your readers, particularly in complex cases—as long as you don't do it constantly. The lawyers for an appellant did this in a complex challenge to surface mining regulations, *In Re: Permanent Surface Mining Regulation Litigation*, 653 F.2d 514 (D.C. Cir. 1981) (*en banc*), when they wrote:

> The Secretary urges six grounds upon this Court as reason for ignoring the text, the purpose and the history of the Act which we have developed above. Four of those we group together under the inelegant but largely accurate title of "the bootstrap arguments," and discuss in more detail the two specific rulemaking authorities under which the Secretary claims to have acted.

15. Do not use the future tense.

You are not Nostradamus; avoid predicting what will happen. "The other side will not object," writes the lawyer, but if it does, you are the one who looks foolish, rather than the attorneys who reneged on the promise. "The other side has assured me it will not object" is the way to express such thoughts.

16. Don't save anything for the final paragraph.

By the time judges get to the last page of your brief, they're not paying much attention. Use the end to restate your argument in a sentence or two without flourishes. If you want to use a rote phrase such as "For the foregoing reasons, the Court should award summary judgment for the plaintiff," it's okay, but don't say "For all the foregoing reasons." As opposed to what? Seven of the eight foregoing reasons?

III. Writing the Introduction and Headings

Follow these two rules:

1. Always include an introduction of a page or less.

All filings should have a first-page, introductory summary, whether the rules require one or not. In this introduction, you want to frame the case and issues in the ways most favorable to your side.

Since this is the first thing a judge reads, it is often the most significant part of your brief. To be sure, selecting one theme out of many in a complex case can be tough. Without an initial focus, however, it is difficult for judges to get a handle on where the case is heading.

Because the Supreme Court rules are strict about such matters, professors Laurence Tribe and Kathleen Sullivan placed their "introduction" at the beginning of the argument section in their High Court brief in *Bowers v. Hardwick*, 478 U.S. 186 (1986). Even though this introduction is a good deal longer than you will want to make most of yours, its impact is obvious (footnotes omitted):

In Section 16–6–2, the State of Georgia has criminalized certain sexual activities defined solely by the parts of the body they involve, no matter who engages in them, with whom, or where. Georgia threatens to punish these activities with imprisonment even if engaged in by two willing adults—whether married or unmarried, heterosexual or homosexual—who have secluded themselves behind closed doors in their own home, as Michael Hardwick did. All that is at issue in this case is whether a state must have a substantial justification when it reaches that far into so private a realm.

The Eleventh Circuit held only that the Constitution indeed requires such heightened scrutiny for a law like the one challenged here. That court never reached the question whether the State might be able to meet such a standard, nor has the State yet had any opportunity in this case to try to do so. The Eleventh Circuit simply ruled that, because Section 16–6–2 criminalizes activity that is "quintessentially private and lies at the heart of an intimate association," the district court's dismissal of the complaint must be reversed, and the case remanded for a trial at which "the State must prove, in order to prevail, that it has a compelling interest in regulating this behavior and this statute is the most narrowly drawn means of safeguarding that interest." App. 26.

The State of Georgia urges this Court to overturn that ruling and declare that a law reaching into the bedroom to regulate intimate sexual conduct is to be tested by no stricter a standard than a law that regulates the community environment outside the home: namely, a standard of minimal scrutiny. In the State's view, the most private intimacies may thus be treated as public displays, and the sanctum of home and bedroom merged into the stream of commerce—all subject to regulation whenever there is any conceivable "rational relationship" to the promotion of "traditional" or "prevailing" notions of "morality and decency."

But our constitutional tradition does not permit such casual state control of our most private realm. Rather, this Court's precedents direct that the intrusion of Georgia's criminal law into the intimate, consensual activities prescribed by Section 16–6–2 be examined more carefully than the State would have it. The Statute should be tested for a close relationship to a compelling state interest, as required by the court below. See App. 22, 26. But even if this Court should deem such scrutiny too strict, the statute should, *at the very least*, be tested for a "fair and substantial relation" to a legitimate governmental objective. *See, e.g., Zablocki v. Redhail*, 434 U.S. 374, 400, 402 (1978) (Powell, J., concurring in judgment). For the State has sought through that statute to control an area of life so removed from the public sphere that "the mere [invocation] . . . [of] the controversial realm of morals cannot [suffice as] justification." *See Poe v. Ullman*, 367 U.S. 497, 545 (1961) (Harlan, J., dissenting).

2. Make your headings specific and persuasive.

Argument headings should convince readers by themselves. "The Due Process Argument" does nothing for a reader, nor does "Smith's Due Process Rights Were Violated," since it makes no memorable argument that applies only to your case. What you want to say is something like "Smith's Due Process Rights Were Violated When She Was Fired as a Teacher Without Being Given Notice or a Hearing."

If you're using the "CRAC" style accurately, your heading should be a pithy synopsis of the first paragraph of the argument that follows. This is repetitive, but there's no harm in repeating the point of a section. Some judges may not read the heading or, worse, may read only the heading, without the argument to follow.

While you want to be argumentative, you also want to be evenhanded. Use few adverbs in headings, and use only those adjectives you need to state the argument accurately. Headings can be more than a sentence if necessary, though a paragraph is too long.

This is one of the rare places where humor and a bit of overstatement can work, as long as you're accurate. In a 1993 Georgia Appeals Court brief, I saw one heading that read: "THEY'VE HAD A HEARING AND A HEARING AND A HEARING... AND THEY STILL WANT ORAL ARGUMENT." I wouldn't try this in the Supreme Court, but I thought it worked in this context.

IV. Work Habits for Litigators

For even the best writers, the method of writing the brief is important. In addition to the crucial points from Chapters 1 and 2, here are a few reminders and additional points to remember.

1. No briefs should be written by a committee.

At most, you want two authors with compatible styles writing a brief in close consultation with each other. You can use others for specific research projects ("What is the standard of review?"), but when the drafting starts, a brief needs a unitary style.

2. Writers should do most of their own research.

It's fine to farm out discrete projects to others, but the process of research inevitably involves a consideration of how the argument will be structured. If someone else does this work, the overall product suffers. Remember that we use our research not only to figure out what we should say but how we should say it. Style is inseparable from substance.

3. Be careful of Web research.

Be wary of what you find on the Web. After all, it was Abraham Lincoln who said, "The trouble with quotes on the Internet is that you never know if they were genuine."

4. In office litigation divisions, separate the writers from the speakers.

Law offices would be better off creating two litigation divisions, one for the trial lawyers who appear before juries and whose main skills are speaking and acting, and another for those whose strength is writing and appear mostly before judges. (This is the basis of the British separation between barristers and solicitors.) The two skills often don't go together. A person can be both a good speaker and a good writer—Dr. Martin Luther King, Jr., comes to mind—but it's rare. In my experience, litigation divisions are usually dominated by jury lawyers because they have commanding personalities. Such lawyers are often poor writers, because they mistakenly think they can charm their way through a brief as they do through a trial.

In any trial, at least two attorneys should be assigned to the case—one who is strong in writing and one whose skills lie on the oral side. The main author of a brief, however, should be the person who makes the oral argument to a judge, since he or she knows the case better than anyone else.

Lawyers who handle appeals should be conversant with everything that went on in the lower court. Many judges have complained to me about appellate attorneys who answer questions by saying, "I didn't try the case below, so I can't say."

5. Always try to read a good brief in your substantive area before writing one.

We learn by emulation. Part of the necessary preparation for writing is reading what has worked before in similar contexts. In the age of the Internet, these documents are more available than ever.

CHAPTER 8

Writing Trial and Appellate Briefs, as Well as Affidavits

I. The Overview: Know Your Court, Know Your Case

II. Six Rules for Writing Better Trial Briefs

1. Keep things short.

2. Use judicial quotations more than in appellate briefs, perhaps in an appendix.

3. Keep in mind the areas of the law in which the facts are particularly critical.

4. If you are going to trial, try to give the judge a short pretrial memorandum, whether one is required or not.

5. When defending against summary judgment motions, remember Vetter's four rules.

6. In briefs before administrative panels, longer filings may be appropriate.

III. Ten Ways to Improve Your Appellate Briefs

1. It helps to have a new lawyer come in at the appellate level to look at the issues raised below from a different angle.

2. On appeal, don't write your facts by strictly relating what the witnesses said at trial.

3. In your "questions presented" section, clearly state your position, be specific, and keep it short.

4. Make your summary of the argument a reformulation of your argument headings.

5. Show respect for the lower court, even while questioning its ruling.

6. It is usually better to appeal on narrow grounds than on broad ones.

7. Tell the court whether the errors you're raising were objected to below.

8. Arguing sufficiency of the evidence is often a loser.

9. In appealing criminal convictions, keep the court's skepticism in mind.

10. In appealing administrative decisions, stress the facts even more than usual.

IV. Two Suggestions for Improving Reply Briefs and *Amicus* Briefs

1. Make your reply briefs short and responsive.

2. With *amicus* briefs, focus on what you can argue that's new.

V. The Six Elements to Remember When Composing Affidavits

1. Rely on short words.

2. People usually don't speak directly or sometimes even in sentences.

3. Compensate for the lack of the visual and aural element in written dialogue.

4. Speakers tend to reflect their gender in the way they talk.

5. Speakers also tend to reflect their age, educational level, geographical place, and class in the way they speak.

6. Speakers tend to reflect their view on the matter at hand in the way they speak.

I. The Overview: Know Your Court, Know Your Case

The differences between writing in trial and appellate practice are often exaggerated; what makes a good brief doesn't differ significantly from forum to forum. Still, two principles do guide the differences in writing for these two types of courts. First, *the lower you are in a court system, the more you should rely on precedent to make the argument.* In the U.S. Supreme Court, lawyers rely on precedent, of course, but that Court, if it so chose, could throw out most of their prior case law tomorrow morning and start again. Lower courts are different; they're bound by the law of their jurisdiction. You should change your style of argument accordingly.

Second, *the lower you are in a court system, the more you should rely on your facts, not the law, to make the case.* This isn't to suggest that the facts aren't important in higher courts as well. It's just that the higher up you go, the less the courts tend to rely on the facts to rule on specific points of law. The U.S. Supreme Court, for example, essentially grants *certiorari* on debating issues: Should the Court overrule a doctrine or change a rule? That doesn't leave as much room for arguing the facts, except on procedural grounds such as standing and ripeness. In lower courts, however, the facts have far greater importance in framing the issue.

II. Six Rules for Writing Better Trial Briefs

In a trial court, lawyers must file a wide variety of motions and briefs. While these vary in style, depending on the circumstances of your case and the rules and habits of your local courts, here are six suggestions for improvement.

1. Keep things short.
Enough said.

2. Use judicial quotations more than in appellate briefs, perhaps in an appendix.
Many trial judges have no clerks and thus little opportunity to verify your assertions easily. In those instances, use more quotes while keeping in mind our rules from before. In many briefs, you can attach the quotation or even the entire case to the back of your brief (perhaps with the key part highlighted).

3. Keep in mind the areas of the law in which the facts are particularly critical.
The facts are always important in trial briefs, but they are even more important when you are dealing with vague standards or areas that aren't easily reviewable. Most discovery disputes, for example, are rarely appealable until after the trial is over; judges can do almost anything they want. Thus, in those cases, you want to base your briefs on the facts and common sense, since precedent does not particularly matter.

Similarly, most family law cases turn almost entirely on the facts, since legal standards such as the "best interests of the child" are vague.

4. If you are going to trial, try to give the judge a short pretrial memorandum, whether one is required or not.

Judges like to feel in control of their courtrooms. A good pretrial memorandum helps judges to achieve that command by giving them something like a program at a sporting event. In an article, "The Trial Brief—The Lawyer's Battle Plan and Ammunition," Charles W. Joiner advised lawyers to draft a similar document for themselves:

> The trial brief must give you fingertip and eye flash control over preparation without giving the appearance of a lawyer who overtries his case. This will require a document or file full of information arranged in such a way that any bit of information can be found at any time, but also arranged in such a way so as not to antagonize the judge or jury. The arrangement must be such as will prevent a lawyer from forgetting any old ideas but will not stifle new ideas as they come up.

While the style of a document you will give to a judge can vary greatly, depending on your strategy, the rules, and the dictates of particular courts, others have written that you should try to include:

a. An introductory paragraph that summarizes your position;

b. A quick preview of the facts (or story) you plan to present, making it clear that these particulars haven't been introduced into evidence yet but have probably been produced already through discovery;

c. A list of witnesses you plan to call, with a one-sentence summary of what you expect them to say;

d. A short list identifying any out-of-the-ordinary evidentiary problems that may arise, stating your position in a sentence or two;

e. A brief summary of your argument;

f. A short list of any problems the judge may have to confront during the trial.

The question always arises of whether you want to tip off the judge and the other side about strategy and problems that may arise. In general, there are few surprises in most trials, and judges don't like them anyway, so at this point in the proceedings, you should probably err on the side of disclosure.

5. When defending against summary judgment motions, remember Vetter's four rules.

In his excellent book *Successful Civil Litigation*, George Vetter recommends four ways to oppose a summary judgment motion:

a. Demonstrate an issue of fact;

b. Expose the invalidity of materials supporting the other side's motion (for example, mistakes in the affidavit);

c. Illustrate how the case hinges on something else that needs to be assessed, such as credibility;

d. Show the moving party's exclusive control of the facts.

A party moving for summary judgment will have to counter all these potential lines of attack. This area may be among the most important parts of civil practice today.

In these cases, you may want to list your facts in a more chronological fashion.

6. In briefs before administrative panels, longer filings may be appropriate.

When assembling a record before an agency that is hearing the matter for the first time, you will often have to write more voluminously, if only to preserve issues for appeal. When required to do so, make sure you have a pithy introduction, and take many of the steps outlined in Chapter 11 about improving technical writing.

III. Ten Ways to Improve Your Appellate Briefs

An appellate brief presents a somewhat different set of challenges from a trial brief. Your facts are determined by the record and findings of the lower court. As always, you must follow your local rules about how to organize the brief.

Here are ten suggestions on how to deal with specific questions and areas.

1. It helps to have a new lawyer come in at the appellate level to look at the issues raised below from a different angle.

Lawyers who do their own appeals are often wedded to their original theories and unable to notice the minor issues below that should become major ones above. Moreover, on appeal, oral argument—and therefore oral skills—count for less than they do at the trial level. For these reasons, having a different set of lawyers handle the trials and appeals within an office can improve performance, as long as everyone is familiar with the record below.

2. On appeal, don't write your facts by strictly relating what the witnesses said at trial.

In many appellate briefs, the litigator takes us on a chronological tour of the trial, relating witness by witness what the facts are. ("The first witness testified about the gun. . . . The second witness testified where the body was found. . . . At that point in the trial . . .")

Most of the time, this is not a good way to write your facts. Your job is to take the facts and make them into a story, highlighting those you want us to remember the most. While you are bound on appeal by both the rules and the record of the court below—which means that you can't relitigate the facts—you are not a stenographer, whose job it is to relate what happened in the precise order it occurred.

If, however, you are focusing on specific events in a trial—arguing, say, sufficiency of the evidence or the legality of a judge's instructions—then you should obviously take your readers through the relevant part of the trial, often verbatim.

3. In your "questions presented" section, clearly state your position, be specific, and keep it short.

The rule on how to set out questions presented for argument varies from court to court. Some jurisdictions require the appellants to submit their version of the questions within weeks of appealing their case. Others simply ask that the questions be included in the brief. In both cases, the same rules tend to apply. Writing questions presented is a lot like writing argument headings. As with those headings, you want your questions to frame the issue in a way that makes your argument.

It's tougher, however, for a reader to digest a long question than a long statement. Therefore, you should strive to make your questions twenty words or less. To make this easier, don't be afraid to divide your questions into sections, as in

> Were Smith's due process rights violated when she was
> a. fired as a teacher,
> b. never given notice, and
> c. never provided a hearing?

Of course, lengthier questions can be made to work occasionally, as this one did, filed by the Washington lawyers Andrew L. Frey and Roy T. Englert, Jr., in *Los Angeles Land Co. v. Brunswick Corp.*, 6 F.3d 1422 (9th Cir. 1993):

> Whether defendant can be labeled a "monopolist" under Section 2 of the Sherman Act because it owned the only bowling center in a small area, even though uncontradicted evidence showed that defendant lacked power to exclude competition or control price.

While you don't want to ask too many questions—this dilutes your core argument—dividing a question into parts can strengthen the assertions within. Defense lawyers may particularly want to use this tactic in criminal appeals, where all it takes for a reversal is one fundamental mistake. By highlighting three or four points within the context of a major one, you may make that reversal more likely, and you will keep your argument focused.

4. Make your summary of the argument a reformulation of your argument headings.

If you have to provide the court with a summary of the argument, write this section last. The easiest way to do so is to assemble all of your argument and subargument headings. Once you have done that, rework the narrative so it makes sense as a short essay that can stand on its own, in case the judge decides to read nothing else. At this point, you should have a cogent summary.

Though it could have been divided into several paragraphs, a fine summary of the argument comes from an *amicus* brief filed by the American Civil Liberties Union in the U.S. Court of Appeals for the D.C. Circuit in *United States v. Nofziger*, 878 F.2d 442 (D.C. Cir. 1989). The case concerned the review of a conviction for violating the Ethics in Government Act:

> This case is ultimately quite easy. Congress enacted a statute imposing criminal sanctions for petitioning the government in particular circumstances. This statute is, at minimum, ambiguous with respect to whether the government must show that the defendant knew of these circumstances when making his petition. In fact, as we explain below, the more natural reading requires the prosecution to show knowledge of each element of the offense. But unless the statute is clear, the question whether any ambiguity should be resolved for or against the accused can

have only one answer. Due process considerations embodied in a number of well-established principles, including the rule of lenity and the presumption against imposing criminal sanctions on a strict liability basis, point clearly to an interpretation that favors the accused. Moreover, the force of these "time-honored rule[s] is all the more compelling when First Amendment rights are involved." *Schwartz v. Romnes*, 495 F.2d 844, 849 (2d Cir. 1974). . . .

5. Show respect for the lower court, even while questioning its ruling.

Judges don't like to reverse their colleagues; they know how much it hurts when it happens to them. Nothing in most of our professional lives as lawyers resembles the sting of a public rebuke from a higher authority. As Judge Kozinski has noted:

> Chances are I'll be seeing that district judge soon at one of those secret conferences where judges go to gossip about the lawyers. I find that you can always get a real chuckle out of the district judges by copying the page where he is described as "a disgrace to the robe he wears" or as "mean-spirited, vindictive, biased and lacking in judicial temperament" and sticking it under his nose right as he is sipping his hot soup.

This fact should inform the writing of all appellants. While you don't want to be obsequious, you should raise your points, in Shakespeare's phrase, more in sorrow than in anger. When recounting judicial errors at trial, be direct and stick to the facts. "Do not say 'the district court failed' to consider, or anything like it," U.S. Court of Appeals judge John Minor Wisdom used to warn his clerks. "Treat district judges tenderly."

If you can do it well, take the lower court's language and use that to your own benefit. In their Supreme Court brief in *Hawaii Housing Authority v. Midkiff*, 467 U.S. 229 (1984), Laurence Tribe and his co-counsel began their argument with this sentence:

> The State of Hawaii's effort in the Land Reform Act to liberate the royal lands of Hawaii's former monarchs for ultimate purchase by the tenantry upon those lands, far from inaugurating the "Huxleyan" Brave New World denounced in the concurring opinion below, 702 F.2d at 807 (A37), simply extends to our fiftieth state the New World of our Constitution's framers.

6. It is usually better to appeal on narrow grounds than on broad ones.

As Judge Wald has pointed out, courts are frequently divided on philosophical grounds. The narrower your appeal is, the likelier it is that you will win agreement and not provoke a dissent and a possible *en banc* reversal. As she suggests, phrases such as "This case is not like . . ." and "This case will not require breaking new ground" can help you.

7. Tell the court whether the errors you're raising were objected to below.

Issues raised for the first time on appeal have a higher hurdle to clear for a court to rule in your favor. Therefore, always tell a court how the issue was handled below, if it was.

8. Arguing sufficiency of the evidence is often a loser.

Appellate courts usually reverse on errors of law. These errors should be the focus of your appeals.

9. In appealing criminal convictions, keep the court's skepticism in mind.

Judges who rule for criminal defendants know they may be putting a putative lawbreaker back on the streets. This doesn't make them especially enthusiastic about ruling for such defendants.

A criminal defense lawyer must deal implicitly with this issue by stressing the broader value involved in upholding a defendant's constitutional rights. You should do this in a way that treats law enforcement gingerly. Putting the police on trial may work as a technique with some juries, but it is unlikely to appeal to judges, many of whom once worked as prosecutors.

Conversely, it never hurts prosecutors to remind an appellate court of the suspect's conviction below.

10. In appealing administrative decisions, stress the facts even more than usual.

As noted earlier, the standards in administrative cases are notoriously vague—"arbitrary and capricious" or "substantial evidence." Therefore, your facts tend to make these cases. Take the way the lawyers for this appellant framed their arguments in a D.C. Circuit challenge to regulations issued by the secretary of the interior in a case cited previously, *In Re: Permanent Surface Mining Regulation Litigation*, 653 F.2d 514 (D.C. Cir. 1981) (*en banc*):

> The Secretary in his regulations has vastly expanded the already detailed statutory provisions. Parts 778–784 of 30 C.F.R. define the information that the applicant must submit with any application for a surface or an underground mining permit. They occupy 18 triple-column pages of the Federal Register, 44 Fed. Reg. 15353–370, and 33 double-columned pages of 30 C.F.R. 1041–1073. They far exceed in volume, in detail, and in burden the requirements of any comparable regulation known to us.

These factual descriptions drive the argument.

Since many administrative matters involve complex areas

that are confusing to judges, you need to simplify your issues in these cases as much as possible. Once you have done this, it also helps to let the court know in some fashion why the expertise of an agency in its area should be disregarded.

IV. Two Suggestions for Improving
Reply Briefs and *Amicus* Briefs

Some special rules apply to reply and *amicus* briefs.

1. Make your reply briefs short and responsive.

Many judges have told me that a reply brief rarely makes a difference in a case. They also have said that if a reply seems to be rearguing points made in earlier filings, they pay it little or no attention. Keep in mind that nothing says you have to file a reply brief if you have nothing new to offer.

On the other hand, Mike McKee has cited Justice Scalia, who claimed that in researching his book on better writing, many judges told him that they read the reply briefs first, presumably because they're shorter.

When you do file a reply brief, you want to keep it focused and short—rarely more than five pages, no matter how numerous or complex the issues. Anything longer risks being tossed immediately onto the never-to-be-read pile. In your first paragraph, you can review the principal points you made in your earlier filing, but it's not required. The key is to use the first or following paragraph to summarize the two or three principal contentions you plan to answer in the reply. Focus on major themes and new points rather than on answering cases and rearguing old ones.

Though they didn't follow this form exactly, the lawyers at the Washington firm of Dickstein, Shapiro, and Morin began the argument section of their reply brief for one of three defendants in *United States v. Wilson*, 26 F.3d 142 (D.C. Cir. 1994), with these pithy statements:

> Citing the wrong standard of review and relying on facts out-side the record, the government argues that DOJ's investigation was properly authorized under the Ethics in Government Act ("the Act"). There is not a shred of support for that view.

The only exceptions to the precepts outlined above are a complex case and the rare instance in which the appellee or defendant has raised a new issue you didn't foresee that has the potential to obliterate your arguments. In such instances, tell the court calmly in the first paragraph that you are filing a longer-than-usual reply because "of the serious and unexpected nature of the arguments." Such a phrase is no guarantee that a judge will read what is to follow, but at least you've noted that you recognize you're doing something extraordinary.

However, never introduce a new argument in a reply brief. Judges will ignore the argument, and they can sanction the at-torney for raising it.

Replying to a reply brief is not only a waste of time, most courts won't allow it. Don't do it unless requested to do so.

2. With *amicus* briefs, focus on what you can argue that's new.

When you file an *amicus* brief, you are presumably doing so to raise an institutional interest in a case, bringing to the court's attention some area of expertise. Once you've secured permis-sion to file an *amicus* (check your local rules on how to do so), concentrate on your unique contribution. The more you repeat what has been argued by others, the more the court discounts what you write.

In your introduction, highlight who you are, what your inter-est is, and why the judges should pay particular heed to your different perspective. Take the excellent statement filed by the American Civil Liberties Union in the *amicus* brief cited earlier in *United States v. Nofziger*, 878 F.2d 442 (D.C. Cir. 1989) (footnotes omitted):

> The American Civil Liberties Union (ACLU) is a nationwide, nonpartisan organization of over 250,000 members, dedicated to the protection of civil rights and civil liberties. The ACLU has a long history of promoting individual rights, including the Fifth Amendment right to due process of law and the First Amendment right to petition the government.
>
> Defendant has been convicted of violating 18 U.S.C. §207 (c), which prohibits former high-ranking government officials from lobbying for one year after they leave government service. This prohibition is limited, however, to communications made under particular circumstances. The district court interpreted §207 (c) to impose criminal sanctions on persons who were unaware of the factual circumstances that subjected their communication to the statutory prohibition. This interpretation ignored well-established principles of statutory construction that reflect concerns embodied in the due process clause. These due process concerns, moreover, are exacerbated by the context of this case. Any regulation of lobbying, a form of petitioning the government, must be judged in light of First Amendment standards. Because the district court ignored these constitutional concerns, the ACLU respectfully submits this brief as *amicus curiae*.

The facts are generally conveyed by the principal party, so pay them little heed unless you want to highlight a different point specific to your interest. In the argument, you can restate the arguments of the principal litigant in a sentence or two, but then move quickly to the different areas in which you can bring special knowledge to the case.

One of the best examples of a helpful set of *amicus* briefs came from the doctors and medical organizations that joined the *Roe v. Wade* abortion rights litigation in the early 1970s. By concentrating on their areas of expertise, these *amici* had a major impact on the majority opinion of Justice Harry Blackmun.

As the principal lawyer in a case, don't forget that contribution from an influential *amicus* can often be a key component of appellate strategy.

V. The Six Elements to Remember When Composing Affidavits

Writing affidavits is a key part of legal practice. In a case in the U.S. Court of Appeals for the D.C. Circuit, *Animal Legal Defense Fund, Inc. v. Glickman*, 154 F.3d 426 (D.C. Cir. 1998) (*en banc*), the entire case turned on whether an affidavit filed in support of a complaint protected it from dismissal for lack of standing. (It did.)

An affidavit, of course, is supposed to be the words of the person offering it. Yet we all know that many lawyers draft affidavits for their clients, and sometimes even for supporting witnesses.

The ethics of the practice aside, the problem with creating affidavits this way is that they often don't sound credible. Truck drivers sign affidavits in which they attest that "the other vehicle had the last clear chance to avoid the collision." If judges can tell that a lawyer has drafted the document, they tend to discount it.

So for good writing reasons as well as ethical ones, you want the affidavits you file to sound like the people who signed them. This is far easier said than done. To write good dialogue, you have to know how people speak in general, and how written dialogue differs from the real thing. Equally important, characters reveal themselves by the way they speak—disclosing their gender, class, educational level, and other key aspects of who they are. It's an art and one few lawyers have mastered.

So, taking each in turn:

1. Rely on short words.

When people speak, they tend to use the short Anglo-Saxon words we talked about in Chapter 2. Pico Iyer of *Time* magazine once noted how Alice Munro, the Canadian short story writer, used thirty-eight one-syllable words in a typical exchange of thirty-nine words. Follow her example.

2. People usually don't speak directly or sometimes even in sentences.

When we read a deposition transcript it often sounds like the ravings of a lunatic—and even then the transcriber has probably edited it. Part of that is because we use our voice and gestures to convey meaning, which isn't going to be captured on the written page (though we have to try, as we'll see in a bit).

Moreover, Americans, at least, don't tend to speak in complete sentences; everything is strung along with a collection of "ands," "buts," or just pauses. Our speech isn't nearly as organized as written expression; it rambles, circling points as much as addressing them. People also don't tend to just come out and express their feelings; these, too, they talk around. "Actual speech tends to be dribblingly repetitive, and relatively nonfigurative, nonpictorial," the critic James Wood once wrote in *The New Yorker*. Good dialogue must capture these qualities to avoid sounding canned.

"Despite all the words at our disposal, words tend to fail us at key moments, and even when we know what we want to say we spend a whole lot of time trying to describe and articulate what we feel without being quite able to do it properly," Nathan Bransford has written. He went on:

We misunderstand, overemphasize, underemphasize, grasp at what we mean, and conversations go astray. So when two characters go back and forth explaining precisely what they are feeling or thinking to each other, it doesn't seem remotely real. Good dialogue is instead comprised of attempts at articulation.

Having said all this, written dialogue does make some allowances for the printed page. It becomes more concise, and characters do tend to speak in complete sentences. The key—and it isn't easy—is to do those things yet still capture the spontaneity of spoken speech.

How do you do this? Skillful writers of dialogue such as George V. Higgins or Ernest Hemingway were masters at it. Their characters may be expressing themselves in something that looks like sentences because there's punctuation, but frequently what we're getting are fragments or, better yet, interruptions as two or several people converse. Still, as the poet John Ashberry has said, "[W]e are most ourselves when we are talking, and we talk in a very irregular and antiliterary way."

3. Compensate for the lack of the visual and aural element in written dialogue.

Gestures can be described rarely, if at all, in dialogue and affidavits ("he slammed the table"), and efforts to capture tone of voice usually fall flat. (Avoid "he said angrily" and the like.) The key instead is to use words to convey emotion. A person who's upset might stutter or repeat things ("I—I don't really want it."). Or she might repeat herself several times or address the questioner. ("Are you listening?") All of these are permissible in an affidavit, even if lawyers currently don't use them.

4. Speakers tend to reflect their gender in the way they talk.
Sociolinguist Deborah Tannen and others have written extensively on the ways in which women and men tend to express themselves differently—keeping in mind that there are some men who sound more feminine in their speech patterns and vice versa. To reduce a complicated analysis to a sentence, men tend to use speech to create hierarchies and organize data; women tend to use it more to make personal connections.

Of course, you will have the advantage of knowing your characters and how they actually speak, but keep in mind the following differences described briefly:

a. Women tend to use more qualifiers than men in their speech patterns.
Eager to reinforce their place in the upper echelons of hierarchy, men tend to make pronouncements, even expressing opinions as fact—"The Steelers are going to win the Super Bowl!" Women often express facts as opinions, hedging far more in an urge to draw out their listeners.

b. Women may answer questions with questions of their own, while men will even argue with a question.
As part of the same impulse described above, if a woman is asked a question, "What time will John be here?", she will often answer it with a question of her own, "About six?"—even if she knows exactly when he will arrive. A man is more apt to say, "He's arriving at six-twelve"—even if he has little idea of the arrival time. Again, betraying a lack of knowledge is not what men tend to do, and they will frequently argue with a questioner in their response.

c. Women tend to use more modifiers or repetition in their speech.
A man will tend to ask for a "big hamburger." A woman might ask for a "really, really big hamburger." In Hemingway's "Hills

Like White Elephants," the exasperated woman finally tells her boyfriend, "Would you please please please please please please please stop talking." A man wouldn't say that—at least that way.

d. Women tend to complete sentences for people with whom they're conversing.

Both genders tend to interrupt frequently (it's part of American communal speech patterns). But with men, it's more to change the subject ("enough about me—let's talk about me"). In contrast, a woman tends to complete sentences for people—not to change the subject but to communicate the notion that she is listening so much that she knows what you're going to say. It's intended as a mark of friendliness and even respect.

e. Men tend to focus on outcomes; women on feelings and process.

Women don't just focus on outcomes; they tend to give detail and narrative to get there because the journey is as important as the result. In describing a friend's mood, a woman won't tend to say, "Susan was sad." She'll more likely say, "I ran into Susan at the store and I could tell she wasn't her usual self and at first she didn't want to tell me," and so on. When women don't do this, it can sound abrupt and unnatural.

f. Women tend to put more observable detail into what they say.

This is related to the previous point. Women tend to focus more on the context—what people were wearing or what the weather was like. Men are more bottom-line oriented. An answer or a story has a point, and to go beyond that is considered a waste of time.

5. Speakers also tend to reflect their age, educational level, geographical place, and class in the way they speak.

Speakers reveal not only their gender but lots of other personal characteristics. Children obviously speak differently than adults, and adolescents have their own slang and take on the world—a perspective perhaps never captured better than by J. D. Salinger with Holden Caulfield in *Catcher in the Rye*. Obviously the more educated you are, the more you know about the world—though keep in mind that even intellectuals tend to dwell in the domain of two-syllable Anglo-Saxon English when they speak. Professionals will use the jargon of their profession (Doctors—excuse me, "physicians"—deal with "fractures," not "broken bones," and so on.) The novelist Richard Price is a master at capturing the phrases and style of the police and their world. Old-style Yankee New Englanders and residents of the northern Midwest tend to be more laconic than westerners and southerners. We reveal ourselves in our speech patterns and what we speak about. In order to sound credible and realistic, your affiants should too.

6. Speakers tend to reflect their view on the matter at hand in the way they speak.

A father and mother talking about their child in a child-custody dispute are going to reveal different perspectives. We know what doctors tend to think about lawyers, so their statements in a malpractice proceeding might well expose their feelings of antipathy in the way they speak. To be credible, your affidavits should too.

"They look like white elephants," the woman says in Hemingway's "Hills Like White Elephants." The scene continues:

> "I've never seen one," the man says, and drinks his beer.
> "No, you wouldn't have."
> "I might have," the man says. "Just because you say I wouldn't have doesn't prove anything."

From that dialogue alone, we can read a lot into the emotions of the characters. You should try to do the same.

CHAPTER 9

Writing Complaints and Answers

I. The Overview: A Complaint Is Your Opening Shot—
Make It a Strong One

II. The Thirteen Rules of Complaint Writing

1. Do your research effectively.

2. Always begin with an introduction.

3. When describing the parties, don't be afraid to include a few relevant details.

4. Organize your facts so they are easy to understand.

5. Don't be afraid to make your factual allegations detailed.

6. Write in Anglo-Saxon English.

7. Avoid adjectives, adverbs, and subjective words.

8. Use short sentences and paragraphs.

9. Use frequent argumentative headings, both in the facts and in the causes of action.

10. Be specific about the relief you are seeking in cases concerning injunctive or declaratory relief.

11. Avoid legal jargon.

12. If permitted, don't be afraid to attach a few relevant documents to your complaint.

13. Think of the consequences if a judge converts a dismissal motion into one for summary judgment.

III. Writing Your Answer to Point Your Case in the
Right Direction

I. The Overview: A Complaint Is Your Opening Shot—
Make It a Strong One

Few pay much attention to the quality of writing in pleadings and complaints. Thanks to the widespread revisions of the federal and state procedural rules more than a half-century ago, which disposed of antiquated forms of pleading, almost anything that looks like a complaint will be treated as a complaint, though this has changed somewhat in recent years, thanks to the Supreme Court decisions in *Bell Atlantic v. Twembly* 550 U.S. 544 (2007) and *Ashcroft v. Iqbal* 556 U.S. (2009). Now plaintiffs are held to a higher standard in the specificity of their factual pleading. (The specific ramifications will not be dealt with here.)

Still, even if the rules require less, a complaint is the first litigation document in a lawsuit; it should . . . well, complain. Moreover, like all good litigation writing, a complaint should inform and persuade the reader that the party filing the document should prevail. This has become particularly important, as courts are moving to resolve an increasing number of cases on motions to dismiss. Despite the plain wording of Rule 8 and supporting case law that a complaint should survive a motion to dismiss unless it appears "beyond doubt that the plaintiff can prove no set of facts in support of his claim," courts have been moving to tighten that standard. According to a study of litigation in the mid-1990s in the U.S. District Court for the District of Columbia, 42 percent of all cases were terminated by dismissal—about twice the number terminated by summary judgment.

As we have learned, first impressions leave lasting impressions, and a complaint is often the first filing a judge reads in a case. It is certainly the first thing the opposing party and lawyers read. And if the case is of interest to the public, it is often read by reporters and outside parties. Why waste the opening shot by firing a blank?

Each of these interested readers is looking for something different in the complaint, so an advocate is often writing for a variety of audiences. A good introduction is likely to grab all readers, but especially outsiders, including the press. A detailed recitation of facts tends to impress the other party, since it shows you have done your homework ("They know that?"). Strong legal pleadings impress the lawyers on the other side as well as the judge. Judges also tend to be extremely interested in the request for relief, since it gives them some idea of how soon and in what manner the court may have to become involved.

A detailed complaint has one other advantage. According to Thomas Williams, a Louisville lawyer writing in the 1990s, disclosure requirements under the Federal Rules of Civil Procedure, Rule 26(a)(1), require an answering party to provide the other side, even without a discovery request, "the name and, if known, the address and telephone number of each individual likely to have discoverable information relevant to disputed facts alleged with particularity in the pleadings, identifying the subjects of the information," as well as any documents, data compilations, or "tangible things" in the party's possession that are relevant to disputed facts in the pleadings. Thus, the more specific your complaint is, the more likely it will be that this requirement is triggered.

Having said all this, there has been a lot of recent academic literature urging advocates to use their facts in a complaint to argue their cases in ways similar to what they should do in a brief. This is carrying things too far. Yes, a complaint needs to be persuasive, but its main goal is to make sure you plead what you need to plead to avoid getting your case dismissed. What's more, while detailed factual pleadings have their place, doing so may well run against the goal of making these documents short and pithy—the better to get allegations affirmed. Cases are won or lost on the persuasive power of the briefs. The same cannot be said of complaints to nearly the same extent.

II. The Thirteen Rules of Complaint Writing

After deciding what message you want to send in your introduction, you must decide what your complaint should include. The following rules are not meant to be exhaustive and may, on rare occasions, be inconsistent with the pleading rules of jurisdictions with odd dictates. They also deal solely with how to make complaints read better and don't address the legal requirements of pleading, such as the requirements for pleading fraud or mistake. *So check your local rules before drafting.*

1. Do your research effectively.

Richard Zielinski, writing in *The Practical Litigator*, has outlined a number of steps advocates should take before they begin drafting their complaints. Among other things, he recommends:

a. Researching the facts and law thoroughly;

b. Preparing a chronology of important events;

c. Outlining the causes of action;

d. Identifying the appropriate defendants;

e. Satisfying all conditions precedent;

f. Selecting the proper forum, and

g. Reviewing all applicable rules.

2. Always begin with an introduction.

The beginning of any complaint should summarize the lawsuit in a paragraph or two, explaining what the case is about, why you should win, and what you are seeking. This makes it much easier for the reader to understand what follows, since by necessity complaints are not organized in a way that makes them easy to comprehend.

In particular, judges need to know what kind of case is before them, what shape it is likely to take, and what relief is sought. In a sense, you are writing a long headnote. It's true that such an explanation is not part of a traditional pleading, but I've never seen a rule that prohibits it, and the worst thing the other side can do with such an introduction is to deny it.

A good example is the first page of the complex twenty-eight-page complaint in *Conservation Law Foundation of New England, Inc. v. Harper*, filed in U.S. District Court in Boston in the 1980s. It began:

> 1. This concerns what has been described as "the most extensive transfer of public property and resources to private control in recent American history." The plaintiffs, who represent over 4 million citizens, allege that members of the Administration of President Ronald Reagan are violating the National Environmental Policy Act, 42 U.S.C.A. §§ 4321 et seq. (1977) [NEPA] and other statutes by implementing a massive program to transfer up to 35 million acres of federally-owned land to private ownership without first analyzing the environmental effects of such a program. These environmental effects include an enormous loss of land available to states and localities for park use; creation of sales criteria which favor private commercial development on present federal lands, and a sharp curtailment of the amount of federal money made available to purchase land for conservation purposes.
>
> The plaintiffs also allege that members of the Reagan Ad-

ministration are implementing this program in clear violation of applicable statutes and regulations concerning disposal of federal lands. The plaintiffs ask this Court to enjoin further implementation of this program and for declaratory relief concerning the illegality of the program.

Another helpful example comes from the complaint in *Chere v. Taye*, No. 2:04-cv-06264-SRC-CCC (D.N.J. Dec. 20, 2004), cited in Elizabeth Fajans and Mary Falk's "Untold Stories: Restoring Narrative to Pleading Practice." The second paragraph reads (citations omitted and names changed):

2. Defendants induced Ms. Dunn to come to the United States from Ethiopia through fraudulent means and then held her as an involuntary servant for almost one and a half years. During this time, Defendants forced Ms. Dunn to work in their home for as many as one hundred hours per week without pay. Defendants kept Ms. Dunn in a condition of involuntary servitude and forced labor through threats of serious harm to her person and well-being and through a pattern of behavior that caused Ms. Dunn to reasonably believe that harm would come to her if she failed to continue performing the household duties assigned by Defendants or if she otherwise reported Defendants' conduct to responsible authorities. Ms. Dunn was finally able to escape Defendants' home with the assistance of acquaintances and family.

And, though lengthy, note the way the lawyers for the Department of Justice in the 1990s, aided by David Boies, began their antitrust complaint against Microsoft with a similar general introduction:

1. NATURE OF THIS ACTION

1. This is an action under Sections 1 and 2 of the Sherman Act to restrain anticompetitive conduct by defendant Microsoft Corporation ("Microsoft"), the world's largest supplier of computer software for personal computers ("PCs"), and to remedy the effects of its past unlawful conduct.

2. Microsoft possesses (and for several years has possessed) monopoly power in the market for personal computer operating systems. Microsoft's "Windows" operating systems are used on over 80% of Intel-based PCs, the dominant type of PC in the United States. More than 90% of new Intel-based PCs are shipped with a version of Windows pre-installed. PC manufacturers (often referred to as Original Equipment Manufacturers, or "OEMs") have no commercially reasonable alternative to Microsoft operating systems for the PCs that they distribute.

3. There are high barriers to entry in the market for PC operating systems. One of the most important barriers to entry is the barrier created by the number of software applications that must run on an operating system in order to make the operating system attractive to end users. Because end users want a large number of applications available, because most applications today are written to run on Windows, and because it would be prohibitively difficult, time-consuming, and expensive to create an alternative operating system that would run the programs that run on Windows, a potential new operating system entrant faces a high barrier to successful entry.

4. Accordingly, the most significant potential threat to Microsoft's operating system monopoly is not from a direct, frontal assault by existing or new operating systems, but from new software products that may support, or themselves become, alternative "platforms" to which applications can be written, and which can be used in conjunction with multiple operating systems, including but not limited to Windows.

5. To protect its valuable Windows monopoly against such

potential competitive threats, and to extend its operating system monopoly into other software markets, Microsoft has engaged in a series of anticompetitive activities. Microsoft's conduct includes agreements tying other Microsoft software products to Microsoft's Windows operating system; exclusionary agreements precluding companies from distributing, promoting, buying, or using products of Microsoft's software competitors or potential competitors; and exclusionary agreements restricting the right of companies to provide services or resources to Microsoft's software competitors or potential competitors.

6. One important current source of potential competition for Microsoft's Windows operating system monopoly comes from the Internet, described by Microsoft's CEO, Bill Gates, in May 1995 as "the most important single development to come along since the IBM PC was introduced in 1981." As Mr. Gates recognized, the development of competing Internet browsers—specialized software programs that allow PC users to locate, access, display, and manipulate content and applications located on the Internet's World Wide Web ("the Web")—posed a serious potential threat to Microsoft's Windows operating system monopoly. Mr. Gates warned his executives: A new computer "born" on the Internet is Netscape. Their browser is dominant, with a 70% usage share, allowing them to determine which network extensions will catch on. They are pursuing a multiplatform strategy where they move the key API [applications programming interface] into the client to commoditize the underlying operating system.

7. Internet browsers pose a competitive threat to Microsoft's operating system monopoly in two basic ways. First, as discussed above, one of the most important barriers to the entry and expansion of potential competitors to Microsoft in supplying PC operating systems is the large number of software applications that will run on the Windows operating system (and not on other operating systems). If application programs could

be written to run on multiple operating systems, competition in the market for operating systems could be revitalized. The combination of browser technology and a new programming language known as "Java" hold out this promise. Java is designed in part to permit applications written in it to be run on different operating systems. As such, it threatens to reduce or eliminate one of the key barriers to entry protecting Microsoft's operating system monopoly.

And so on.

3. When describing the parties, don't be afraid to include a few relevant details.

The parties to a lawsuit don't just have names and addresses. Though this is not the place to be exhaustive, you might want to give the reader a sentence or two of background about each, especially if it puts your client in a good light. In an article in the *Yale Law Journal*, Professor Herbert Eastman suggested the following paragraph for a hypothetical civil rights lawsuit:

2. Hattie Kendrick is an African-American, born in Mississippi, who moved to Cairo in the early 1920s. She has taught for decades in the racially segregated Cairo public schools, teaching generations of African-American children that participation in American democracy is their right and their duty. To set an example, she has worked throughout her life to better her community through neighborhood organization, peaceful demonstration, political activity, and litigation. She has paid a price for her dedication: She has been forced out of segregated business establishments, arrested by the police during peaceful marches, and fired by the school system.

4. Organize your facts so they are easy to understand.

Since factual allegations are generally (and should be) numbered, they can't be written as compellingly as facts in a brief. Here, unlike in a brief, you might want to recite the facts chronologically. Or you might want to consider listing them by category—facts involving the accident, the insurance policy, the warranty on the car—using captions above each section. The 1982 *CLF v. Harper* complaint dealing with public land sales discussed earlier divided its facts into three sections—the Federal Land Disposal Scheme, the National Environmental Policy Act, and the Defendants' Program.

5. Don't be afraid to make your factual allegations detailed.

I understand that some lawyers maintain that the best way to litigate a case is to be as vague as possible at the outset, to keep their opponent guessing. In many cases, however, that strategy doesn't work. The more specific you are in your factual allegations, the more prepared you seem. Though it is at times unavoidable, you want to stay away from phrases such as "on or about" and "approximately," because they make you look as if you don't know the underlying facts—a bad impression to convey.

Though your preparation will differ from case to case and you may find instances when you want to file early and then flesh out your allegations through discovery, my advice in most matters is to delay filing a complaint until you can be specific. The more authority you demonstrate in the beginning (particularly if you are seeking an early settlement), the stronger your case will appear. Moreover, by pleading your facts specifically, you trigger the disclosure rule under Fed. R. Civ. P. 26(a)(1), discussed earlier. In fact, you should state at various points in your fact section that your facts are being "pled with particularity as required by Rule 26."

6. Write in Anglo-Saxon English.

Defendants read complaints with an eye toward denying as much as possible. Ambiguity in pleading makes that easier, which is why you want to use words that have the clearest meanings in English. As we've learned, those tend to be short and derived from Anglo-Saxon. If we allege that someone "is running," we all tend to have the same sense of what that means. If, however, we allege that someone "is ambling," reasonable minds can disagree as to what that means. That gives the other side a chance to deny it.

7. Avoid adjectives, adverbs, and subjective words.

As Frank Cooper noted in *Writing in Law Practice*, your opponents can deny subjective declarations far more easily than objective statements. "Jones broke the window because he was careless with a hammer" will almost certainly be denied. "Jones dropped the hammer three times" may not be.

8. Use short sentences and paragraphs.

The longer and more complex your sentences are, the easier it also is for your opponents to deny what you are saying. The goal with most complaints, after all, is to get your allegations admitted. Shorter sentences help achieve that goal.

Don't plead facts you don't need to prove your case. Don't be repetitive, either. When stating your individual causes of action, simply "replead paragraphs 5–17" (if those are the facts you are using) rather than giving the reader the same facts again.

9. Use frequent argumentative headings, both in the facts and in the causes of action.

It is difficult to read something numbered by sentence or paragraph. Therefore, make it easier for your readers by dividing your complaint into several sections. If you have enough sections, provide a table of contents for the complaint after the cover page.

At the beginning of each section, use a heading, as in a brief. These headings make it easier for the reader to follow what's coming, and they emphasize the points of your arguments. For example, for each cause of action, use a heading that summarizes the allegation: "The defendant violated the National Environmental Policy Act when it failed to prepare an Environmental Impact Statement before leasing sites for oil drilling in the Pacific Ocean."

10. Be specific about the relief you are seeking in cases concerning injunctive or declaratory relief.

In cases seeking equitable relief, judges are understandably concerned about what they are being asked to do. The more specific you can be about the relief you are seeking, the better. If, for example, you are asking for a preliminary injunction, you might want to preview in the relief section what the order might look like. In that 1982 *CLF v. Harper* land sales complaint, the plaintiffs specifically enumerated ten preliminary and permanent injunctions they sought ("Issue an injunction prohibiting the defendant Robert Burford from considering the national deficit and federal revenue as a criterion in deciding whether to dispose of federal land").

No one will hold you precisely to that language (as long as you also ask for "any other relief the court finds appropriate"), and it will help the judge understand the case better.

11. Avoid legal jargon.

Like letters and contracts, complaints tend to be a repository of ancient prose. Write these documents in twenty-first-century style. This is, after all, the century in which you are filing your complaint.

12. If permitted, don't be afraid to attach a few relevant documents to your complaint.

Complaints are harder to read than letters or articles. If a document, letter, or newspaper story is relevant to the allegations in your complaint and the rules permit you to attach it, consider doing so. Illustrations also help a case come to life, and they are often read by a judge first. You can be more expansive in what you give a judge here than elsewhere.

Moreover, in many jurisdictions, documents attached to the complaint become part of the record if the opposing party does not object. In administrative cases, attachments to a complaint can supplement the record the agency must provide, if the court permits them.

The danger, of course, is that under the federal rules, a court can convert a dismissal motion to a summary judgment motion if it considers extraneous evidence. If a court does so and renders judgment, that judgment is on the merits and is not just a simple dismissal. So use your discretion and read the next rule.

13. Think of the consequences if a judge converts a dismissal motion into one for summary judgment.

If a court considers extraneous material on a Rule 12(c) motion to dismiss, it is supposed to convert the dismissal motion into one for summary judgment. According to some commentators, courts frequently do this without making the formal conversion, with the result that judgment is rendered without giving the plaintiff a chance to develop a factual record.

All this should prompt you to make your complaints more fact-driven.

III. Writing Your Answer to Point Your Case in the Right Direction

No one reads answers in the same way he or she reads complaints. How you write them, therefore, is of little consequence. Here are six quick suggestions.

1. Occasionally you can include a one-page introduction, just to give the judge and the other side a taste of your interpretation of the case.

2. Similarly, you might want to give your version of the facts when challenging the other side's. You can say something like "The Defendant denies paragraph 7, stating, instead, that the car was traveling only 18 mph."

3. Be as specific and as straightforward as possible. If something is true, admit it.

4. In *Successful Civil Litigation*, George Vetter admonishes lawyers never to say, "Neither admit nor deny the allegations of paragraph ___ but leave the plaintiff to his proof." He says some courts have held this not to be a denial.

5. If you don't have the resources to wage an extended discovery war, you may want to be less contentious in challenging the other side's allegations.

6. If your local rules permit it, when addressing allegations, always include the allegation and then your answer, so those concerned can read your answer without referring back to the complaint. (You might put the actual allegation in italics.)

In other words, don't do this:

4. Denied.
5. Denied.
6. Insufficient information to admit or deny.

Do this:

4. Plaintiff's allegation: *The defendant was driving the car at 30 mph.* Defendant's answer: Denied.
5. Plaintiff's allegation: *The defendant had consumed four beers at the ballgame.* Defendant's answer: Denied.
6. Plaintiff's allegation: *The defendant is a Redskins fan.* Defendant's answer: Insufficient information to admit or deny.

These suggestions are obviously not a panacea, nor will they allow litigators to win most cases they otherwise would have lost. Again, the primary role of a complaint and answer is not to convince the court or the other side but to list the legal causes of action and answers in a manner that allows the case to proceed.

However, these suggestions can provide a means to transform complaints from their current status as little more than legal checklists to documents that make some kind of an argument. That is, after all, what litigation is ultimately about.

CHAPTER 10

Writing in Discovery

I. The Overview: Written Discovery Can Have Several Advantages over Depositions

II. Ten Tips for Writing in Discovery

1. Always include an introduction.

2. Try to assemble your questions in a logical order.

3. Try not to use canned questions.

4. Be concise, using basic English when possible.

5. Establish a simple vocabulary.

6. Establish a set of instructions for answering.

7. Use requests for admissions freely, and when doing so, include the converse of the admission as the next submission.

8. Ask pertinent questions that will lead to the discovery of admissible evidence.

9. When answering discovery questions, answer as briefly as possible.

10. If you must object to a question or request, make your objection as specific as possible.

I. The Overview: Written Discovery Can Have Several Advantages over Depositions

Let's face it: Judges rarely read discovery documents—admissions, requests for documents, and interrogatories. And with these matters, you're usually in no mood to make things easier for the opposing side. Nonetheless, making discovery documents more persuasive and concise will make you a better litigator by enabling you to get the information you seek more easily. If a judge does need to look at these documents, effectively written ones will help your case as well.

When lawyers think of discovery, they tend to focus on depositions. The great advantages of depositions are that the answers can't be as well-prepared as with interrogatories, and that lawyers can depose nonparties. Depositions also require parties or witnesses to speak for themselves, not through a lawyer.

Requests for written admissions, documents, or interrogatories can be a more useful way to obtain some kinds of information, however. They can be a better tool for obtaining from the parties intricate or voluminous details that must be gathered by consulting a wide variety of people, as in the case of a corporation and many of its employees under Rule 33(a) of the Federal Rules of Civil Procedure. In some jurisdictions, you can file a request for interrogatories or documents with a complaint, moving the process along early. In fact, written discovery is probably best used as an initial tool to learn facts you don't already know—identifying the other side's witnesses, contentions, or experts. It is also useful in determining whom to depose—though some experts recommend deposing the opposing party before serving interrogatories, if only to tie the other side's story down as quickly as possible.

For lawyers who have to worry about costs, written discovery is also cheaper than depositions. Some litigators have pointed out that interrogatories are helpful in cases in which the deponent does not know the English language well. Finally, written discovery can often be a better tool than a deposition for impeachment at trial. Witnesses can claim they were confused about a deposition question, but it is more difficult to make such a contention in cross-examination about a question that was submitted in writing.

In an article in the *ABA Journal* Patricia Seitz, a Miami lawyer, once compiled a useful checklist of information that interrogatories can collect:

a. The identity of all lay witnesses who have knowledge of the facts of the case;

b. The identity of the people from whom the other side obtained statements;

c. More detail about claims or defenses;

d. A list of all codes or regulations that the opposing side thinks are relevant;

e. The identity of expert witnesses the other side will call at trial, with a listing of the subject of their testimony, their opinions, and the grounds for those opinions;

f. The identity of others liable to the other side;

g. Information regarding insurance coverage;

h. A detailed description of damages or injuries;

i. The identity of those with subrogation interests;

j. Background about the business entity (state of incorporation, number of employees);

k. Personal background of the other side;

l. The "existence, description, custody, condition, and location of documents and tangible things relating to the subject matter"; and

m. The identity of those who were consulted or helped prepare the answers.

Questions about these subjects require information that the other side will usually find difficult to twist. In contrast, questions that ask "why" are generally best saved for depositions.

For information about potential experts (Seitz's item e), Kenneth R. Berman, a Boston lawyer, has suggested a question roughly like this:

For each expert whom you expect to call as a witness at trial, please state:

a. The name and address of the expert;

b. The subject matter on which each such expert is expected to testify;

c. The substance of the facts and opinions to which each such expert is expected to testify; and

d. A summary of the grounds for each such opinion.

One caution: In *Successful Civil Litigation*, George Vetter warns that written discovery can occasionally backfire. He tells a story about a driver who sued another driver who had hit him from behind. The defendant seemed to have no defense, and the insurance company, through its adjuster, seemed quite willing to settle the case for a reasonable amount. Then, for no apparent reason, the plaintiff served interrogatories on the defendant, asking him why he had failed to stop. Lawyers then had to become actively involved for the defense, and when they asked the defendant why he hadn't stopped, he told them for the first time that his car had skidded on a patch of ice. He now had a defense and was less likely to settle.

The moral? Don't ask for information unless you really need it.

II. Ten Tips for Writing in Discovery

If you decide that written discovery requests will serve you well, keep these tips in mind.

1. Always include an introduction.

As with all other types of litigation writing, an introduction makes it easier for the reader to understand what will come next. Such an opening may seem unnecessary, but if the scope and relevancy of your requests come before a judge, an introduction can provide the context behind the questions. For example, you might write:

> These admissions are filed with the purpose of ascertaining exactly what happened on the night of the accident. First, we seek information about road conditions. Then we look for a description of how the car was running . . .

Writing such an introduction will force you to formulate and reveal your game plan for discovery. This isn't a bad thing, since pointless questions don't serve the interests of anyone.

2. Try to assemble your questions in a logical order.

Questions that flow in some kind of narrative order are easier to follow. Try to use queries that build on previous ones, or a chronological approach, or move from the general to the specific. Headings can help too.

3. Try not to use canned questions.

No matter how mundane the subject matter may appear, try to draft your questions from scratch. Prewritten questions can contain technical inaccuracies and make the lawyer asking them look bad. When asking questions of opposing experts, make sure your experts help you draft the inquiries.

4. Be concise, using basic English when possible.

Complex questions (or admissions) have less evidentiary value than simple ones and may confuse both your adversary and a judge. "Please identify all schools the plaintiff has attended" is an example of a good, straightforward request. Using examples can help clarify a demand too, particularly in a request for documents. You are also free to suggest answers or the types of categories you are seeking. Remember, too, that the more complex your language is, the more recalcitrant adversaries can claim they didn't understand your questions.

5. Establish a simple vocabulary.

Any problematic word or term of art should be defined in the text as simply as possible. Yet complex definitions can also get you into trouble, as the lawyers for Paula Jones found out in a slightly different context in their sexual harassment lawsuit against Bill Clinton in the 1990s. The lawyers defined "sexual relations" as follows:

> For purposes of this deposition, a person engages in "sexual relations" when the person knowingly engages in or causes contact with the genitalia, anus, groin, breast, inner thigh, or buttocks of any person with an intent to arouse or gratify the sexual desire of any person.

Thus, by a literal construction, a passive participant in oral sex could claim he had not had sexual relations, but his partner had. Like others, the lawyers for Jones would have been much better off simply adopting a simple definition from the dictionary.

6. Establish a set of instructions for answering.

For your instructions, you should:

a. Ask for an identification of who is answering the questions;
b. Specify a time period for answering the questions, even if it is obvious from the rules;
c. Inform the parties that if they find any term ambiguous, they should define the term for themselves and then answer the question and include the definition in their answer;
d. Tell the parties that if they are unable to answer a question, they should explain in detail why;
e. Tell the parties that if they are unable to answer part of a question, they should explain why and then answer as much as they can;
f. Suggest that parties use Rule 33(c), which gives responding parties the option of supplying written records in lieu of written answers. Going through these records can be time-consuming, but it often provides advocates with some of their best material in discovery. (When seeking documents, always ask for the original.)
g. If asking for documents under Rule 34 of the Federal Rules of Civil Procedure (or the state analogue), ask for a specific identification of any documents being withheld for reasons of privilege or otherwise, and ask for an explanation why.
h. Remind the parties that they have a duty to supplement some facts (information regarding the identity of people with knowledge of discoverable facts) or amend answers found later to be false. Patricia Seitz also suggests reminding parties of their duty under the rules to "provide all information, including that learned through hearsay, which is known by you, your agents, employees, or attorneys, or appearing in your records."

Richard Rosen, a New York lawyer, has suggested using definitions in document requests to eliminate unnecessary repetition and long phrases. In an article every litigator should read, "Making Discovery Tools Work," published in the November 1992 issue of *The Practical Lawyer*, he cites the following definitions, among others, as examples:

> The term "building" shall mean the property located at 211 West 86th Street, New York, New York.
>
> "Offer to purchase" means United Technologies' offer to purchase for cash Sheller's outstanding 13 percent senior subordinated notes due June 15, 2000.

Avoid long or boilerplate instructions as well. Courts have held, for example, that boilerplate instructions "need not be considered in responding," and that overly lengthy instructions can provide an excuse for failing to answer at all. (*See Diversified Products Corp v. Sports Center Co.*, 42 F.R.D. 3, 4 [D. Md. 1967].) Perhaps this court had in mind the document definition Jacob Stein once wrote about in an article:

> The term "document" or "documents," as used in this Request for Production of Documents, means the original or a copy of the original and any nonidentical copy, regardless of original location, of any recorded, written, printed, typed, or other graphic material of any kind, variety, type or character, including, by way of example but not limited to, the following: books; records; contracts; agreements; invoices; orders; bills; certificates; deeds; bills of sale; certificates of title; financial statements; instruments . . .

And so on, for about two hundred more words.

Do not ask, as Berman notes, for "every fact" or "all facts," since it is beyond the power of anyone—even a lawyer—to know everything.

7. Use requests for admissions freely, and when doing so, include the converse of the admission as an alternative submission.

Requests for admissions are the great unused device in discovery, utilized by only around 10 percent of lawyers in their practices, according to one estimate. Nonetheless, this kind of discovery can be properly enlarged to request the admission of any kind of discoverable fact, opinion, or even the application of law to facts. You can use admissions effectively to challenge key claims and defenses and to tie down facts you think you already know, limiting what must be proved at trial. Using an admission in this way can also mean that you don't have to put a weak witness on the stand to testify to these facts.

Richard Rosen suggests using admissions to authenticate documents or overcome possible objections to the hearsay rule, as in these examples:

> It was the regular practice of Comex Clearing to create and retain Daily Trade Registers in the ordinary course of its business in 1979 and 1980 in the form of Documents CX 1 through CX 602.
>
> Documents CX 1 through CX 602 are business records of Comex Clearing within the meaning of Fed. R. Evid. 803 (6).

Keep in mind too that there is no limit to the number of admissions an advocate can file in many courts. (A Massachusetts case approved the use of 704 separate requests!) Moreover, if these requests are not denied within the proper time, they're admitted. Lack of information is no defense for a failure to answer one; the responding party must take reasonable steps to determine the answer. As the venerable Jim McElhaney reminds his trial practice students, admissions can be read to the jury, along with a reminder from the judge and the lawyer that the responding party has admitted that these things are true.

One word of advice, however. Let's say you submit an admission to the other side that states, "The accident occurred at night." You should then submit an admission that states, "The accident did not occur at night." After these two admissions, you should have one admission and one denial.

Doing this may seem duplicative, but it guarantees that you will receive usable evidence. Confronted with these two admissions, some disingenuous adversaries might deny both statements on the grounds that the two cars suffered a "mishap," not an "accident." Better to be exhaustive and safe. Timothy Klenk, a Chicago lawyer, suggests occasionally filing an interrogatory as a follow-up, asking the party why it denied certain admissions.

8. Ask pertinent questions that will lead to the discovery of admissible evidence.

Patricia Seitz suggests that once you have drafted your questions, admissions, or requests following the instructions above, and after you have edited them for style, you should go through each, asking:

Could the question be made simpler or shorter?
Can any of these be eliminated?
What helpful information do I hope to get here?
What loopholes are there?

To find loopholes, approach each question as if you were the lawyer on the other side and ask yourself if the language permits you in any way to avoid answering. If you have time, ask a colleague to do the same thing, since drafters are often so close to their material that they can't see the loopholes. This is similar to the drafting process recommended later in Chapter 14.

9. When answering discovery questions, answer as briefly as possible.

There is obviously no cross-examination with an interrogatory. Be forthcoming and honest, but as with anything else in litigation writing, brevity is the soul of wit. Your job is not to guess at or provide information that the other side is not seeking. You also want to restate the question in some fashion, so the answer can be read as a whole. Remember, too, that you are under a continuing obligation to revise your answers if you receive new information.

In *Successful Civil Litigation*, George Vetter provides the following checklist of options you have to respond to interrogatories and requests for admissions:

INTERROGATORIES

1. Answer.
2. "Do not know" but subject to duty of reasonable inquiry.
3. Object with reasons spelled out . . .
4. Move that answer to interrogatory seeking application of law to fact should be deferred until pretrial.
5. Seek a protective order under Rule 26(c).
6. Specify and offer the records from which the answer can be ascertained . . .

REQUESTS FOR ADMISSION

1. Admit, or deny or qualify, in whole or in part.
2. a. Neither admit nor deny, stating reasons.
   b. Statement of lack of information or knowledge sufficient to admit or deny but that the party has made a reasonable inquiry.

3. Object with reasons spelled out . . .
4. Object that answer should be deferred until pretrial.
5. Seek a protective order under Rule 26(c).

10. If you must object to a question or request, make your objection as specific as possible.

Objections need to be as narrow as possible. Once you have done so, keep in mind that a judge's discovery rulings are rarely reviewable at the time, so you want to rely on logic, not precedent, while emphasizing the burden of answering—especially on nonparties.

PART IV

Writing in Legal Practice

CHAPTER 11

Technical Writing

I. The Overview: Yes, Virginia, You Can Make E-mail
and Even Patent Applications More Readable by
Studying Board Games and Cookbooks

II. The Fourteen Rules of Technical Writing: Making
the Incomprehensible Easy to Understand

1. Make sure you understand the material yourself before you begin.

2. Start with the bottom line.

3. After the bottom line, tell your readers how you intend to explain. Give them a written table of contents.

4. Frequently divide your material into sections.

5. At the beginning or end of every section, you may want to summarize where you've been and tell the reader where you're heading.

6. Number your points.

7. Use the second person.

8. Graphics are important.

9. Layout is important too.

10. Be conversational and stay away from terms of art.

11. Don't talk down to your readers.

12. Make the people or entities you're discussing memorable.

13. Refer to common experiences or use narrative.

14. Don't be wedded to the essay format.

I. The Overview: Yes, Virginia, You Can Make E-mail and Even Patent Applications More Readable by Studying Board Games and Cookbooks

Composing something that's complicated or technical is one of the hardest things writers have to do. Legal writers have to do it all the time, whether they're trying to explain a complex factual situation to a judge, a hard-to-follow legal position to a client, or, increasingly, keep things exceedingly short in an e-mail. One reason that drafting something technical is difficult is that law students rarely receive any training in it, even though they must do it all the time. Another is that while good examples of technical writing exist—the *New England Journal of Medicine* and *Scientific American*, to name two—few lawyers are inclined to examine them. Even those who decide to study these periodicals have a problem. An article on, say, nuclear physics may be written so that the average reader can understand the material. Unless one knows a lot about nuclear physics, however, it's hard to figure out how the writer got from point A to B to C.

Having said all that, however, most of us have encountered some examples of technical writing. Consider the directions to board games such as Clue and Monopoly, or a cookbook. Or, as we've already encountered, there are the directions on Google Maps or MapQuest. If you think about it, the writers of these "rules" do a workmanlike job of taking a fairly complex set of facts and explaining them so that anyone can follow them.

Examining how games, directions, and cookbooks describe their "rules" can give lawyers a number of ideas about how to proceed with their own technical writing. Of course, not all of these will be applicable every time a writer sits down to draft something complicated. Four or five, however, usually will come in handy. Here, then, are fourteen rules of technical writing that lawyers should remember.

II. The Fourteen Rules of Technical Writing: Making the Incomprehensible Easy to Understand

1. Make sure you understand the material yourself before you begin.

This is an obvious rule, but that doesn't mean that lawyers don't violate it all the time. The most embarrassing violations tend to come in oral argument. "Your Honor, the marginal cost analysis of this study shows—" the lawyer will begin.

"Counselor, what do you mean by 'marginal cost analysis'?" asks the judge.

There is a pause. "We mean the cost of the analysis, Your Honor."

"In laymen's terms, what do you mean by that phrase?" the judge asks again.

"If you analyze the margin and the cost, what you find . . ." And later that same afternoon we know as little about the phrase as we did before.

That lawyer, like many others in similar situations, hadn't a clue as to what the phrase meant. She just copied it from some record or testimony without bothering to figure it out first. The rule here is, can you put the concept in your own words? If you can't, you probably don't understand it. Ludwig Wittgenstein once said, "What can be said at all can be said clearly." Follow his thought, if not his example.

2. Start with the bottom line.

This is our rule from Chapter 1. It's important to repeat it here, because writers of technical material often get so anxious about what they're going to write that they dive right into the material without giving the reader the core idea. Just as the instructions for board games tell players the object of the game first, you should tell readers your basic idea.

This is what the appellants' lawyers did in *Conservation Law Foundation v. General Services Administration*, 707 F.2d 626 (1st Cir. 1983), a complex environmental case. The brief begins (citations omitted):

> This is a case about a governmental decision to sell surplus land. The government insists that in sales of property to the public, its only task is to get the highest prices it can for the property. The plaintiffs—citizens and environmental groups—maintain, however, that under the National Environmental Policy Act and the Federal Properties and Administrative Services Act, the government has an obligation to take environmental factors into account in its land sales decisions. At a minimum, the plaintiffs maintain that an Environmental Impact Statement analyzing the land sales must address specifically what will happen to the lands after sale.

3. After the bottom line, tell your readers how you intend to explain. Give them a written table of contents.

With complex material, readers need a written table of contents before they begin. To go back to our road trip analogy, if you're driving for the first time from San Francisco to Los

Angeles, you don't want to sit in the car and take orders. You like to look at a map first. The same principle applies here: Giving readers the game plan from the start makes them feel in control. (Remember that Wikipedia does something similar.) This not only makes the rest of the text easier to follow, it allows readers to skip to the parts they want to read—an increasingly essential attribute of prose in an Internet age that empowers readers to decide just what they want to read or not.

In their Supreme Court brief in the flag-burning case, *United States v. Eichman*, 496 U.S. 310 (1990), Charles Fried and Kathleen Sullivan provided just such a written table of contents in the "Summary of Argument":

> In this brief, we shall show (Point I) that what the Act forbids cannot be relegated to the fringes of the First Amendment assigned to low value speech . . .
>
> Next, we shall show (Point II) that the prohibitions of the Act are wholly and inescapably content-based . . .
>
> Finally, we draw the inescapable conclusion (Point III) that since no other purpose than the suppression of political activity is available to justify the Act . . .

At other times you may be presenting your information in an unusual way. That too should be pointed out to your readers at the outset, as Charles Alan Wright and others did in their famous brief for the appellants in *San Antonio Independent School District v. Rodriguez*, 411 U.S. 1 (1973):

> Because of the unusual background of this case, and of the constitutional principles it announces, it does not lend itself readily to the usual form of appellate brief, in which Roman-numbered topic sentences proceed in syllogistic splendor to the inevitable conclusion.

4. Frequently divide your material into sections.

The more complex a document is, the more you need to break it into sections to give readers a chance to consolidate the information. A complex document should be broken up every four double-spaced pages or so, occasionally more often. Remember, when dividing your document, to label the sections as simply as possible—I, II, II(A), II(B), III. Anything subdivided more becomes confusing.

The purpose of sectioning is to simplify the material for the reader, not to reflect its complexity. If Charles Dickens could write *Great Expectations* with simple chapter numbers, you can take your most complex material and do the same.

5. At the beginning or end of every section, you may want to summarize where you've been and tell the reader where you're heading.

Earlier I said that lawyers tend to be too repetitive, and that's true. However, in technical writing you want to repeat your principal ideas often. Readers of complex information frequently forget what they just read. When I was in law school, I would often read several pages of a case before I'd come upon a passage I recognized and realize that I had read the same case the night before. That happens to readers of technical material all the time.

These readers are also anxious readers; they need reassurance. Every few pages or so, remind them what you've been saying and what you'll say next. To continue our road trip analogy, if you've never driven from New York to Philadelphia, it helps to see signs every few miles indicating that you're on the right road. They don't put I-95 signs up every mile or so just to give convicts something to do on work release. Road designers understand that drivers need reassurance. So do your readers.

This technique is what the environmental lawyers adopted in *Conservation Law Foundation v. General Services Administration* to describe the series of complicated arguments the appellate court could use to justify the lower court's decision (footnotes omitted):

> GSA's argument that it is exempt from NEPA in public land sales can be refuted in any of three ways. This Court can find:
>
> (1) that the command in §484 (e) (2) (C) to consider the "public interest" when it sells land to the public does not preclude a consideration of environmental factors. The district court adopted this position;
>
> (2) that the command in §484 (e) (2) (C) to consider factors other than price when it sells land to the public does not preclude a consideration of environmental factors; or
>
> (3) that the command to accept fair market value in land sales to the public does not preclude a consideration of environmental factors.

6. Number your points.

As we've seen, Internet map services, as well as game rules and cookbooks, number their points and with good reason: Giving the reader five specific points makes those points more memorable than just reciting them paragraph by paragraph. It also makes them easier to read, and tends to be more succinct than an essay. Of course, if you're making thirty-seven points, numbering isn't going to do much good, unless you're writing for devotees of our favorite philosopher, Wittgenstein, who wrote in numbered paragraphs. In moderation, however, the technique works.

7. Use the second person.

Let's remind ourselves how you give directions. You don't say, "One should make a left on Green Street. One then goes a half-mile." What you say instead is "Make a left on Green Street. Go five blocks to the gas station and make another right." You use the imperative—the second person. So does Monopoly: "Go directly to jail. Do not pass Go. Do not collect $200."

There's a lesson in this. Ideas expressed in the second person are often much easier for readers to understand. This is one reason that law professors use hypotheticals so much. They want to put you metaphorically in the shoes of the concept they're explaining, to make it easier to grasp.

As a corollary to this rule, don't be afraid to talk to your readers directly. If you were explaining a difficult concept to someone out loud, you would provide a context from time to time. "The reason I'm going to explain the legislative history of NEPA now is that without this background, you can't understand the next argument," you might say. For some reason, however, legal writers are afraid to provide that guidance in their written prose. Don't make that mistake.

8. Graphics are important.

We live in a visual age; a picture can be worth the proverbial thousand words. Giving judges or clients a drawing can make it far easier for them to grasp the nuances. Graphs, timelines, bar graphs, and other visual representations help too. Make sure your graphics are accurate and look good. In this visual age, readers have high expectations for their illustrations.

9. Layout is important too.

I once heard about a study in which the participants were given two virtually identical sets of contracts to read. One set contained the usual contracts—single-spaced, poorly organized, without highlights. The second set of contracts was laid out far more attractively, with points highlighted in italics, the text double- and triple-spaced in parts, with wide margins.

By an overwhelming majority, the study participants said the contracts in the second set were better written. Of course, they weren't; they were just better packaged. Yet the principle holds: In a world where writers can easily use computers to present their material in appealing fashion, you should use these tools too. As we mentioned in Chapter 2, don't be afraid to vary your fonts or use color, as long as you do so in moderation. Lots of white space helps too. In litigation you must follow court procedures, and many of these rules are quite strict about layout. In other contexts, however, use your imagination.

10. Be conversational and stay away from terms of art.

The more complex your ideas are, the simpler and more conversational your prose should be. Paragraphs and sentences need to be short in technical writing. "See Spot run" is first-grade prose. "See Spot claim estoppel" sounds less so, and with good reason.

We must occasionally use terms of art, which should be defined. So be it. However, try to avoid using words that have to be defined. (Drafts of contracts and rules, where definitions are essential, are an exception to this edict.) Keep your definitions to a minimum: Children can play Monopoly even if they don't understand what mortgages are. Remember that most readers don't read definitions, and even if they do, they seldom remember them.

Judge Posner made the same point in *Indiana Lumbermen's Mutual Insurance Company v. Reinsurance Results, Inc.*, 513 F.3d 652 (7th Cir. 2008):

> Reinsurance is a dauntingly complex, esoteric field of business and the briefs in this case are correspondingly complex and esoteric. But the facts relevant to the appeal are actually rather simple, and the forbidding jargon of reinsurance ("ceded unearned premium," "aggregate excess of loss," "under-ceded reinsurance loss," "reinsurance treaty," and the rest) can be dispensed with.

A good example of a piece of technical writing striving to be conversational comes from this opinion written by the Federal Energy Regulatory Commission (FERC):

> So, the logical questions with which to begin are: "How important is this subject to consumers? How much do they have at stake? Do they have anything at stake?"
>
> The answers are clear.
>
> For the contemporary American consumer, the most significant thing about the oil pipeline rate controversy is its utter insignificance. On an overall, industry-wide basis, the pipeline charge came to 61 cents a barrel in 1981. Since there are 42 gallons in a barrel, that is approximately 1.5 cents a gallon. No great cause for perturbation there.

11. Don't talk down to your readers.

Computer manuals tend to suffer from this malady. "This is easy!" they announce cheerfully, and an hour later, when you still can't figure out what the manual is talking about, you stop trying. Nothing is easy. However, avoid the temptation to announce repeatedly how difficult a task is. That will only intimidate the reader. Just get the chore of explanation done and go home.

12. Make the people or entities you're discussing memorable.

With complex information, readers tend to organize the material around the characters. If those characters are indistinct, the reader is lost from paragraph one. Take any movie, short story, or novel; the characters tend to be introduced slowly. Otherwise, the writer has created a crowd scene.

Find a way to introduce your main actors and actresses slowly and memorably. This is a particular problem in legal writing, because so many corporate names sound alike, or are at least forgettable, to the first-time reader. Keep in mind that using initials as a way to make corporate or agency names memorable doesn't usually work either.

Another useful bad example comes from the decision by the U.S. Court of Appeals for the Second Circuit in *Ryder Energy Distribution Corp. v. Merrill Lynch Commodities Inc.*, 748 F.2d 774 (2d Cir. 1984):

> The following facts cannot be found in the complaint: REDCO's previous dealings with TOI, REDCO's reasons for conducting an EFP, Merrill's inability to find REDCO an EFP partner, REDCO's introduction of TOI to Merrill, Hutton and NYME's lack of knowledge of TOI's default until June 11, and NYME's instigation of a rules compliance investigation after June 11.

Here is another example of what not to do, provided by courtesy of Judge Kozinski:

> LBE's complaint more specifically alleges that NRB failed to make an appropriate determination of RPT and TIP conformity to SIP.18.

I often receive complaints from corporate clients who say they get letters like this from lawyers: "Under the APA and NEPA, you must file an EIS, ASAP, with DOI, as well as a FOIA exemption." Understandably, they're baffled. Call these entities "agencies" or "Interior." Don't use initials, except in rare cases.

13. Refer to common experiences or use narrative.

When I was a judicial law clerk, we had a case that required us to understand something about how oil wells work. The lawyer began by comparing these wells to bicycles, a device we all understood better.

That was a good strategy. If you can get your readers feeling comfortable with a concept, it's far easier to move on to something more complicated. That's why many technical writers begin with a story or a striking example.

In intellectual property matters, as we've noted, often it's far better to explain why an invention or development is unique by telling the story of how it originated, rather than detailing its constituent parts. Engineers often do the latter, much to their detriment.

A wonderful example of this technique came in a brief filed by several San Francisco lawyers in the U.S. Court of Appeals for the Ninth Circuit in *Lewis Galoob Toys v. Nintendo*, 964 F.2d 965 (9th Cir. 1992). In the brief, the story that makes the technicalities come alive is laid out by the lawyers at Howard, Rice, Nemerovski, Canady, Robertson, and Falk in, of all things, the "questions presented" section (names changed):

It is Saturday, somewhere in Los Angeles. Lying on her bed, Abby, age 11, picks up the book she has checked out of the school library, *Charlotte's Web*. Although she has only read through page 61, this morning she finds herself wondering how it ends. Furtively she flips through the book and glances at the last two pages. Relieved to discover that Wilbur has not been made into bacon, she returns to page 61.

Later in the morning, Abby comes down the stairs to find an empty living room. Her older brothers, both in high school, are at the beach. Abby slips a videocassette of her favorite movie, *Casablanca*, into the family VCR, and starts the tape. As Rick and Ilsa embrace, Abby frowns, and hits "fast forward" until more suitable action appears on the screen.

Suddenly, Abby notices the ordinarily occupied Nintendo game sitting temptingly on the coffee table in front of the television. Seizing on the opportunity, Abby turns off the movie and slips the game cartridge for "Super Mario Bros. 3" into the control deck; on reflection, she removes it, attaches the Game Genie video game enhancer, and reinserts the cartridge. She keys in the code "AEKPTZGE," which according to the instructions will give Mario nine "lives" instead of the usual three. That, Abby thinks to herself, will make up for her inexperience at the game her brothers have managed to monopolize. She also keys in the code that will start Mario in "world four" rather than at the beginning in world one; in previous attempts, Abby has never gotten past world three. Pushing the "Start" button, Abby begins to play "Super Mario Bros. 3." At the end of the game, she turns off the television set and the Nintendo control deck. The game cartridge is as it was before she played, unaltered in any respect. She has made no copy of the mysterious software in that cartridge, nor has she recorded in any form the game she played or the video displays that entertained her.

Has Abby infringed the copyright in *Casablanca*? The book author's copyright? And—as Nintendo asserts in this case and the district court seems to have found—has she infringed Nintendo's copyright in "Super Mario Bros. 3"? To answer that ultimate question, the Court will need to resolve the following questions.

14. Don't be wedded to the essay format.

In litigation writing, we write rarefied essays because that's what the rules require. In other contexts, however, writers need to be more creative about their prose models. When Heloise or Dear Abby a generation ago wanted to discourse on a subject, they didn't write a lengthy essay; they answered questions, told stories, or made a list.

You should try similar approaches. If you have to explain a new tax regulation to a client, rather than writing a traditional memo, you might want to consider drafting a two- or three-sentence summary. Then tell your reader, "Here are five questions you're likely to have about these new regulations" and go on to answer them. Your material will probably be easier to understand presented in this format.

No one wants to suggest that explaining the intricacies of patent or environmental law is easy. But by keeping your writing simple and clear, you give the reader a much better chance of understanding your point of view as well as the technical aspects of the matter at hand.

CHAPTER 12

Writing E-mail and Letters

I. The Overview: The Importance of E-mail

II. The Sixteen Rules of Writing E-mail

1. As always, lead with your conclusion, rephrasing questions with your first sentence.

2. Keep it short: the presumption is 150 words or less.

3. Write in the second person.

4. Write in Anglo-Saxon English.

5. Avoid formal salutations and sign-offs.

6. Forget the exclamation point!!!

7. Play it straight.

8. Make sure your heading line summarizes the subject of the e-mail.

9. Assume unknown readers.

10. Think before you send.

11. Because the Internet has virtually obliterated the notions of confidentiality and privilege, be careful about what you put in writing.

12. If you're writing anything privileged, confidential, inflammatory, or contentious, put the names of the recipients into the "To" box last, after everything has been checked and edited.

13. Beware the "reply all" button.

14. Avoid questionable phrases or sentences.

15. When you edit an e-mail, print it with no paragraphing before you begin.

16. Don't overuse e-mail.

III. The Eight Rules of Letter Writing

1. Keep it short and lead with your conclusion.

2. Don't pick a fight.

3. Be specific.

4. Each letter should stand on its own.

5. Stay away from jargon.

6. Design your letters so they'll be understood.

7. Be careful about what you put in writing.

8. Make sure an opinion letter lets the reader know the complete basis for the opinion.

I. The Overview: The Importance of E-mail

Even though writing e-mail is now the bread and butter of lawyering, having replaced formal letters in many instances and memos in others, attorneys frequently underestimate the importance of this type of correspondence. Don't make that mistake. Many clients, foes, and other lawyers get their first view of you through e-mail. You're also dealing with a tough audience: The average person now gets so much e-mail that the tendency is to read a few lines and then lose interest, especially because e-mail is often read while the recipient is doing something else at the same time. If you want people to read your electronic communications—and I assume you do—you have to take steps to make them readable.

Writing e-mail is still a new area with undefined rules. It's a place where writers feel they can be personal and informal, and that can actually free some writers to be more creative. For both of these reasons, treat these suggestions as just that: things are changing rapidly.

Following these rules should help:

1. As always, lead with your conclusions, rephrasing questions with your first sentence.

Of course, the heading above begs the question: *What* should be the conclusion of most e-mails? Two things, really. First, you want to tell your readers *why* you're writing them. Most lawyers do this well. Second, you need to tell them specifically *what you want them to do in response*. Most lawyers do this poorly, if at all.

True, often you're telling your readers something they don't want to hear or do. The desire to bury such information is understandable, and it often seems rude to give orders to your readers in the first paragraph.

In the e-world, however, you don't have much choice. Back into your conclusions and your readers likely never get to them. At least once a month, I find myself exchanging e-mails with someone who asks me why I haven't responded to something they requested. The reason is usually that the request was buried in the eighth paragraph of a 1,000-word e-mail and I never saw it. I don't think I'm alone in failing to notice.

What if your e-mail isn't asking someone to do something? Ask yourself why you're sending it at all and then, maybe, don't. The modern lament is rarely that we don't get enough e-mail and feel lonely as a consequence. It's that we're drowning in it. Restricting much of your e-mail to requests for action and their consequences allows you to lessen the load of unnecessary reading for others. Get yourself noticed in different ways.

Remember, too, that readers don't want to reread what they sent you, even if your e-mail program provides that opportunity. If you are answering a question about an assignment, say something like "You asked when I'll finish the assignment and my best guess is Tuesday." Otherwise, the reader is initially trying to remember the original question and figure out the point.

2. Keep it short: the presumption is 150 words or less.

Write anything longer than five sentences or so and you strongly risk having the remainder unread or forgotten. Of course, we often have to convey more information than that electronically. The suggestion here is to attach a longer document as a PDF, and then use the e-mail both to summarize the document and tell your readers to print the document and read it in hard copy. Maybe they won't, but at least you've warned them. To do otherwise is to send along a pile of information that will rarely be digested.

3. Write in the second person.

Informal? Yes. Easier to understand? That too. We've already discussed how the second person makes prose easier for a reader to absorb. It also helps the writer comply with the next rule.

4. Write in Anglo-Saxon English.

When we speak, we use the shorter, simpler words that are easier to grasp without reflection. Writing in the second person puts the e-mail writer in the role of a speaker and makes that transition easier.

5. Avoid formal salutations and sign-offs.

In the informality that is e-mail, you rarely need to start off with a "Dear So-and-so." Just write "To: John Jones," or "John Jones:" or "John:" or just start with no salutation at all; usually you don't need it.

As to how you end, just signing the e-mail with your name is fine. If you want to say something more, keep it simple with "Sincerely." Anything more is too formal for this medium.

6. Forget the exclamation point!!!

Exclamation points don't look professional. You may think they convey warmth or approachability. Instead they convey that you think like a fourteen-year-old. F. Scott Fitzgerald likened them to laughing at your own joke. Avoid them.

7. Play it straight.

In their tendency to write informally, e-mail writers often try their hands at humor. Avoid that too. Daniel Goleman has written how "we tend to misinterpret positive e-mail messages as more neutral, and neutral ones as more negative, than the sender intended. Even jokes are rated as less funny by recipients than by senders."

Your recipients are reading your e-mail in a very utilitarian manner. If they don't get the joke, they'll often think you're insulting them. That's not a good idea, to say the least.

8. Make sure your heading line summarizes the subject of the e-mail.

Often we're answering an answer of an e-mail (and so on) and we keep using the same subject line. That's a mistake. You want your subject line to cover what you're writing about in that specific message, if only because we receive so many e-mails that we delete some without reading, based on what we see in the subject line. If the subject line is inaccurate, you risk having that happen to your message. And, even if the message is read, it's irritating to be misled from the outset.

It is also annoying to get the seventh e-mail in a trail that has covered many subjects and have it titled "Re: Re: Re: Saturday," etc.

9. Assume unknown readers.

Much of our e-mail is passed on to others, many of whom we don't know. In the old days—like ten years ago—if we sent a document to a client or another lawyer we could safely assume that its chances of disclosure to others were slim. First, there weren't a boatload of copies floating around. Second, even if someone unexpected got hold of the document, there wasn't that much he or she could do with it if the press wasn't interested in disseminating the information.

That obviously isn't the case today. E-mail makes it easy for anyone to pass anything on to whomever they want (and sometimes by accident). Once an unforeseen reader has the document, he or she can post it on the Internet—and the whole world has access.

That dictates an approach in which e-mail writers should essentially assume that anything they write could be read by anyone, because in many cases it will be. "You have zero privacy," Scott McNealy, a co-founder of Sun Microsystems, said way back in 1999. "Get over it."

That means a few things. First, don't be too informal. Many e-mail writers carry informality so far that they misspell words or make grammatical errors. That doesn't make the writer look sharp. Keep in mind, too, that anything you say in an e-mail can be passed on to someone else or read by a snooper, even if you think you've erased it. It may even be discoverable.

Moreover, assume as you write that the document is going to be read by people you didn't anticipate—even adversaries. Caution is your watchword.

Finally, see the next rule—and then the one after that.

10. Think before you send.

Because e-mail is so easy to dash off, writers often send it before they're ready. Proofread what you plan to send. And if you're at all angry with the recipient, hold the e-mail for at least an hour or so.

"On email, people aren't quite themselves," David Shipley and Will Schwalbe write in what I think is the best guide to writing e-mail, *Send: The Essential Guide to Email for Office and Home.* "They are angrier, less sympathetic, less aware, more easily wounded, even more gossipy and duplicitous. Email has a tendency to encourage the lesser angels of our nature."

11. Because the Internet has virtually obliterated the notions of confidentiality and privilege, be careful about what you put in writing.

By the time they graduate, all law students have learned the rules of privilege, whether they stem from the "work product" rule, the attorney-client privilege, or some other source. And yes, the privileges still exist. In reality, however, they mean far less than they did. I love the e-mails I get from law firms that always have a warning at the end (where no one will read it anyway), warning me that the information I've just received is confidential. Want to bet?

Abraham Lincoln used to ask his audiences, "If you call a tail a leg, how many legs does a sheep have?" People in the audience would yell back, "Five." "No," Lincoln would answer. "Four. Calling a tail a leg doesn't make it one."

Similarly, calling a document "privileged" doesn't make it so.

Of course, lawyers are often under a professional obligation to tell an adversary if they have received privileged communication from the other side (and they are supposed to read only as much of the communication as they need to determine it is privileged). Still, all anyone has to do is hit a button and that "confidential" data belongs to the world. What's more, many foreign jurisdictions don't have the same privilege protections that we do.

The e-age dictates an approach in which lawyers are increasingly selective about what they put in writing. Some things are better said to others, rather than put in written form. As the old Boston political boss Martin Lomasney supposedly once said, "Never write if you can speak, never speak if you can nod, never nod if you can wink." This isn't to imply that what you're telling your readers is illegal or unethical, but only that if it exists in writing, someone may see it who could disclose it and cause problems. Even deleting it on your computer offers no assurances that a researcher can't retrieve it from your

hard drive, much less that of others. Sure, an oral communication to a client is likelier to be misunderstood or forgotten.
But the alternative—a written message—carries its own set of
risks too.

There isn't a week that goes by where some publication carries a story about some poor soul who sent an e-mail he or she
should never have sent. A few headlines are enough to convey
the substance:

**DID LAWYER'S E-MAIL GOOF LAND $1B SETTLEMENT
ON NYT'S FRONT PAGE?**

**11 EMBARRASSING WALL STREET EMAILS TO REMIND
YOU WHY YOU SHOULD NEVER USE EMAIL AGAIN**

**MISDIRECTED E-MAIL SET THE STAGE FOR
CLEAR CHANNEL SUIT**

**LAWYERS SANCTIONED FOR E-MAIL INSULTS,
INCLUDING "SCUM SUCKING LOSER" COMMENT**

It's true that the ABA's *Rules of Model Professional Conduct*
require lawyers who have received an accidental e-mail to notify
the sender. But they're not required to destroy it and the rest of
the world obviously isn't bound by the rule. Even "privileged"
documents may not be as protected as they seem, because the
privileges that protect documents are broader in theory than
in application. Let's say you write a memo in which you tell
clients that they are apt to be sued unless they clean up a waste
site. The clients are later sued for not cleaning up. Somehow
the other side asks to see your memo in discovery as part of
a sweeping request for documents. Based on attorney-client or
work-product grounds, you claim that the document is privileged. Even if you're right, in many cases, the judge still has to

read the document *in camera* before deciding on the claim of privilege.

The problem, of course, is that once a judge has read your memo advising a cleanup, he or she isn't likely to forget it, even if the memo is ruled to be protected. If this case is being tried before that judge, not a jury, you have a rough burden to bear. You would have been far better off simply telling the clients to clean up rather than putting it in writing.

That said, don't go to your office and start destroying files. In the future, just be careful about what you put in writing.

12. If you're writing anything privileged, confidential, inflammatory, or contentious, put the names of the recipients into the "To" box last, after everything has been checked and edited.

Yes, composing and editing in this fashion is time-consuming. But it's worth it, because frequently we send messages way too soon, if only because we hit the wrong button. Moreover, follow the next rule.

13. Beware the "reply all" button.

This is the source of countless mishaps, as lawyers fail to be careful, hit the "reply all" button, and send confidential or sensitive information to unknown readers and even the other side. If you can, disable it or get some kind of software that sends a warning before sending. If not, the best advice, as before, is to draft first, edit, and put in the names last. Otherwise, one day you're bound to hit the wrong button, with all the chaos that will ensue.

14. Avoid questionable phrases or sentences.

Roger Matus writes an entertaining blog—*Death by E-Mail*. He warns to avoid the following phrases or sentences, among others:

- "Delete this e-mail immediately."
- "I really shouldn't put this in writing."
- "We're going to do this differently than normal."
- "I don't want to discuss this in e-mail. Please give me a call."
- "Don't ask. You don't want to know."

Elizabeth Chartus of Cataphora, a provider of e-discovery software, lists some others, including:

- "I could get into trouble for telling you this, but . . ."
- "Is this actually legal?"
- "Don't tell So-and-So." Or, "Don't send this to So-and-So."
- "She/He/They will never find out."

Another set of examples comes from the website The HR Specialist. "The 'e' in email stands for eternal evidence and it doesn't go away," the blog quoted attorney Mindy Chapman, author of the HR Specialist's *Case in Point* blog. It went on:

Chapman gave examples of real-life email blunders that cost employers big in court, including managers who included these beauties in their email:
- "We would like to accommodate you, but we're not set up for blind people." (an $8 million verdict)
- "I don't care about the FMLA, shmeflma!"
- "I'm sick of always having to accommodate her."

15. When you edit an e-mail, print it with no paragraphing before you begin.
Why this advice? Because on many devices, this is the way what you wrote will be read.
Keep in mind that much e-mail doesn't get formatted, with

the result that everything comes in one strung-along paragraph. Writing electronically is closer to writing telegrams (with a premium on every word because you pay for every word)—or even texting—than it is to writing essays.

16. Don't overuse e-mail.

Many professionals are drowning in e-mail. One study showed workers spending more than a third of their time writing and answering—time that used to be better spent on other tasks. More than a few partners have complained to me that they are hounded by e-mail questions that their associates would never think of asking either in person or on the phone. "We're working in an interruption-driven workplace," one corporate manager has said. "You can't finish the product, finish the thought."

It's true, as Michael Kinsley once pointed out, that e-mail encourages egalitarianism. He wrote that e-mail is

> another blow to the old corporate culture in which Mr. Bigshot dictates letters and memos and the secretary types them, folds them, mails them, opens them at the receiving end, files them, and so on. . . . Refusing to use a keyboard will soon be as anachronistic as, say, refusing to speak on the telephone.

Still, the democratic nature of e-mail has caused its own set of problems. "The ease of e-mail encourages unnecessary exchanges," wrote Shipley and Schwalbe, understating the matter considerably, warning on another occasion that "[t]he fact that e-mail defies time zones also means that it can defy propriety." What Naomi Baron, a professor of linguistics at American University in Washington, D.C., said about communication with all mobile devices applies here. "What [people] . . . like about their mobile devices is that they can reach other people," she said. "What they like least is that other people can reach them."

My basic rule here is that if you would contact the recipient either in person or by phone and e-mail is simply the most efficient way to do so, you should use it. If, however, the question wouldn't warrant a personal contact, it likely isn't worth an e-mail message either. Put the message in hard written copy instead or, if it's worth the time, call.

If you are sending an e-mail that doesn't require an answer, consider ending your e-mails with a "No Need to Respond." That helps everyone.

III. The Eight Rules of Letter Writing

Thanks to e-mail, letters are used far less in legal practice and business than they were even a decade ago. Today, a letter conveys a formality that e-mail doesn't and tends to be used when that's called for. Following the rules below should help you keep your letters readable.

1. Keep it short and lead with your conclusion.

As with e-mail, the biggest problem with most legal letters is that they don't present the conclusion first, violating our cardinal rule from Chapter 1. Of course, the bottom line in a letter can vary greatly, depending on the circumstances. Generally, however, someone who receives a letter from a lawyer wants to know two things right up front, just as in e-mail.

Why are you writing to me?
What do I have to do?

Follow the example of Abraham Lincoln, who wrote to his brother-in-law beginning: "Your request for eighty dollars, I do not think it best to comply with now."
I understand that legal letters frequently bring bad news,

and, as we said before, lawyers tend to want to bury that news in the body of the letter, after buttering up the reader with an explanation or a series of minor congratulations. This technique rarely works, however. If you have to deliver unpleasant information, it's usually far better to say it at the outset and go on to explain. Otherwise, the letter ends up looking disjointed, and insincere to boot.

As to length, try to keep these documents two pages or less. That's around 800 words—more than enough to express most things.

2. Don't pick a fight.

Many legal letters are threatening to the point of offensiveness. Even a demand letter should be understated and unquestioningly gracious, giving readers a gentle out if they want to take it. Don't mention "your unproven assertions" or say "You have the facts wrong." As Robert Smith points out in his estimable book *The Literate Lawyer*, which has an excellent chapter on letter writing, it's better to say something like "the facts are disputed" or "despite your assertion, we have found . . ." Even demand letters can be polite. As it says in the Bible, "A soft answer turneth away wrath, but grievous words stir up anger."

After all, it is far more difficult to deescalate a fight than it is to escalate one. In my interviews with lawyers, many have confessed that some of their more embarrassing moments in practice have come when they have dashed off an angry exchange to an adversary, only to revisit the text a day or two later and cringe. (The instantaneous nature of e-mail has, unfortunately, worsened the problem.) It has always surprised me that lawyers would never dream of *saying* the kinds of things that they freely *write* in a letter. Once sent, that letter can be shown to a judge, photocopied, scanned, or simply posted on a wall to provoke the recipient. I'm not suggesting that you start insulting people verbally, but it is usually far better to express your negative thoughts that way than to put them in writing.

Anytime you compose a letter that could be construed as even remotely hostile or threatening, put it aside for at least twenty-four hours. If you want to send it after a day, that's up to you. Often, with a cooler head, you won't.

3. Be specific.

In letter writing, as in e-mail drafting, there is little room for nuance. Recipients of letters don't pore over them the way they might read James Joyce's *Finnegans Wake* or the Bible. If they understand the letter after quickly reading it once, great. But if they don't, they're not going to lose any sleep over it.

Either express your thoughts clearly and concretely or don't bother to express them at all. Ideas "implied" in a letter are rarely understood. I've often read letters from lawyers that are incomprehensible. "What were you trying to say?" I'll ask the writer. "Well, I was trying to hint subtly that we're tough and won't settle," she'll say. In this case, you have two choices. Either tell the reader directly, "We're tough—we won't settle," or say nothing at all. Say what you mean; otherwise, the thought is likely to be lost and you'll confuse the reader.

4. Each letter should stand on its own.

I hear constant complaints from clients that they are tired of reading letters that incorporate other documents or letters by reference. Recipients should be able to understand each letter without referring to anything else. Otherwise, you've drafted a letter that reads like the tax code.

A reader should be able to tell from the outset exactly what the letter is about. "In reference to our conversation of August 23" does a reader little good, because he might have had sixty conversations on that date and not be able to remember the one with you. What you should write is "In reference to our conversation of August 23, in which we discussed the imminent filing of an intent to sue letter . . ." Now the reader knows what you're talking about and can read on with confidence.

5. Stay away from jargon.

A letter should be conversational, and its style should be as contemporary as possible. Unfortunately, if there is a major repository for anachronistic prose in the legal profession outside of wills and contracts, it is the letter. Within this domain, perfectly normal attorneys either turn on the dictaphone or start writing, and it's as if they stepped into a time machine and started composing in the styles of centuries past. Phrases such as "wishing to state" and "hoping to hear" don't belong in letters.

When the Clinton administration decided to implement a plain-language rule in government writing in 1998, it found letters like this one from the Veterans Benefit Administration:

> If evidence is not received before June 28, '98, which is one year from the date of our first letter, benefits, if entitlement is established, cannot be paid before the date of receipt of the evidence.

In its place, the revised letter read:

> We'll have to turn down your claim if we don't get your documents report by June 28.

Lawyers assume archaic and convoluted styles because they want to impress on their readers that they really are attorneys, and they figure the way to do this is to write in stereotypically lawyerly language. It's unnecessary, though, and it creates a barrier between you and your readers. Anyone who gets a letter with all those names at the top and the fancy printing is going to know it came from a lawyer; you don't need the antiquated language.

6. Design your letters so they'll be understood.

Lawyers often forget how difficult letters are to read. Here computer design doesn't help. The form of business letters dictates that they should be single-spaced, with an extra space between paragraphs. That means that a four-page letter is really an eight-page document, presented in a way that is difficult to digest.

This suggests two approaches. First, if you are drafting a letter that is going to be longer than two pages, try to find a way to get it out of the letter format. There's no reason that long opinion letters have to be letters. If you make them into opinion memoranda, you can double-space them, add a table of contents, and use other techniques to make them easier to follow. Similarly, I have seen lawyers file letters with administrative agencies or courts that go on for pages, sometimes with footnotes. Do these attorneys really think anyone is reading these documents past page 2?

If you find yourself in a situation where you have to write a letter of more than two pages, consider adopting some of the techniques we discussed in Chapter 11, on technical writing. The more you can take a long document and break it into sections, make the paragraphs short, or make lists, the easier it will be for readers to follow what you are saying.

Always keep in mind that letters are not the best forum for an exchange of serious, complex ideas. If you have a thought that is going to take a while to explain, search for another means to do so.

7. Be careful about what you put in writing.

Letters are used to make a record. Though you may not intend them to be public records, once you send them, as with e-mail, you have little control over where they land. Anything confidential should often be expressed in another way.

8. Make sure an opinion letter lets the reader know the complete basis for the opinion.

In his book *Drafting Legal Opinion Letters*, M. John Sterba, Jr., suggests that you include the following items, among other things, in an opinion letter:

Role and independence of counsel
Reason for opinion
Limitations as to particular laws
Reliance upon opinions of other counsel
assumptions
Extent of investigations
Undertakings as to subsequent events

Above all, be honest and precise. Don't give opinions about matters you were not asked to comment on. This is the place where qualifications are necessary if you are uncertain or the law is. As we discussed in Chapter 2, tell the reader the reason for the uncertainty: "The events underlying this transaction may change soon," or "Some courts have begun to apply a different test."

In an article in *The Practical Lawyer*, the New York attorneys Harold Segall and Jeffrey Arouh suggested the addition of this paragraph to opinions concerning litigation, when appropriate:

The view expressed above should not be construed in any sense
as a guarantee or unqualified prediction of the result. Litigation
is inherently a risky undertaking and for that reason the possi-
bility always exists that, contrary to expectation, the claim will
[or will not] be successful.

CHAPTER 13

Writing Memos

I. The Overview: Memos Are Now Frequently E-Documents

II. Seven Sections Around Which to Organize Your Memos

1. Question for Research
2. The Answer or Conclusion
3. The Written Table of Contents
4. The Facts
5. The Analysis
6. Future Questions for Research
7. Bibliography

III. The Politics of Memos

1. Give or get your assignments in writing.
2. Make sure everyone understands how long the project should take.

I. The Overview: Memos Are Now Frequently E-Documents

In the new age of e-writing, lawyers still write research memos, though their form has changed. Yet attorneys rarely give much thought as to how those memos will read and how they should be organized. Lawyers are so intent on thinking about the principles they present that they forget how important the presentation of those principles is. Before you begin writing any memo, try to remember these four starting points:

1. With clients, focus on what they have to do, not why they have to do it. Remember that non-legal readers are far less interested in legal theories and rationales than attorneys are. Most of the issues memos address ultimately deal with concrete issues that demand tangible resolutions. Don't give these readers law review articles.

2. Organize the material to make it accessible. Remember that in the e-age, Wikipedia and MapQuest are our formatting templates. Use executive summaries, lists of cases rather than essays about them, and don't be afraid to include links if the document is to be read electronically.

3. When writing for lawyers, remember that a memo is less of an advocacy document than a brief. Yes, advice is a form of argument. Yet that has to be balanced against the notion that the purpose of a brief is to convince; the purpose of most memos is to dissect.

When analyzing for other lawyers, brevity is sometimes not the soul of wit. A memo can present both sides, often presenting the analysis in more than enough detail. Footnotes are far more permissible in a memo than in a brief, since memos are research documents.

New lawyers who are asked to combine the functions of an analytical memo and an argumentative brief ("Just write me the first draft of this argument") often get into trouble. A brief doesn't present every conceivable argument, and even those it does offer, it frequently presents in condensed form.

4. *As with e-mail, be careful about what you put in writing.* As we said before in Chapter 12, the notions of privilege and confidentiality don't mean what they once did. As with e-mail, assume readers you don't know may read your memos and act accordingly.

II. Seven Sections Around Which to Organize Your Memos

Here are some general suggestions about how to organize memos. Any long memo should probably include all of the following sections, though the days of such lengthy documents may be numbered.

1. Question for Research
In a sentence or two at the beginning, state the question you were asked to research.

2. The Answer or Conclusion
Immediately answer that question, in a sentence or two at most. Even if the answer is not a yes or no but descriptive, answer the question as briefly as possible ("The legislative history of Section 1983 covers three areas. First . . .").

If you are asked more than one question, state the first ques-

264 Writing to Win

tion, then answer it; state the second, answer that one, and so on. Otherwise, the reader can't figure out which answers apply to which questions.

Remember, too, that with clients, the answer should usually be a practical one—"we need to do X," not why you need to do it.

3. The Written Table of Contents

Here, in a paragraph or two, set out how you intend to organize your discussion. This makes it easier for readers to assemble the densest material in the memo before they begin that section. How you choose to organize a memo is frequently unimportant, as long as you tell your readers first what the organization is. As with Wikipedia, in an e-memo, you can provide links with the sections, so readers can skip the parts they don't want to read. With a hard copy, provide the page numbers of the forthcoming sections.

4. The Facts

Most memos should contain some description of the facts, however brief, even if you think the facts are too simple or that all your readers know them. If your readers don't want to be bothered with these details, they can skip the section. This section is usually the easiest way for future readers considering similar issues to determine how relevant your memo is to the research they are doing. Besides, you don't know who is going to read the document.

5. The Analysis

This is the heart of the memo—its reasoning. Take as much space as you need, but be careful to create new sections every few pages to break up the monotony of the document. Here, as in a brief, use conclusory headings for each section. This tends to make the memo easier to digest. Long quotes are more acceptable here too. Remember the saying of Wilson Mizner, a turn-of-the-century dramatist: "When you steal from one author, it's plagiarism; if you steal from many, it's research."

You don't need to restate the conclusion. And, depending on the audience, don't necessarily bind yourself to the formal rules of citation, which mean nothing to non-lawyers.

6. Future Questions for Research

Often a junior lawyer who has spent a lot of time on an issue in a case has noticed other areas that should be researched or examined further. This section is an opportunity to note those areas, so they won't be forgotten in the crush of subsequent proceedings.

7. Bibliography

All legal memos should have a bibliography, and I have never been able to figure out why most don't. Often the first question lawyers have when reading a memo is "What did the writer rely on?" It's impossible to tell from reading most of these documents. Moreover, if readers want to follow up on the research provided (as on Wikipedia) and the writer isn't around, they have to backtrack if there is no bibliography. Providing this section also saves the writer time. Rather than spending pages going through all the research that yielded no results, the writer can use the bibliography to take the reader through the "dry holes" quickly in a few lines.

Do not provide an exhaustive bibliography; a memo is not an academic paper. Instead, label the section "Selected Bibliography" or "Annotated Bibliography" and list the main books examined and the principal cases read. Provide links with an e-memo. Putting your cites in footnotes is fine too.

With a shorter memo, you can probably skip Sections 4 (written table of contents) and 6 (future questions for research). You will also be able to cut your recitation of the facts (Section 3) to a sentence or two.

III. The Politics of Memos

From my experience, office discord between senior and junior lawyers often arises in the assignment and handling of memos. Having been on both ends of that exchange, I think it's the responsibility of the senior lawyer giving the assignment to make sure the task is properly understood. In the office world, though, that's not how the politics usually play out. When something goes wrong, the associate takes the rap.

Therefore, to protect everybody, keep these two rules in mind.

1. Give or get your assignments in writing.

Instructions given casually and verbally are frequently misunderstood. Moreover, a written assignment is apt to be thought through a good deal more than a spoken one. No magazine writer would undertake an article without written instructions from an editor. The same rule applies here: The more specific an assignment is, the better it is.

Of course, if a partner gives a verbal assignment, it's not easy to snap back, "Excuse me, could you put that in writing?" What you can do, however, is ask, "Do you mind if I put that in an e-mail and run it past you?" Few senior lawyers will object to that, and it ensures that everyone is beginning on the same page. I would attach the written assignment page to the memo, as either the first page or an appendix.

If you get an assignment in writing, you ensure that the memo won't look silly when you finally complete it. Often young lawyers are given a task and by the time they return with an answer, the question has changed or has been rendered moot. That isn't the writer's fault, and an assignment in writing absolves the researcher from appearing to be behind the curve.

2. Make sure everyone understands how long the project should take.

A written assignment should include a description of how long the memo should be and how long the lawyer or paralegal has to complete the assignment. This doesn't simply ensure that the project gets the proper number of billable hours; a lawyer who is given twenty hours to complete a project should produce a better memo than one who is given only six hours.

In many cases memo writers should indicate at the beginning of a memo and on the assignment sheet how long they were given to complete a project. This enables readers to evaluate how complete and reliable the information is.

CHAPTER 14

Drafting Contracts and Rules

I. The Overview: When Bad Writing Might Be Acceptable but Is Still Avoidable—Drafting Contracts and Rules

II. The Ten Basic Rules of Drafting

1. Use familiar words and short sentences.

2. Use the active voice and the present tense.

3. Try to use Anglo-Saxon words.

4. Don't use "shall"; use "will" or "must."

5. Be careful how you use adjectives and adverbs.

6. Try not to put mental states or subjective language into a contract.

7. Express the same ideas in the same way.

8. There's no need to say "the parties agree."

9. Be concise.

10. Avoid jargon.

III. The Eleven Steps of Drafting

1. Do your basic research.

2. Ask specific legal questions.

3. Develop a blueprint for action.

4. Write a strong introduction.

5. Draft a detailed outline of the contract or law.

6. Write the document.

7. Compose the definitions.

8. Edit the document yourself initially.

9. Then, have at least two other lawyers and, if possible, the client edit the document.

10. Try out some hypotheticals within the draft.

11. Do your final editing.

I. The Overview: When Bad Writing Might Be Acceptable but Is Still Avoidable—Drafting Contracts and Rules

find it difficult to say that bad writing is ever acceptable. After years of practice and teaching, however, I have to concede that good writing is less important in one context than in others.

Writing contracts, agreements, and laws is different from the other types of writing covered in this book. With a brief, e-mail, or memo, good writing is always the goal. If these documents read poorly, you're less likely to win your cases or be an effective lawyer.

This isn't as true with contracts (private rules governing behavior) and laws and regulations (public rules governing behavior). Like others, I would always prefer to read a well-written contract or statute than a badly composed one. Two centuries ago, Thomas Jefferson was complaining about how the law, with its "tautologies, redundancies, and circumlocutions," was "unintelligible to those whom it most concerns." Furthermore, many states have enacted plain-language laws, and the Securities and Exchange Commission in the late 1990s undertook an initiative to require better-written corporate disclosure documents.

Nevertheless—and I realize this is controversial in a book promoting better writing—poorly written agreements can still be serviceable ones if they promote your client's interests. (I would not say the same about disclosure documents, given the SEC initiative.) For better and often for worse, few people evaluate agreements on the basis of their readability. We just assume that an essay, such as the Declaration of Independence, will read well, while an "agreement," such as the Constitution, won't.

That's true for several reasons. First, e-mail and briefs are read for their plain meaning. In contrast, people read agreements or rules differently—often with an eye toward getting out of them. This forces the drafters of such utilitarian documents to try to explain away as much of the ambiguity inherent in the language as they can. That leads to repetitive and stale writing.

For example, the tax code is so complex primarily because people don't like to pay taxes. Tell taxpayers to pay Uncle Sam 35 percent of their income and they start playing language games, explaining why their fringe benefits aren't income. So someone has to define "income," and then "fringe benefits," and so on.

Second, the drafters of contracts, and especially laws, seek to be ambiguous at times, if only to get the other participants to agree to the terms of the document. In the regulatory area, legislatures have adopted a whole style of drafting intentionally vague laws and then letting others worry about the details.

Third, most ordinary documents are written by an individual, or should be; laws and contracts are, in theory, written by at least two people, and often by hundreds. In writing, too many cooks do spoil the broth.

Finally, the drafters of statutes and contracts are attempting to use language to control future behavior. To do so, they must try to envision a wide range of circumstances that could arise and then deal with them in the document. Complicated laws and contracts are reflections of complex societies. As problems become more technical, so do solutions. That, too, leads to rather expansive prose.

Because these documents are scrutinized so carefully, even a slight change of a word or of punctuation can change the meaning. For that reason, lawyers frequently end up copying the format and language of what has worked before in similar circumstances, no matter how badly written it is. To be honest, when I have been in such situations in legal practice, I have occasionally done the same thing. Good writing is important, but risking an agreement worth millions just to reach that goal isn't.

All this may be changing as more states and agencies adopt plain-language requirements. What's more, if you have time to edit a prior document or you have to draft a document from scratch, you have an opportunity to create a much cleaner model and you may eliminate a number of ambiguities. Below you will find some general suggestions about how to do so. Because there is a whole set of rules governing the interpretation of these unusual documents, you have to know these rules, as well as the substantive law governing the area in which you are working. A contract or law drafter has to consult and master a number of specialized treatises, such as Reed Dickerson's *The Fundamentals of Legal Drafting* and Becker, Becker, and Savin's *Legal Checklists: Specially Selected Forms.* These can save you time in the initial stages of writing a commercial agreement, and they have helped me formulate the suggestions that follow.

II. The Ten Basic Rules of Drafting

Before drafting anything, review the ten rules in Chapter 2. While there are dozens of specific rules of drafting that control how you must write individual documents, here are ten basic points to remember that apply in many drafting situations.

1. Use familiar words and short sentences.

As with all legal writing, the more complicated the idea you're conveying is, the shorter you want your sentences and words to be. The less you have to define, the better.

The first winner of the "No gobbledygook plain language award," given by Al Gore in 1998 when he was vice president, went to Marthe Kent of OSHA for changing this regulation.

Before:

This paragraph applies to all operations involving the immersion of materials in liquids, or in the vapors of such liquids, for the purpose of cleaning or altering the surface or adding to or imparting a finish thereto or changing the character of the materials, and their subsequent removal from the liquid or vapor, draining, and drying. These operations include washing, electroplating, anodizing, pickling, quenching, dyeing, dipping, tanning, dressing, bleaching, degreasing, alkaline cleaning, stripping, rinsing, digesting, and other similar operations.

After:

(a) When does this rule apply?

(1) This rule applies to operations using a dip tank containing any liquid other than water:

(i) To clean an object;

(ii) To coat an object;

(iii) To alter the surface of an object; or

(iv) To change the character of an object.

(2) This rule also applies to drying or draining an object after dipping.

2. Use the active voice and the present tense.

Contracts written in the passive voice are hard to follow. Even the future tense is confusing to readers ("Borrowers will be required to return their books"). You are giving commands, and as in the military, it is best to be laconic ("Don't fire until you see the whites of their eyes").

Many contract drafters write their contracts in the future tense because the duties are going to kick in at a future date. But a contract exists from the moment it is signed and ratified, meaning that the duties exist in the present, unless, for the most part, we're dealing with a condition that triggers a future action.

3. Try to use Anglo-Saxon words.

We've already covered this rule earlier with complaint writing, but it has special application here. The goal in a contract is to pick words about which there is as little dispute as possible as to their meaning. Words that came into the language largely through Latin (or its derivatives, such as French or Spanish) are often more ambiguous or conceptual than their Anglo-Saxon counterparts. There's a reason French is the language of diplomacy. Its inherent abstractness allows enemies to sit at the same table, since they can, in a sense, talk past one another.

4. Don't use "shall"; use "will" or "must."

Contract drafters, employing an archaic style, use "shall" throughout their documents, much as the creators of the King James Bible did. But they shouldn't, because it is a word capable of two constructions and you don't want to confuse the two. If I write, "You *shall* cross the street at 2 pm," I could be saying, "You *will* cross the street at 2 pm"—that's a prediction. On the other hand, I could be saying, "You *must* cross the street at 2 pm"—that's an obligation. Those are two enormously different things. Bryan Garner has noted that in some instances "shall" can even mean "should."

Thus, if you are setting forth an obligation, use "must." Otherwise, use "will." The objection I sometimes hear is that "must sounds too strong; the parties will think they have to fulfill this duty." Of course, they do—that's why we're signing the contract.

5. Be careful how you use adjectives and adverbs.

This, too, is related to a rule we discussed before. To one side of a contract, a duty couched with an adjective or adverb makes it more flexible. That's because, as we learned before, adjectives and adverbs are opinions; they tell but don't show. If goods must be delivered whenever it's "cold," the contract is difficult to enforce unless few would dispute that label. On the other hand, if we say the goods must be delivered "whenever the temperature falls below thirty-two degrees Fahrenheit," there is little dispute about what the duty means.

True, adjectives and adverbs are often placed in contracts to please one side of the deal; otherwise the party wouldn't sign. And some are part of the standard accepted lexicon of contracts, as in "best efforts." But many of them are also there simply through poor drafting. An adjective or adverb attached to a duty is like a loose thread in a suit. Pull on it and often the whole contract becomes essentially unenforceable.

6. Try not to put mental states or subjective language into a contract.

This is a frequent mistake of drafters. A contract deals with the real, tangible world, because those are things we can define and enforce. Mental states are largely unenforceable, because we don't know what people think; we only know how they act.

Thus, requiring the parties to "cooperate" is largely meaningless, because it involves a mental as well as a real obligation. How do we determine if someone is cooperating? The more unenforceable terms you put in a contract, the less serious the contract becomes and the more a reader needs to parse the actual obligations in the contract from the useless admonitions. That's a recipe for trouble.

7. Express the same ideas in the same way.

This is not the place to be creative. If you express the same idea in different ways, courts will interpret the phrases differently on the theory that "if they had wanted to say the same thing, they would have said it the same way." Be repetitive if it's called for.

8. There's no need to say "the parties agree."

Contracts often state duties so that they read, "The parties agree to deliver the goods." The "agree" part is superfluous, and not only because it involves a mental factor. Of course, the parties agree—that's why they signed the contract. Just say, "The parties must deliver the goods." A further problem is that often, some of the terms in a contract have "the parties agree" clause and others don't. Under our prior rule requiring consistency in contracts, that creates a loophole, since a judge or arbitrator is instructed to read those clauses differently because they're constructed differently.

9. Be concise.

Under the rules of contractual and statutory interpretation, all words will be given meaning. Therefore, any unnecessary words you use can change the meaning of whatever you draft and make it harder to understand.

This is a rule frequently violated in legislative drafting. The original personal income tax law, passed in 1913, was fourteen pages, according to John Steele Gordon, writing in the *Wall Street Journal*. The health care bill passed by Congress in 2010 was over 2,400 pages. Yes, it dealt with complex issues. But as Gordon points out, maybe unreadability and ambiguity were the goals.

10. Avoid jargon.

Yes, drafted documents have a place for formality that doesn't exist in other legal writing. Still, attorneys inevitably overdo things. When OSHA redrafted some regulations in 1998, it changed this:

> Ways of exit access and the doors to exit to which they lead shall be so designed and arranged as to be clearly recognizable as such. Hangings or draperies shall not be placed over exit doors or otherwise so located as to obscure any exit. Mirrors shall not be placed in or adjacent to any exit in such a manner as to confuse the direction of the exit.

to this:

> An exit door must be free of signs or decorations that obscure its visibility.

Even that, as Al Gore once pointed out, can be improved to "Don't put up anything that makes it hard to see the exit door." It is better to be understood than to sound like a lawyer.

III. The Eleven Steps of Drafting

Here is the way I recommend approaching drafting.

1. Do your basic research.

To draft a good rule or contract, you have to know thoroughly:

a. *The factual areas your agreement or rule covers.* Since you are dealing with future contingencies in an effort to control them, you must know enough to anticipate them. This is by far the major focus of your research. With legislation, committee staff or hearings can do much of this work, but with a contract, it's usually up to the lawyers and their far more limited staff.

b. *The law in all the areas your document will deal with and what laws will govern the contract.* This should include any tax or other subsidiary legal implications.

c. *The needs and desires of your client.* Obtaining this information accurately may well be the most important part of your initial research. In his classic, *Fundamentals of Legal Drafting*, Dickerson wrote:

The draftsman pumps the client for information. He finds out specifically what the client wants and how much the client wants to leave to the draftsman's discretion. He points out any substantive inconsistencies that he thinks he sees in the idea.

2. Ask specific legal questions.

In his book *Writing in Law Practice*, Frank Cooper suggested pondering the following questions before drafting:

a. Will the proposed contract be valid and legally enforceable?

b. Is a question likely to arise as to the capacity of the parties?

c. If there are several promissors, should their obligations be joint, several, or joint and several?

d. Should provision be made as to the right of the parties to make assignments?

e. How about the time of performance? When is delay to be excused?

f. Should there be a limit on the duration of the contract?

g. Should provision be made for liquidated damages?

h. Would it be wise, practically and legally, to include a recital that all the terms and conditions of the agreement between the parties have been included in the written contract?

i. Will one party desire to examine the books and records of the other?

3. Develop a blueprint for action.

Once you have done your research, write down what is supposed to happen: *Who* will do *what* to *whom* and *when*. Then write down this information in a paragraph. This will form the basis of the document's introduction, and indeed, the contract itself.

4. Write a strong introduction.

As with any other document, form is important. Though many contracts still lead with a recital clause, such beginnings don't do much for the reader. Instead, use your first paragraph to summarize what the contract or law is about and to whom it applies. With detailed documents, tell the reader right away the basis of what is to follow. You can rewrite this paragraph later if your document changes as it is drafted, but it's important to begin with your conclusion. Otherwise, your drafting will drift.

Keep in mind, too, that many readers examine laws and contracts with one question in mind: What do I have to do? These obligations are usually scattered throughout the document. Try to organize a section for each party (or, for the public, with a regulation or law) where you lay out specific obligations. If you are unable to do so in the formal document, at least present your client with such an outline separately as an informal primer to the document.

5. Draft a detailed outline of the contract or law.

Drafting a law or agreement requires a good outline even more than with other types of writing. It's like building a house: If you don't start with comprehensive plans, you're likely to run into trouble during construction.

Using your introduction as a basic blueprint, plan the sections—referring to a treatise on drafting or local legislative rules to determine what sections to include. Though it may be difficult, try to establish a logical flow to the document—from the general to the specific or chronologically, depending on how the parties will carry out their obligations.

In a sweeping article on drafting contracts, University of Richmond professor Peter Swisher suggested the following checklist of possible sections. You don't have to follow it exactly or comprehensively, but it does suggest some starting points.

Short Title
Statement of Purpose or Policy
Application of the Document
Definitions
Provisions
General Exceptions
Sanctions or Penalties
Temporary Provisions
Assignability and Application to Others
Choice of Law Governing the Document
Entire Agreement Clause
Modification Clause
Effective Date and Duration
Severability Clause
Advice of Counsel Clause
Signatures and Notarization

6. Write the document.

With your detailed outline in hand, draft the document. Since you will be going back to edit your product many times, don't be anxious about getting everything right on the first try.

7. Compose the definitions.

Definitions are an integral part of any agreement or law. "Sexual harassment is prohibited in the workplace" is an edict that anyone can draft in less than a minute. The key questions are: What is harassment? How is sexual harassment different from other forms? What constitutes a workplace? All these questions are definitional ones.

You have several ways to define your terms. Looking in the dictionary is never a bad place to start, nor is finding a simpler or more precise term. If that doesn't help, try comparing your word or terms to others, use examples, or describe your terms by means of their components and purpose ("A microwave is a home appliance that contains the following parts . . .").

Keep your definitions as short as possible. Don't define words that don't require definition. Don't put definitions in the substantive parts of a document; they get their own section. Don't define words differently from the way they are defined in the real world, because that creates confusion ("By rice, we mean rice and pasta"). Finally, include no substantive rules in your definitions.

8. Edit the document yourself initially.

At this point you are ready to begin editing. Unlike an ordinary document, which you can edit quickly, drafting requires writers to review every word and passage exhaustively, as if they were the lawyers on the other side. You should ask yourself, is there any way I can construe these words to evade the obligations of the agreement? If so, you must change the wording.

In drafting, a good self-editor should go through this process several times.

9. Then, have at least two other lawyers and, if possible, the client edit the document.

As an editor of your own work, you are bound to miss things. Thus you must have at least two others review the draft exhaustively as well. If other legal disciplines touch on this document, a lawyer from those areas must review it too. Clients obviously need to review it too, both to see that the contract does what they want and to provide their informational input.

Finally, you want a lawyer who is not an expert in the substance of the agreement or its areas of law to edit the draft. This ensures that the original drafters have not lost the proverbial forest for the trees. Since judges and arbitrators who know little about the substantive area a contract or law concerns may be called on to examine the document, you want someone who approaches it as they would to review your draft.

10. Try out some hypotheticals within the draft.

When you have finished the draft and the editing, get some colleagues together and try creating dozens of imaginary situations that could arise under the agreement or law. Does the document cover them adequately? Often a draft will look great on paper but breaks down when put into practice.

11. Do your final editing.

At the final stage, look for unnecessary words that you can cut, sentences that you can shorten, or inconsistent expressions of identical details. Be careful, however, not to change the meaning of what you have drafted.

The Real Damage of Bad Legal Writing

By now it should be clear that legal writing can use a lot of improvement. There is more to becoming a better legal writer than just learning the rules, though, or adapting to the Internet age. There's something about the culture of the law that produces terrible writers—which is why most law students say, accurately, that they graduate as less accomplished writers than they were when they arrived at law school. In part, lawyers write badly because that promotes their economic interests. More important, poor writing is as much a consequence of the way lawyers look at the world as is their ability to read a contract and find consideration. Lawyers write poorly not only because they know too little but because they know too much.

For example, lawyers are frequently concerned that if they stop "writing like lawyers," they might have trouble charging as much for their work. Every time attorneys confound their clients with a case citation, a "heretofore," or an "in the instant case," they are letting everyone know they possess something the nonlegal world does not. As anyone who has ever been "subject to a molar extraction" by a dentist knows, lawyers are not alone in using professional double-speak. You don't have to be a Marxist to understand that jargon helps professionals convince the world of their occupational importance, which leads to higher payment for services.

All professions indulge in this linguistic self-preservation, but the legal profession is far worse than most, and with good reason. Doctors can explain fairly easily the skill they learned in medical school: how to heal people. But the task of definition is more difficult for lawyers. Exactly what did they learn in law school? Professors are fond of telling us that we learn to "think like lawyers." Thinking like a lawyer, however, is an elusive concept, and even those who can define it have a lot of trouble explaining why it's worth hundreds, or even thousands, of dollars an hour.

Therefore, to convince themselves and others they are erudite, lawyers embrace a different language and write poorly. That parlance, acquired by law students beginning on the first day of classes, has become the way the outside world distinguishes genuine practitioners from charlatans. That's certainly what prisoners arguing *pro se* think; their briefs are so full of legal jargon that they read as if they were produced by Wall Street firms gone wild. Sad to say, a lawyer in our society has become someone who sounds like a lawyer.

Why should this be so? If legal discourse had no purpose besides communication, there would be no apparent reason for it to read poorly. But a language and a way of writing are more than simply words; they both reflect and determine a way of viewing the world. As Ludwig Wittgenstein observed, language "earmarks the form of account we give, the way we look at things." If lawyers speak and write differently, it is not only because they use their language as a form of self-promotion but also because they do view the world differently. A lawyer who doesn't realize this—and fails to deal with it—will never become a proficient writer.

Take, for instance, the Supreme Court's decision in a now mostly forgotten case, *Rummel v. Estelle*, 445 U.S. 263 (1980). The Court held that a Texas statute requiring life imprisonment upon a third felony conviction ("three strikes and you're out") did not, as applied, violate the Eighth Amendment. One lawyer explaining the case to another would relate it in much the same way that I have and would go on to recite the issues, describe how the Court framed the questions before it, and analyze the Court's use of precedent. There would be little or no mention of Rummel, the prisoner who now faced a life sentence for committing three thefts involving a total of less than $250.

A nonlawyer would tell a different story in another language, however. The average reader or listener would want to know what Rummel did, what he thought about his sentence, and whether it was fair to sentence him to life imprisonment for stealing less than $250. In fact, we could argue that only a lawyer could find that Rummel's sentence did not violate the Eighth Amendment; other people would always find a life sentence for stealing less than $250 "cruel and unusual." Legal language thus limits what lawyers can see.

But what do lawyers see, and how does what they see affect their writing? In this book, we've discussed some of these attributes. First, lawyers see a world dominated by precedent. It is one of the law's timeless truths that everything is merely an extension or alteration of what has appeared before. Thus, in their briefs and legal opinions, lawyers constantly explain things in terms of the past; they reason that they are doing nothing new and only following existing precedent.

In contrast, most other writers try to convince their readers that they are doing something new, even if they are not. The theme in Ernest Hemingway's *The Sun Also Rises* may be as old as the verse in Ecclesiastes that provided the book's title, but Hemingway strives for a new message, or at least a new way of expressing that message. A lawyer writing that novel would have cited the biblical passage and left it at that. Legal writing is not supposed to create new truths or even recast old ones; it must only apply them. That limited objective often leads to uninspired prose.

The use of precedent also leads to repetitive writing. A system founded on precedent requires a form of logic in which rules are restated repeatedly and altered only incrementally. Because what changes most from case to case is the facts, not the laws or precedents, judicial opinions keep their discussion of facts to a minimum. In imitation, lawyers also write about rules, not facts.

Anyone who writes about rules and not facts, however, is going to have a difficult time composing an appealing piece. As we have learned, most readers are intrigued by stories about people, and a story is usually the development of a character. In contrast, many legal writers feel they must ignore the attractive part of the story and be content instead to discuss the application of rules in a way that tells others what doctrines they should follow. Even Mark Twain would have trouble doing much under these constraints.

The law also purports to be a search for objective truths—rules that are rational, have universal application, and seem fair. Legal writing, as bad as it is, makes the task easier. For starters, we use labels to objectify and simplify; Jennifer Jones or Patrick Smith become tortfeasors or lessees. We resort to a style of writing replete with dozens of footnotes designed to show the objectivity of the process. Finally, because legal language aspires to objectivity, it often refuses to recognize troublesome concepts such as hope, candor, and even love. If the legal doctrine of standing to sue means anything, it must be that certain perceived hurts are not recognized in conventional legal discourse, perhaps because in an objective world they can have no universal meaning.

There is nothing illegitimate about any of these devices, but as we have learned, good legal writers must learn to overcome them. They must also deal with the fact that many of the ordinary writer's tricks of the trade are unavailable to them. Nonlawyers, after all, can always tell a joke and some can even make things up. Lawyers, in contrast, feel sentenced to tell their stories one step at a time, in workmanlike and often ponderous language. Even their personal experience must be banished from the written page—a clear invitation to resort to the "institutional passive" voice, which further separates writer from reader. "It could be argued," write most lawyers, never pointing out that there is an "I" doing the arguing. As a consequence, very little legal writing reveals much about the author.

Perhaps most damaging, however, is lawyers' frequent use of language as a deception. Face it: If we have a losing case—and at least half the time we do—confusing the issue may be the best we can do for our clients. Indeed, attorneys are the culture's most respected con artists. Our job in many cases is to try to make something out of nothing.

Again, there is nothing necessarily wrong with that; lawyers may simply be victims of the role society has created for them. But lawyers recognize their role as deceivers and understand that language is the means through which they work their magic. After a while, they begin to lose faith in the honesty of words, and their writing suffers. Language is a human invention, one designed to bring people closer together. But after a lifetime of using words to strangle communication, lawyers begin to view speech as a barrier that separates them from others and others from the truth. Once they begin to despise their language—and many of them eventually do—their distaste is reflected in poorly written prose. Why bother to write clearly if communication itself is a lie?

Thus, in the end, the problem with legal writing has as much to do with lawyers themselves as it does with writing. After all, the outside world has lived with poor legal writing for centuries and has survived intact. Lawyers may not be so lucky. As children, we learned that sticks and stones can break our bones but words can never hurt us. But we learned incorrectly: Words *can* hurt us. To write like a lawyer, at least in traditional terms, is to choose a perspective that cheapens language and forces us to relate to a narrow world of rules, not people. It's true that part of the purpose of legal training is to enable lawyers to think and write in just this way. But perhaps this book has convinced you that lawyers lose more than they gain by acquiring this "gift" of legal vision. The lifelong struggle of learning to write well is a way to regain your humanity as a lawyer. It is a constant reminder that complaints about legal writing are never just laments about craftsmanship; they are cries that lawyers no longer can see.

The Sixteen Rules of Professionalism in Legal Writing

General Rules

1. Never lie, under any circumstance.
2. Don't plagiarize.
3. Don't use euphemisms to disguise the truth.
4. If it's not required, hedging is a form of dishonesty.
5. Avoid the use of hyperbole to distort the truth of your assertions.
6. Ghostwriting is a form of dishonesty.
7. An affidavit should be the assertions of the person who signs it.
8. Always cite accurately.

Additional Rules in Litigation

9. Don't engage in personal attacks.
10. In a brief, you must deal with key unfavorable facts and case law in that jurisdiction.
11. Don't argue or editorialize in your fact statements.
12. Adjectives are usually not facts but opinions about them, and they don't belong in your fact statements. Show, don't tell.

13. Don't restate the other side's arguments or cases in a way that is unfair to what they argued.

14. Don't guess. If you are asked about something and you don't know or are unsure, say so.

15. Do not misstate the facts or the law.

16. Remember Rule 11: An attorney who drafts pleadings must ensure they are supported by the facts and law.

Of all the changes in the culture since the last edition, this bibliography may well reflect the biggest.

A dozen years ago, sources on good legal writing weren't terribly numerous. Today, thanks to the Internet, a legal writer is engulfed by thousands of sources and suggestions. As with so much else in the culture, the problem now is not of too little information but too much.

What that means is that inevitably in what follows below, I've failed to note or credit a number of worthy sources for follow-up—not intentionally but because I just missed them. My apologies. What follows is not intended to be the last word on the subject.

In the first section of the bibliography, I've listed those invaluable works on which I relied most frequently in writing this book, or those I think would be most helpful to those pursuing further study. A more detailed chapter-by-chapter bibliography of major sources follows. For each chapter, I've listed books first, then articles. Again, if I missed anything, my apologies.

I must make special mention again of several works that I found particularly useful throughout: Bryan Garner's *A Dictionary of Modern Legal Usage* and Frederick Wiener's *Briefing and Arguing Federal Appeals*, as well as the annual *Green Bag Almanac*, a yearly collection of exemplary legal writing. Any litigator will benefit greatly, as I did, by watching or reading Bryan Garner's numerous interviews with justices, judges, and lawyers (they're available on the Web). In the Internet world, I relied heavily on the always excellent Twitter sources—

Quotes4Writers and Marilyn Bush LeLeiko's *LawWriting*—as well as Wayne Schields's *Legalwriting.net* blog, and John Winokur's *Advice to Writers* at www.advicetowriters.com. For those interested in further study of the rules of grammar and writing as they apply specifically to lawyers, the late Irving Younger wrote a wonderful column in the *ABA Journal* in the 1970s and 1980s.

Discerning readers of this bibliography will note that I have not followed strict Blue Book form in the cites. This book, after all, is not a court filing, and my goal was to get the information to the reader in the most straightforward way possible. For those offended by such informality, my apologies. Throughout the book, I have tried to follow *The Chicago Manual of Style* on capitalization, which is the standard for trade books. All professional titles are lowercase when they are used as identifiers or stand alone. The standard in trade publication is to change capitalization and punctuation within quotations to conform to this style, as long as the meaning isn't changed. As in many fields, those in the law like to capitalize things to make them look important, but it makes for difficult reading.

Principal Sources Used and Books of Great Interest

The Chicago Manual of Style, 14th ed., University of Chicago Press, 1993.
The Economist Style Guide, Tenth Edition, Wiley, 2010.
NLRB Style Manual, 2000.
A Plain English Handbook: How to Create Clear SEC Disclosure Documents, SEC, 1998.
Alterman, *Plain and Accurate Style in Court Papers*, American Law Institute of the ABA, 1987.
Barzun, *Simple and Direct*, Harper & Row, 1975.
Cohen, *Creative Writing for Lawyers*, Citadel, 1991.
Cooper, *Writing in Law Practice*, Bobbs-Merrill, 1963.
Copperud, *American Usage and Style*, Van Nostrand Reinhold, 1980.
Freeman, *The Grammatical Lawyer*, American Law Institute of the ABA, 1979.

Garner, *A Dictionary of Modern Legal Usage*, Oxford University Press, 1987.

Goldfarb and Raymond, *Clear Understandings: A Guide to Legal Writing*, Random House, 1982.

Goldstein & Lieberman, *The Lawyer's Guide to Writing Well*, McGraw-Hill, 1989.

Gopen, *Writing from a Legal Perspective*, West, 1981.

Hurd, *Writing for Lawyers*, Journal of Broadcasting and Communications, 1982.

Johnson, *Historic U.S. Court Cases 1690–1990: An Encyclopedia*, Garland, 1992.

Kane, *The Oxford Guide to Writing*, Oxford University Press, 1983.

Levenson, *Bill Bernbach's Book: A History of the Advertising That Changed the History of Advertising*, Villard, 1987.

Noonan, *Person and Masks of the Law: Cardozo, Holmes, Jefferson, and Wythe as Makers of the Masks*, Farrar, Straus and Giroux, 1976.

Plimpton, *The Writer's Chapbook*, Viking, 1989.

Ray and Cox, *Beyond the Basics*, West, 1991.

Rodell, *Woe Unto You Lawyers*, Berkley, 1980.

Smith, *The Literate Lawyer*, Michie Butterworth, 1995.

Stein, *Legal Spectator*, George Psalmanazer, 1981.

Strunk and White, *The Elements of Style*, Macmillan, 1979.

Weihofen, *Legal Writing Style*, West, 1980.

Weisberg, *When Lawyers Write*, Little, Brown, 1987.

Wiener, *Briefing and Arguing Federal Appeals*, BNA Incorporated, 1961.

Williams, *Style: Ten Lessons in Clarity & Grace*, Scott Foresman, 1981.

Winokur, *Writers on Writing*, Running Press, 1986.

Wydick, *Plain English for Lawyers*, Carolina Academic Press, 1985.

Zinsser, *On Writing Well*, HarperPerennial, 1990.

"The Act of Geat Writing," bighow.com.

Bashman, "How Appealing," www.howappealing.law.com.

Goldstein and Lieberman, "Writing like pros(e)," 6 *California Lawyer* 43 (January 1986).

Introduction

White, *The Legal Imagination*, University of Chicago Press, 1973.

White, *Trials and Tribulations: Appealing Legal Humor: A Collection*, Catbird Press, 1989.

Willette, "Memo of Masochism (Reflections in Legal Writing)," 17 *Nova Law Review* 872 (1993).

Chapter 1. Organizing Your Material

Goldstein and Lieberman, *The Lawyer's Guide to Writing Well*, McGraw-Hill, 1989.

Agger, "How We Read Online," *Slate*, June 13, 2008.

Bilton, "The American Diet: 34 Gigabytes a Day," *New York Times*, December 9, 2009.

Buckman, "E-Mail's Friendly Fire," *Wall Street Journal*, November 27, 2010.

Carr, "Is Google Making Us Stupid," *The Atlantic*, July–Aug. 2008.

Frey and Englert, "How to Write a Good Appellate Brief," 20 *Litigation* 6 (Winter 1994).

Goleman, "E-Mail Is Easy to Write (and Misread)," *New York Times*, Oct. 7, 2010.

Kakutani, "Texts Without Context?" *New York Times*, March 17, 2010.

Kozinski, "How You Too . . . Can Lose Your Appeal," 23 *The Montana Lawyer* 5 (October 1997).

Prosser, "English as She Is Wrote," *7 J. Legal Educ.* 155 (1954).

Siegel, "E-Filing Holds Promise and Peril for Appellate Attorneys," *Texas Lawyer*, December 7, 2010.

Chapter 2. The Rules of the Road

The Economist Style Guide, www.economist.com/research/styleguide/

Barzun, *Simple and Direct*, Harper & Row, 1975.

Baugh and Cable, *A History of the English Language*, Routledge & Kegan Paul, 1951.

Biskind, *Simplify Legal Writing*, Arco, 1975.

Garner, *A Dictionary of Modern Legal Usage*, Oxford University Press, 1987.

Goldfarb and Raymond, *Clear Understandings: A Guide to Legal Writing*, Random House, 1982.

Goldstein and Lieberman, *The Lawyer's Guide to Writing Well*, McGraw-Hill, 1989.

Holmes, *The Common Law*, Dover, 1991.

Kane, *The Oxford Guide to Writing*, Oxford University Press, 1983.

Kilpatrick, *The Writer's Art*, Andrews, McMeel & Parker, 1984.

Kluger, *Simple Justice: The History of Brown v. Board of Education and Black America's Struggle for Equality*, Vintage, 1977.

McCrum, Cran, and McNeil, *The Story of English*, Penguin, 1993.

Mellinkoff, *The Language of the Law*, Little, Brown, 1963.

Mellinkoff, *Legal Writing: Sense & Nonsense*, West, 1982.

Ogilvy, *Confessions of an Advertising Man*, Atheneum, 1983.

Ogilvy, *Ogilvy on Advertising*, Vintage, 1985.

Orwell, *Politics and the English Language*, Typophiles, 1947.

Strunk and White, *The Elements of Style*, Macmillan, 1979.

Wiener, *Briefing and Arguing Federal Appeals*, BNA Incorporated, 1961.

Williams, *Style: Ten Lessons in Clarity & Grace*, Scott Foresman, 1981.

Zinsser, *On Writing Well*, HarperPerennial, 1990.

"The Legaldegook Awards," *Scribes Journal of Legal Writing*, 107 (1993).

"Pursuant to Long-Winded Legalese A Stock Offer (as Defined Herein)," *Wall Street Journal*, July 15, 1998.

"Requirements and Suggestions for Typography in Briefs and Other Papers," www.ca7.uscourts.gov/rules/type.pdf.

Collett, "Art of the Police Report," *Writer's Chronicle*, February 25, 2011.

Falcicchio and Wolfe, "Accentuate Your Argument and Increase Your Persuasive Power with a Hyperlinked Brief," *The Jury Expert*, 2010.

Flammer, "Persuading Judges: An Empirical Analysis of Writing Style, Persuasion, and the Use of Plain English," 16 *Legal Writing* 184 (2010).

Garner, "On Legal Style," 74 *ABA Journal* 104 (October 1988).

Gerhardt, "Improving Our Legal Writing: Maxims from the Masters," 40 *ABA Journal* 1057 (1954).

Haslett, "The Art of Good Writing," *Financial Times*, January 21, 2011.

Howe, "Nine Essential Hotel Contract Clauses," *Meetings & Conventions*, May 1998.

Johnson, "Airlines," *The Economist*, May 16, 2011.

Lacher, "Great Literature Retitled to Boost Web Traffic," *McSweeney*, www.mcsweeneys.net/links/lits/27lacher.html.

Larkin, "Forget the Wind Up and Make the Pitch," www.ontariocourts.on.ca/coa/en/ps/speeches/forget.htm.

Madrigal, "What's in a Typeface?" *The Atlantic*, January 27, 2011.

McGrum, "To Cut a Long Story Short, Brevity Is Best," *Guardian*, March 20, 2011.

McPhee, "The Art of Nonfiction," No. 3, *Paris Review*, April 2010.

Nolan, "The Enemies of Language," *Boston Globe*, August 22, 1998.

Schiess, "Does the Quality of Writing Matter? Answer 2," *Legalwriting.net*, March 15, 2011.

Shafer, "Washington Wire," *Wall Street Journal*, February 10, 1995.

Smith, "Making Sense: Some Reflections on Legal Writing," 56 *Oklahoma Bar Journal* 2563 (1985).

Sorkin, "The Art of Euphemism," 82 *Illinois Bar Journal* 103 (February 1994).

Welton, "What Happens in Vagueness Stays in Vagueness," *City Journal*, Winter 2011.

Willette, "Memo of Masochism (Reflections in Legal Writing)," 17 *Nova Law Review* 872 (1993).

Wineapple, "Voices of a Nation," *American Scholar*, Summer 2010.

Wydick, "Plain English for Lawyers," 66 *California Law Review* 727 (1978).

Younger, "In Praise of Simplicity," 62 *ABA Journal* 632 (May 1976).

Younger, "Romancing the Verb," 72 *ABA Journal* 94 (Feb. 1986).

Younger, "Skimming the Fat Off Your Writing," 72 *ABA Journal* 92 (March 1986).

Zinsser, "Visions and Revisions," *American Scholar*, Spring 2009.

Chapter 3. The Mechanics of Editing

Barzun, *Simple and Direct*, Harper & Row, 1975.

Brooks & Pinson, *Working with Words*, St. Martin's, 1989.

Bryson, *The Penguin Dictionary of Troublesome Words*, Penguin, 1984.

Lanham, *Revising Prose*, Macmillan, 1992.

Ross-Larson, *Edit Yourself*, W. W. Norton, 1982.

Stein, *Legal Spectator*, George Psalmanazer, 1981.

"The Legaldegook Awards," 3 *Scribes Journal of Legal Writing* 107 (1992).

Deighton, "Facing the Hard Questions Before Chapter One," *Wall Street Journal*, April 27, 2011.

Ross, "Copyediting at The New Yorker Magazine. An Interview with Mary Norris," *Red Room*, September 20, 2009.

Chapter 4. The Art of Argument

Coffin, *On Appeal: Courts, Lawyering and Judging*, W. W. Norton & Co., 1994.

Douglas, *The Court Years*, Random House, 1980.

Goldstein and Lieberman, *The Lawyer's Guide to Writing Well*, McGraw-Hill, 1989.

Harvard University Law School Board of Student Advisers, *Introduction to Advocacy*, Foundation Press, 1991.

Heath and Heath, *Made to Stick: Why Some Ideas Survive and Others Die*, Random House, 2007.

Higgins, *The Art of Writing Advertising: Conversations with William Bernbach, Leo Burnett, George Gribbin, David Ogilvy, Rosser Reeves*, Advertising Publications, 1965.

Hornstein, *Appellate Advocacy*, West, 1984.

Johnson, *Historic U.S. Court Cases 1690–1990: An Encyclopedia*, Garland, 1992.

Levenson, *Bill Bernbach's Book: A History of the Advertising That Changed the History of Advertising*, Villard, 1987.

Ogilvy, *Confessions of an Advertising Man*, Atheneum, 1983.

Ogilvy, *Ogilvy on Advertising*, Vintage, 1985.

Spence, *How to Argue and Win Every Time*, St. Martin's Griffin, 1995.

Wiener, *Briefing and Arguing Federal Appeals*, BNA Incorporated, 1961.

Zinsser, *On Writing Well*, HarperPerennial, 1990.

Amsterdam, "Clinical Legal Education—A 21st Century Perspective," 34 *J. Legal Education* 612 (1984).

Droga, "Sweating Ad Copy Like 'Mad Men,'" *Wall Street Journal*, June 11, 2011.

Eastman, "Speaking Truth to Power: The Language of Civil Rights Litigators," 104 *Yale Law Journal* 763 (1995).

Littleton, "Advocacy and Brief-Writing," 10 *Practical Lawyer* 41 (December 1964).

Meyer, "Vignettes From a Narrative Primer," 12 *Journal of the Legal Writing Institute* 229 (2006).

Ordover, "Teaching Sensitivity to Facts," 66 *Notre Dame Law Review* 813 (1991).

Chapter 5. The Role of Narrative in Argument

French (ed.), *The Copywriter's Guide*, Harper Brothers, 1959.

Noonan, *Persons and Masks of the Law: Cardozo, Holmes, Jefferson, and Wythe as Makers of the Masks*, Farrar, Straus, and Giroux, 1976.

Phillips (ed.), *Ernest Hemingway on Writing*, Scribner's, 1984.

Madden, *Revising Fiction: A Handbook for Writers*, New American Library, 1988.

Guilford, "Legal Writing: A contract between the reader and writer," *California Bar Journal* (November 2010).

Gumport, "Ighijenia in Forest Hills: Anatomy of a Wonder Trial by Janet Malcolm—Review," *Guardian* May 19, 2011.

McElhaney, "Trial Notebook: The Right Word," 7 *Litigation* 43 (Spring 1981).

McLemee, "Storytelling," *Chronicle of Higher Education* (August 25, 2010)

Younger, "What Happened in Erie," 11 *Litigation* 43 (Spring 1985).

Chapter 6. Writing the Facts

Higgins, *The Art of Writing Advertising: Conversations with William Bernbach, Leo Burnett, George Gribbin, David Ogilvy, Rosser Reeves*, Advertising Publications, 1965.

Levenson, *Bill Bernbach's Book: A History of the Advertising That Changed the History of Advertising*, Villard, 1987.

Peck, *Writing Persuasive Briefs*, Little, Brown, 1984.

Wellman, *The Art of Cross-Examination*, Garden City, 1948.

Wiener, *Briefing and Arguing Federal Appeals*, BNA Incorporated, 1961.

Frey and Englert, "How to Write a Good Appellate Brief," 20 *Litigation* 6 (Winter 1994).

Kaufman, "Bessie Cohen, 107, Survivor of 1911 Shirtwaist Fire, Dies," *New York Times*, February 24, 1999.

McElhaney, "Trial Notebook: The Right Word," 7 *Litigation* 43 (Spring 1981).

Raphael, "Frederic Raphael's Top 10 Talkative Novels," *Guardian*, March 10, 2010.

Ricks and Istvan, "Effective Brief Writing Despite High Volume Practice: Ten Misconceptions That Result in Bad Briefs," 38 *University of Toledo Law Review* 113 (Summer 2007).

Chapter 7. Writing Arguments

Gale and Moxley, *How to Write the Winning Brief*, Section of General Practice—American Bar Association, 1992.

Gaylin, *The Killing of Bonnie Garland: A Question of Justice*, Simon & Schuster, 1982.

Hornstein, *Appellate Advocacy*, West, 1984.

Lacarova (ed.), *Federal Appellate Procedure*, BNA, 2008.

Ogilvy, *Confessions of an Advertising Man*, Atheneum, 1983.

Ogilvy, *Ogilvy on Advertising*, Vintage, 1985.

Peck, *Writing Persuasive Briefs*, Little, Brown, 1984.

Re, *Brief Writing and Oral Argument*, Oceana, 1987.

Vetter, *Successful Civil Litigation: How to Win Your Case Before You Enter the Courtroom*, Prentice-Hall, 1977.

Wiener, *Briefing and Arguing Federal Appeals*, BNA Incorporated, 1961.

"The Legaldegook Awards," 4 *Scribes Journal of Legal Writing* 107 (1993).

Ginsburg, "Introduction for Dolley Lecture," Loyola University School of Law, October 13, 1988, unpublished.

Joiner, "The Trial Brief—The Lawyer's Battle Plan and Ammunition," 29 *Wisconsin Bar Bulletin* 31 (April 1956).

Kozinski, "How You Too . . . Can Lose Your Appeal," 23 *Montana Lawyer* 5 (October 1997).

Liptak, "Justices Are Long on Words but Short on Guidance," *New York Times*, November 17, 2010.

Posner, "Effective Appellate Brief Writing," *Appellate Procedure Journal* (Spring 2010).

Pregerson, "The Seven Sins of Appellate Brief Writing," 34 *UCLA Law Review* 431 (1986).

Scanlan, "Appellate Advocacy: Building the Framework," 5 *Trial* 19 (August 1979).

Weiss, "Why Words Can Be Like Ugly Cravats: Justices Dish on Legal Writing," *ABA Journal*, March 10, 2008.

Chapter 8. Writing Trial and Appellate Briefs, as Well as Affidavits

Re, *Brief Writing and Oral Argument*, Oceana, 1987.

Bransford, "Seven Keys to Writing Good Dialogue," www.blog.nathan bransford.com/2010/09/seven-keys-to-writing-good-dialogue .html.

Frey and Englert, "How to Write a Good Appellate Brief," 20 *Litigation* 6 (Winter 1994).

Godbold, "Twenty Pages and Twenty Minutes—Effective Advocacy on Appeal," 30 *Southwest Law Journal* 801 (1976).

Herr and McCarthy, "Amici Curiae: Not Just Friends of the Court Anymore," 9 *Practical Litigator* 11 (May 1998).

Iyer, "How to Write a Short Story," *Time*, November 5, 2006.

Joiner, "The Trial Brief—The Lawyer's Battle Plan and Ammunition," 29 *Wisconsin Bar Bulletin* 31 (April 1956).

McKee, "Are Reply Briefs Really Necessary?" *Recorder*, August 1, 2008.

Nordby, "The Craft of the Criminal Appeal," 4 *William Mitchell Law Review* 1 (1978).

Posner, "Effective Appellate Brief Writing," *Appellate Procedure Journal* (Spring 2010)

Purver and Taylor, "The Criminal Appeal: Writing to Win," 87 *Case and Comment* 3 (September–October 1982).

Wald, "Summary Judgment at Sixty," 76 *Texas Law Review* 1897 (1998).

Wood, "Say What?," *New Yorker*, April 7, 2008.

Zinsser, "The 300-Word Challenge," TheAmericanScholar.org, March 11, 2011.

Chapter 9. Writing Complaints and Answers

Cooper, *Writing in Law Practice*, Bobbs-Merrill, 1963.

Vetter, *Successful Civil Litigation: How to Win Your Case Before You Enter the Courtroom*, Prentice-Hall, 1977.

Eastman, "Speaking Truth to Power: The Language of Civil Rights Litigators," 104 *Yale Law Journal* 763 (1995).

Fajans & Falk, "Untold Stories: Restoring Narrative to Pleading Practice," *The Journal of the Legal Writing Institute* 3 (2009).

Kozinski, "How You Too . . . Can Lose Your Appeal," 23 *Montana Lawyer* 5 (October 1997).

Rothman, "Drafting Complaints in the Post-Iqbal World," *Litigation*, Summer 2010.

Wald, "Summary Judgment at Sixty," 76 *Texas Law Review* 1897 (1998).

Williams, "Pleadings as a Discovery Tool," 6 *Practical Litigator* 13 (November 1995).

Zielinski, "How to Draft Effective Complaints," 1 *Practical Litigator* 13 (March 1990).

Chapter 10. Writing in Discovery

Dombroff, *Discovery*, Kluwer, 1986.

McElhaney, *Trial Notebook*, Section of Litigation—ABA, 1994.

Vetter, *Successful Civil Litigation: How to Win Your Case Before You Enter the Courtroom*, Prentice-Hall, 1977.

"Defining Sex," *New York Daily News*, September 22, 1998.

Berman, "Q: Is This Any Way to Write an Interrogatory? A: You Bet It Is," 19 *Litigation* 42 (Summer 1993).

Bruni, "For Starr Probe, the Devil's in the Definition," *New York Times*, August 16, 1998.

Cappello, "Document Discovery in Commercial Cases: Some Common-Sense Tips," 8 *Practical Litigator* 7 (September 1997).

Epstein, "Rule 36: In Praise of Requests to Admit," 7 *Litigation* 30 (Spring 1981).

Kenney, "Making Requests for Admission Work," 4 *Practical Litigator* 19 (May 1993).

Klenk, "Using and Abusing Interrogatories," 11 *Litigation* 25 (Winter 1985).

McBurney, "Written Interrogatories," 38 *Wisconsin Bar Bulletin* 30 (October 1966).

Rosen, "Making Discovery Tools Work," 3 *Practical Litigator* 51 (November 1992).

Seitz, "Get More Information and Less Indigestion Out of Your Interrogatories," 71 *ABA Journal* 74 (March 1985).

Shattuck, "Use Written Discovery More Effectively," 1 *Practical Litigator*
11 (May 1990).

Stein, "The Discoverers," 15 *Litigation* 47 (Fall 1988).

Thames, "Discovery Strategy," *28 for the Defense* 12 (January 1986).

Chapter 11. Technical Writing

Garner, *A Dictionary of Modern Legal Usage*, Oxford University Press,
1987.

Turk and Kirkman, *Effective Writing: Improving Scientific, Technical, and
Business Communication*, E. & F.N. Spon, 1982.

Kimble, "Writing for Dollars, Writing to Please," www.plainlanguage-
network.org/kimble/dollars.htm.

Kozinski, "How You Too . . . Can Lose Your Appeal," 23 *Montana Lawyer* 5 (October 1997).

Maher, "The Infernal Footnote," 70 *ABA Journal* 92 (April 1984).

Chapter 12. Writing E-mail and Letters

Dugger, *Business Letters for Busy People*, National Press, 1996.

Hodgson, *The Dartnell Direct Mail and Mail Order Handbook*, Dartnell
Corporation, 1980.

Shipley and Schwalbe, *Send: Why People E-Mail So Badly and How to Do It
Better*, Knopf, 2008.

Smith, *The Literate Lawyer*, Michie Butterworth, 1995.

Sterba, *Drafting Legal Opinion Letters*, John Wiley, 1988.

Weihofen, *Legal Writing Style*, West, 1980.

Buckman, "E-Mail's Friendly Fire," *Wall Street Journal*, November 27,
2007.

"E Is for Evidence: The HR Risks of Smoking-Gun Employee Emails,"
http://www.thehrspecialist.com/37735/E_is_for__Evidence_
The_HR_Risks_of_Smoking_Gun_Employee_Emails.hr?cat=
employment law, June 28, 2011.

Email Charter, http://emailcharter.org.

Gallagher, "Beware the Evolving Ethics of Reviewing E-Mails," *New Jersey Law Journal*, March 8, 2011.

Gore, "National Small Business Week Awards/Plain Language Announcement," June 1, 1998, http://www.npr.gov/library/speeches/
gorepln.html.

Goleman, "E-Mail Is Easy to Write (and Misread)," *New York Times*, Oct. 7, 2007.

Grimsley, "Message Overload Taking Toll on Workers," *Washington Post*, May 20, 1998.

Kinsley, "The Morality and Metaphysics of E-Mail," *Forbes*, December 2, 1996.

Malcolm, "Pandora's Click," *New York Review of Books*, September 27, 2007.

Matus, "10 Things Never to Put in E-Mail," Death By E-Mail, www.deathbyemail.com, December 2, 2008.

McDonough, "Things You Should Never Put in an E-mail," *ABA Journal*, December 3, 2008.

Naughton, "Personal Privacy Is a Thing of the Past, So You'd Better Get Used to It," *Guardian*, April 24, 2011.

Outing, "Looking into the Future of E-Mail," harvard.net.news, May 26, 1998.

Pogue, "We Have to Fix E-Mail," *New York Times*, June 31, 2011.

Rossman, "Y U Luv Texts, H8 Calls," *Wall Street Journal*, October 14, 2010.

Segall and Arouh, "How to Prepare Legal Opinions," 25 *Practical Lawyer* 29 (June 1979).

Sorkin, "Letters of the Law," 82 *Illinois Bar Journal* 267 (May 1994).

Sharton and Lyons, "The Risks of E-Mail Communication: A Guide to Protecting Privileged Electronic Communications," *Business Law Today*, September/October 2007.

Chapter 13. Writing Memos

Cuff, "Writing Research Memoranda," 9 *LA Lawyer* 21 (October 1986).

Willette, "Memo of Masochism (Reflections in Legal Writing)," 17 *Nova Law Review* 872 (1993).

Chapter 14. Drafting Contracts and Rules

Becker, Becker, and Savin, *Legal Checklists: Specially Selected Forms*, Callaghan, 1977– .

Brody, Rutherford, Vietzen, and Dernbach, *Legal Drafting*, Little, Brown, 1994.

Child, *Drafting Legal Documents*, West, 1992.

Cooper, *Writing in Law Practice*, Bobbs-Merrill, 1963.

Dean and Wallach, *Understanding Plain English—Preparing for the SEC's Enactment, Practicing Law Institute,* 1997.

Dickerson, *Fundamentals of Legal Drafting,* Little, Brown, 1965.

Dickerson, *Materials on Legal Drafting,* West, 1981.

Feldman, *Drafting Effective Contracts: A Practitioner's Guide,* Prentice-Hall Law & Business, 1989.

Garner, *A Dictionary of Modern Legal Usage,* Oxford University Press, 1987.

Statsky, *Legislative Analysis and Drafting,* West, 1975.

Conrad, "New Ways to Write Laws," 56 *Yale Law Journal* 501 (1947).

Cuff, "Drafting Agreements," 15 *Barrister* 41 (Winter 1988).

Dickerson, "How to Write a Law," 31 *Notre Dame Lawyer* 14 (1955).

Dickerson, "Legal Drafting: Writing as Thinking, Or, Talk-Back From Your Draft and How to Exploit It," 29 *Journal of Legal Education* 373 (1978).

Gordon, "The Global Reform Dodge," *Commentary Contention,* May 3, 2010.

Gore, "National Small Business Week Awards/Plain Language Announcement," June 1, 1998, http://www.npr.gov/library/speeches/gorepln.html.

Haynsworth, "How to Draft Clear and Concise Documents," 31 *Practical Lawyer* 41 (March 1985).

Johnson, "One More Round with 'Shall,'" *The Economist,* May 25, 2011.

Sweet, "The Lawyer's Role in Contract Drafting," 41 *Wisconsin Bar Bulletin* 39 (February 1969).

Swisher, "Techniques of Legal Drafting: A Survival Manual," 15 *University of Richmond Law Review* 873 (1981).

ABOUT THE AUTHOR

STEVEN D. STARK is a writer, lawyer, and consultant who teaches courses on writing and speaking to lawyers and other professionals. A former cultural commentator for CNN, National Public Radio, and the Voice of America, he is the author of four books and one eBook and has written frequently for the *New York Times*, the *Los Angeles Times*, *The Atlantic*, and the *Boston Globe*, where he was an op-ed columnist. A former lecturer on law at Harvard Law School, he is a graduate of Harvard College and Yale Law School. His website is at www.stark writing.com.